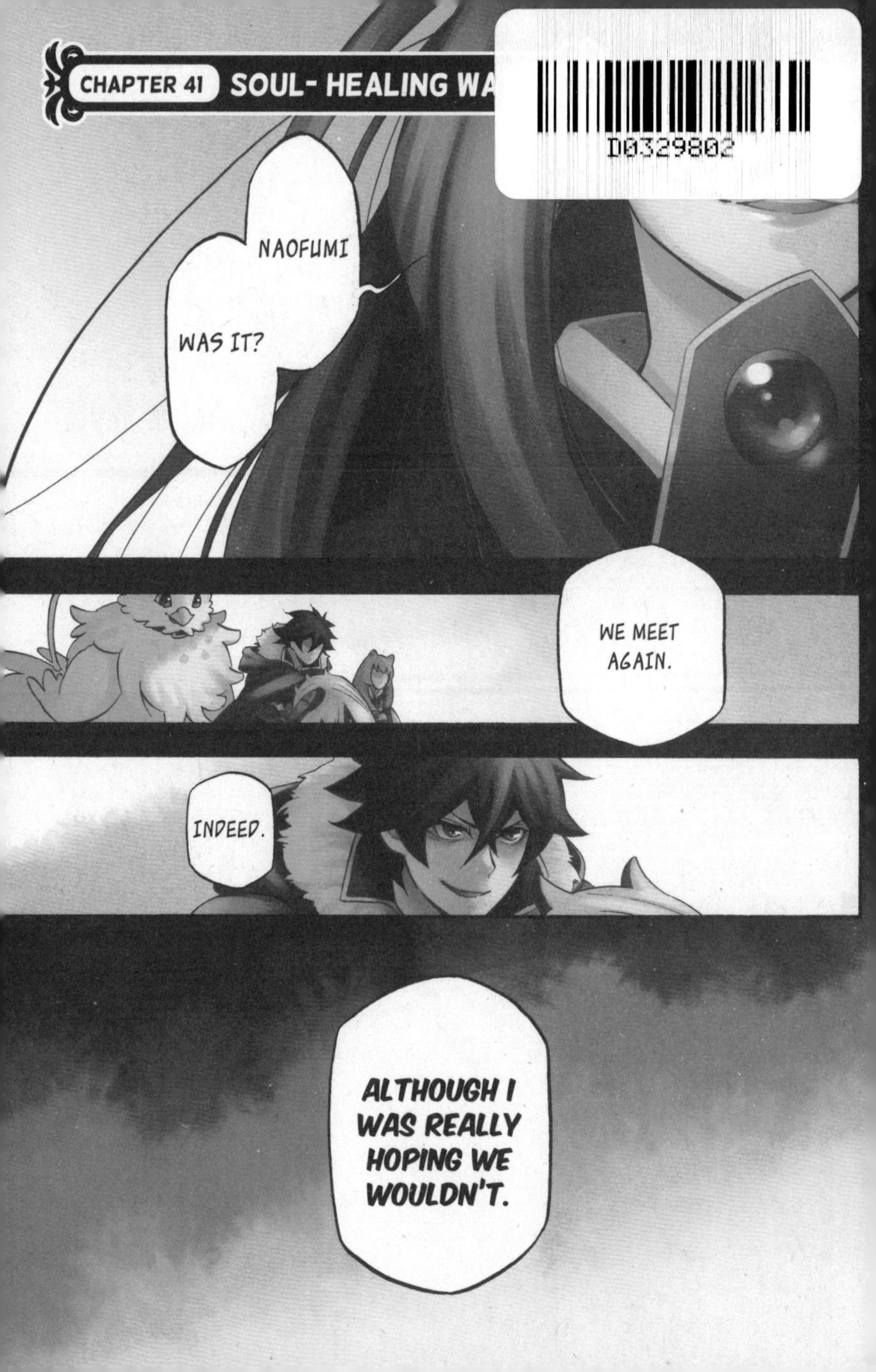
CHAPTER 41
SOUL- HEALING WA
NAOFUMI
WAS IT?
WE MEET AGAIN.
INDEED.
ALTHOUGH I WAS REALLY HOPING WE WOULDN'T.

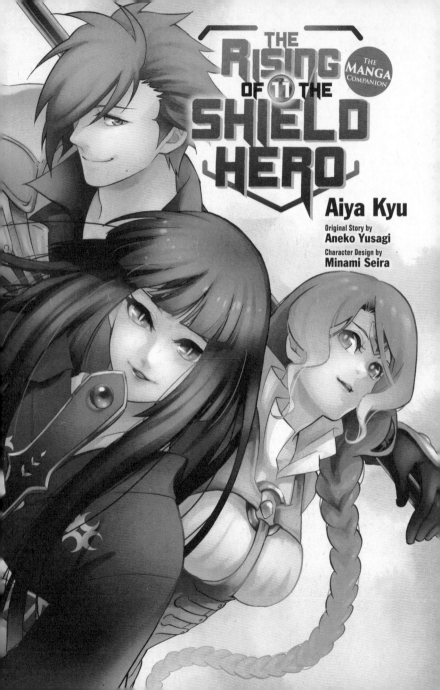

# THE RISING OF THE SHIELD HERO

**THE MANGA COMPANION**

11

## Aiya Kyu

Original Story by
**Aneko Yusagi**

Character Design by
**Minami Seira**

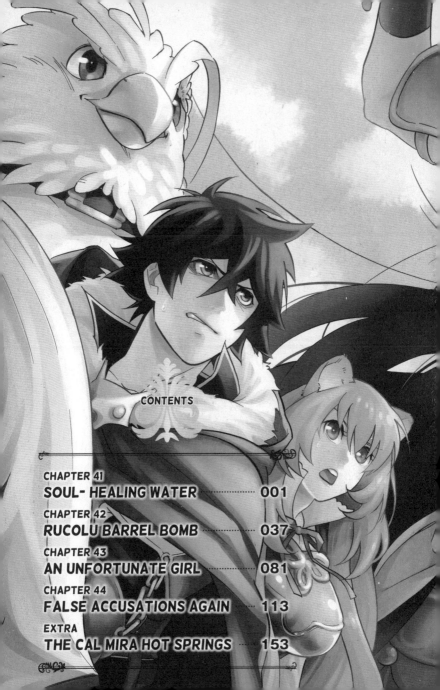

## CONTENTS

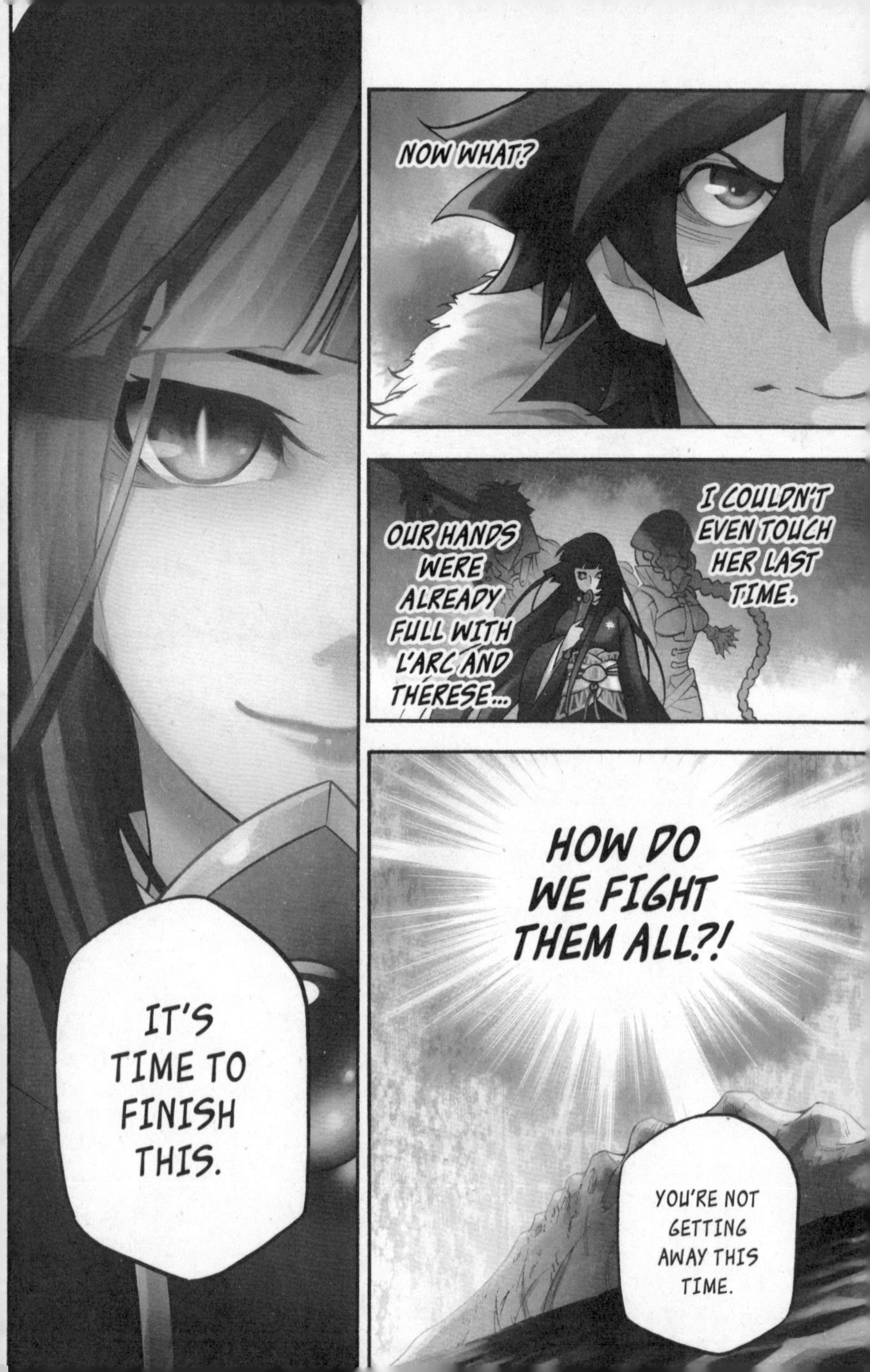
NOW WHAT?
I COULDN'T EVEN TOUCH HER LAST TIME.
OUR HANDS WERE ALREADY FULL WITH L'ARC AND THERESE...
HOW DO WE FIGHT THEM ALL?!
YOU'RE NOT GETTING AWAY THIS TIME.
IT'S TIME TO FINISH THIS.

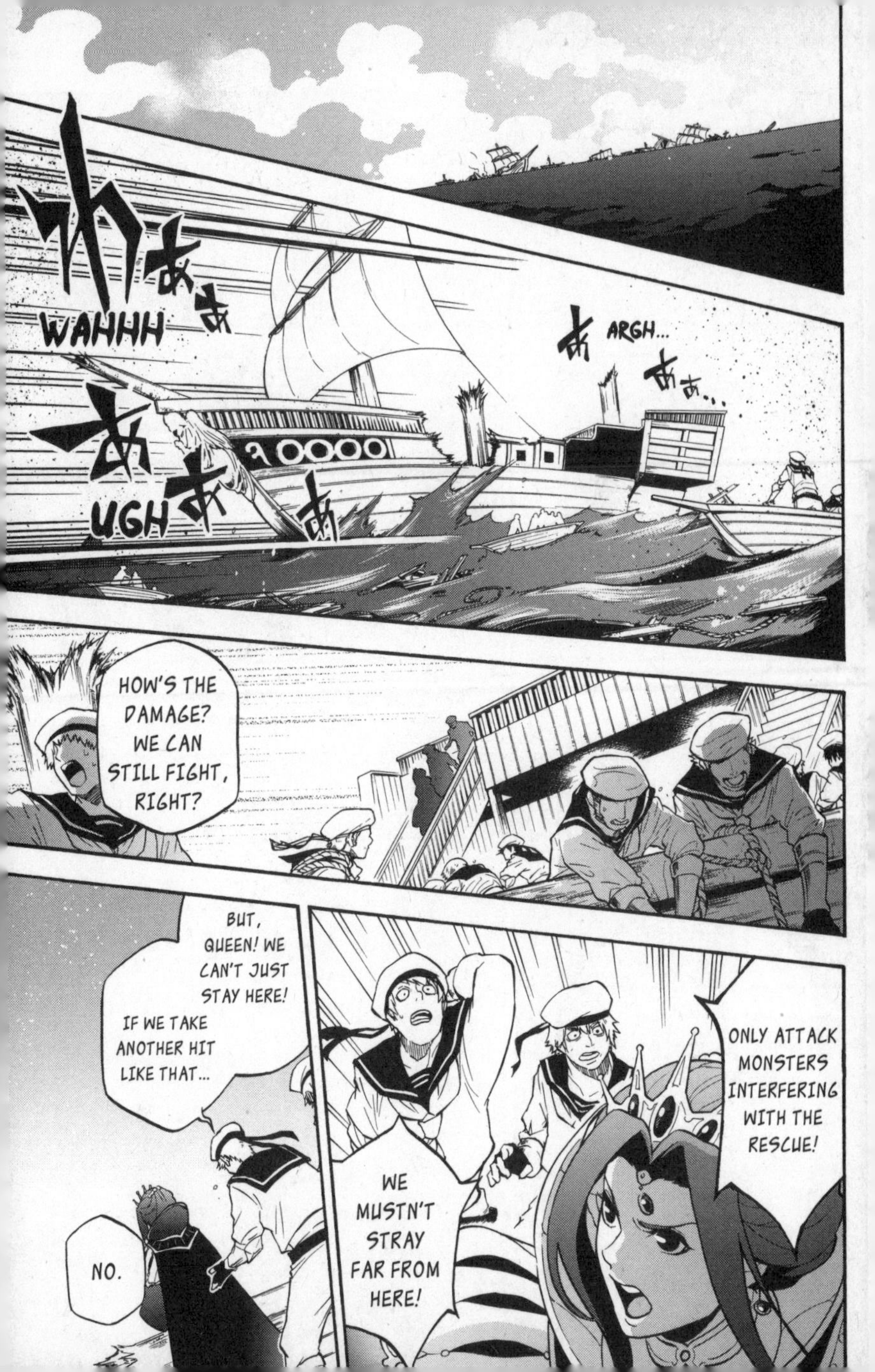
あ ARGH...
あぁ...
わあぁ WAHHH
あ UGH あ あ
HOW'S THE DAMAGE? WE CAN STILL FIGHT, RIGHT?
ONLY ATTACK MONSTERS INTERFERING WITH THE RESCUE!
WE MUSTN'T STRAY FAR FROM HERE!
BUT, QUEEN! WE CAN'T JUST STAY HERE!
IF WE TAKE ANOTHER HIT LIKE THAT...
NO.

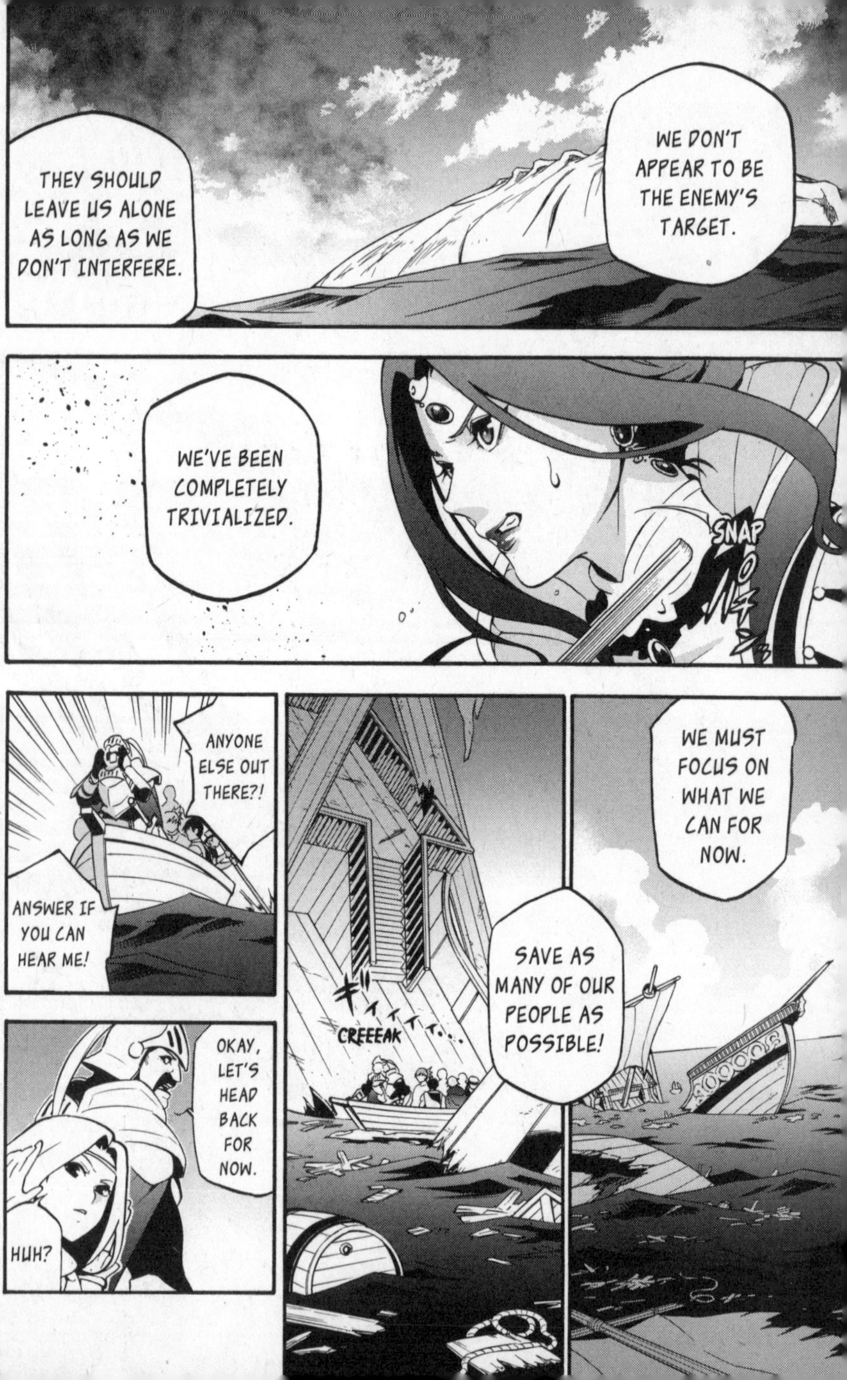
WE DON'T APPEAR TO BE THE ENEMY'S TARGET.
THEY SHOULD LEAVE US ALONE AS LONG AS WE DON'T INTERFERE.
WE'VE BEEN COMPLETELY TRIVIALIZED.
SNAP
WE MUST FOCUS ON WHAT WE CAN FOR NOW.
SAVE AS MANY OF OUR PEOPLE AS POSSIBLE!
CREEEAK
ANYONE ELSE OUT THERE?!
ANSWER IF YOU CAN HEAR ME!
OKAY, LET'S HEAD BACK FOR NOW.
HUH?

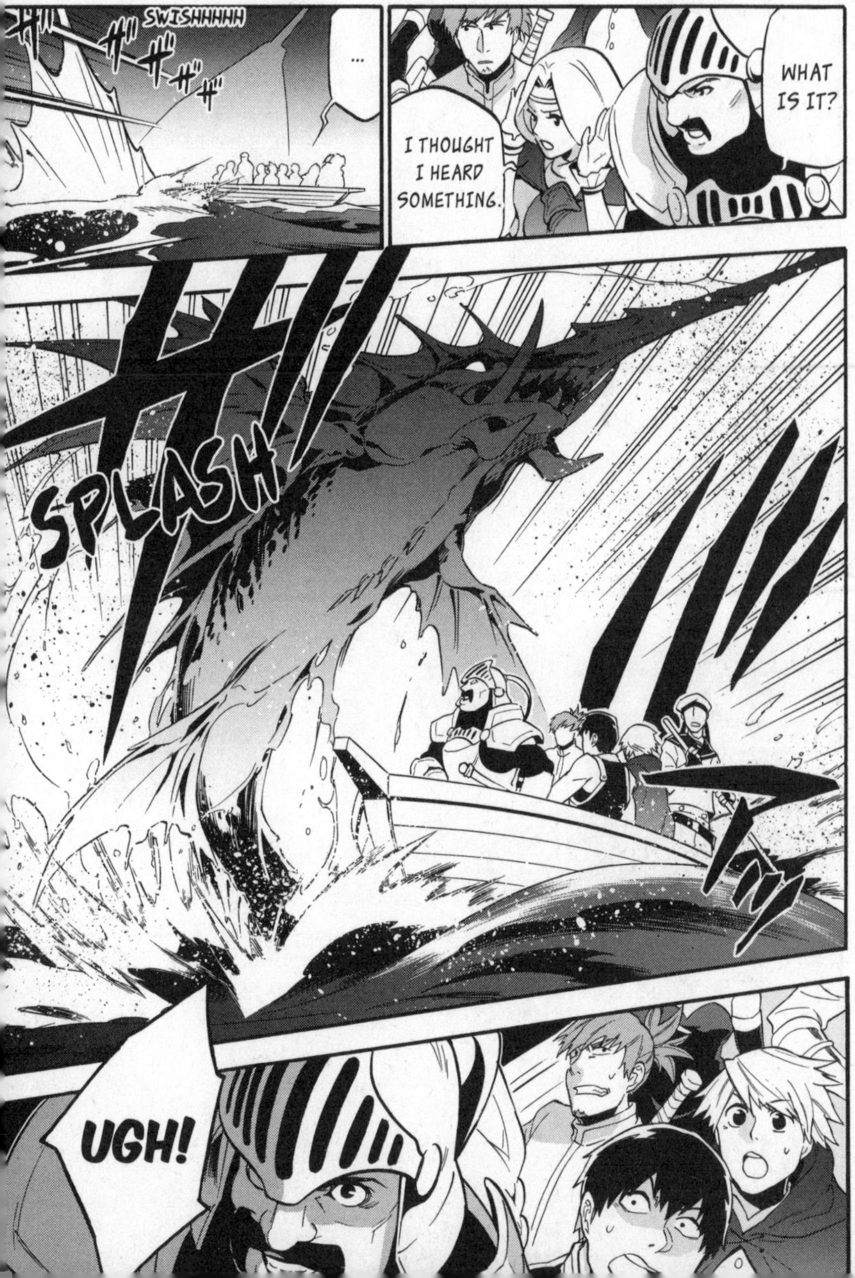
WHAT IS IT?
I THOUGHT I HEARD SOMETHING.
SWISHHHHH
...
SPLASH
UGH!

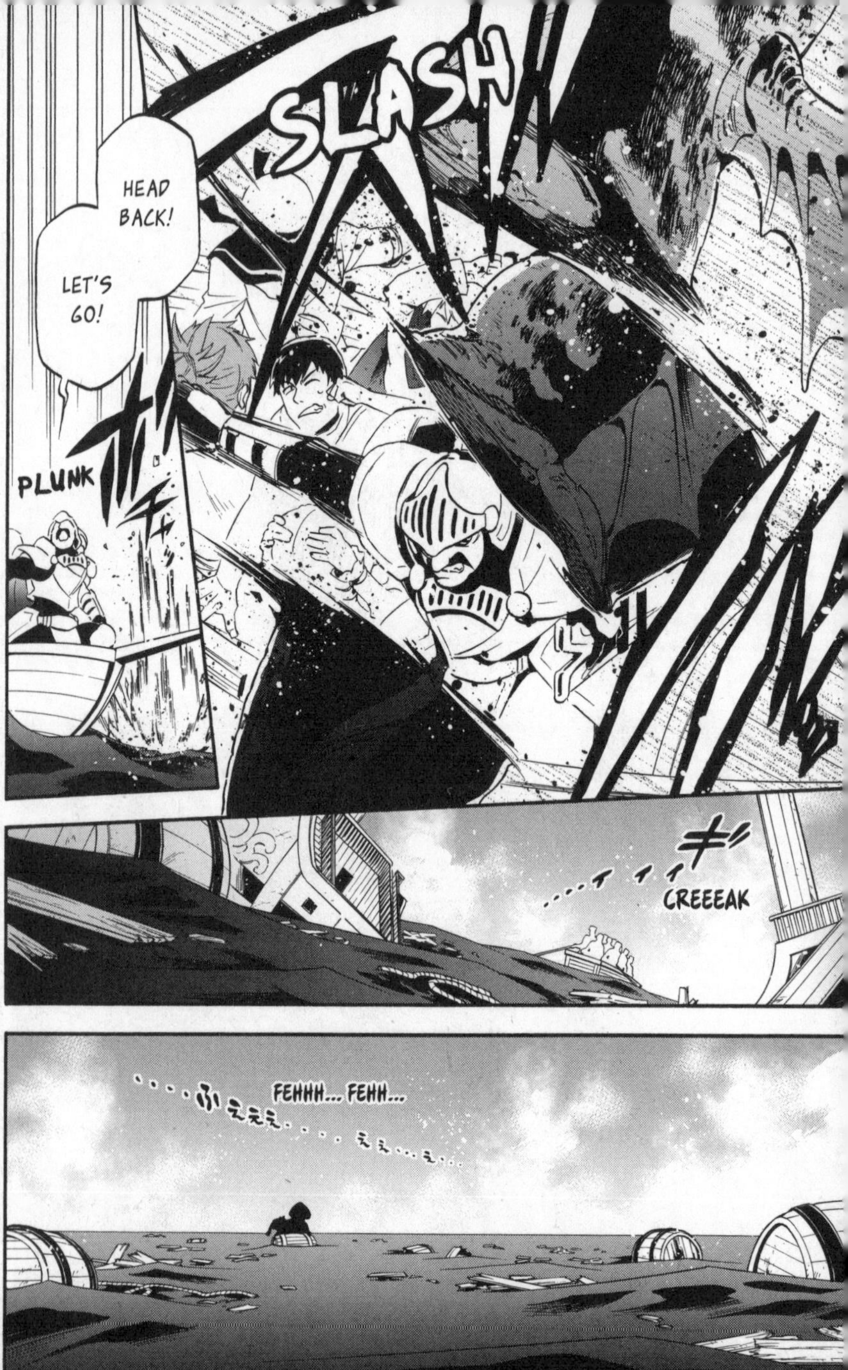
SLASH
HEAD BACK!
LET'S GO!
PLUNK
CREEEAK
FEHHH... FEHH...

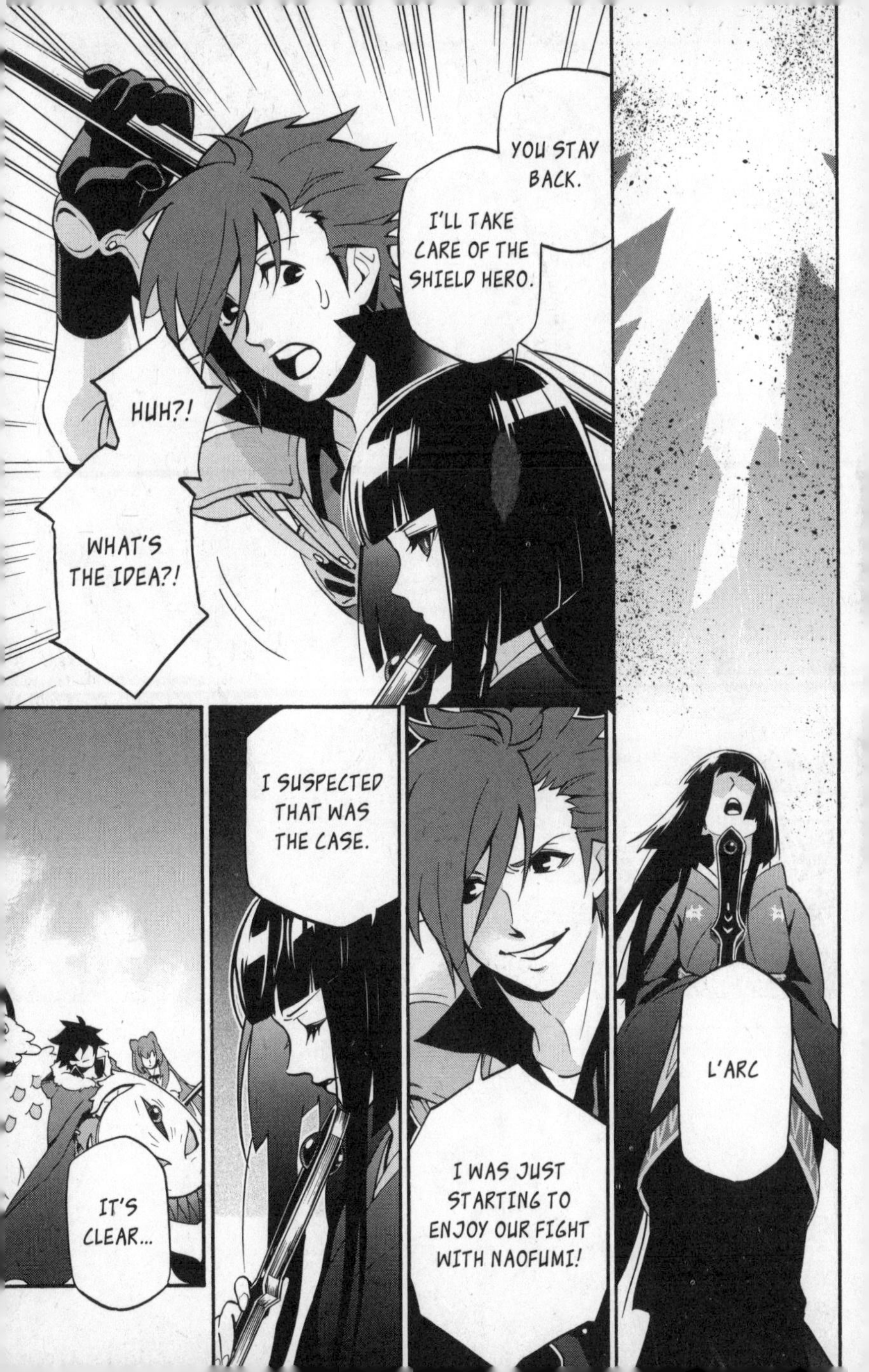

L'ARC
YOU STAY BACK.
I'LL TAKE CARE OF THE SHIELD HERO.
HUH?!
WHAT'S THE IDEA?!
I SUSPECTED THAT WAS THE CASE.
I WAS JUST STARTING TO ENJOY OUR FIGHT WITH NAOFUMI!
IT'S CLEAR...

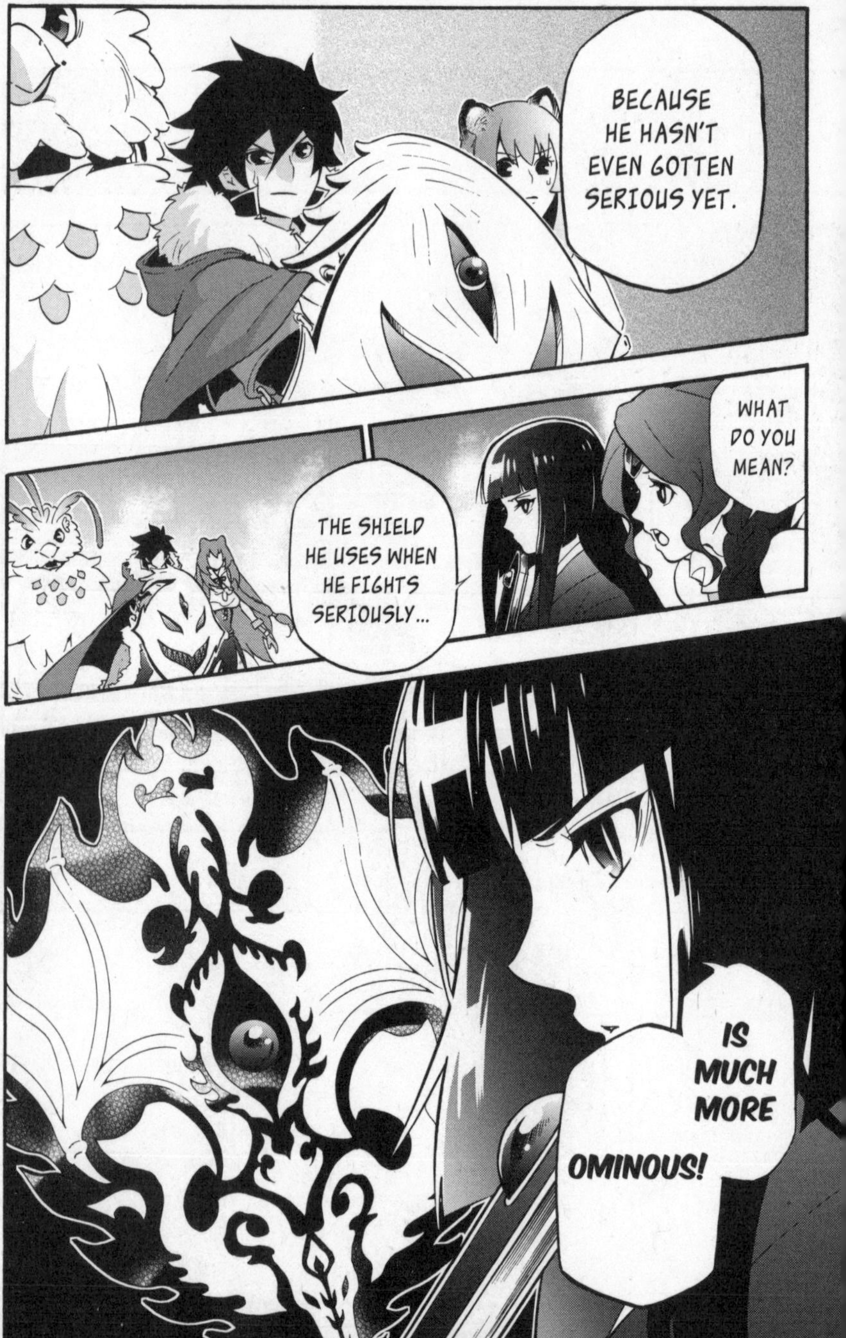
BECAUSE HE HASN'T EVEN GOTTEN SERIOUS YET.
WHAT DO YOU MEAN?
THE SHIELD HE USES WHEN HE FIGHTS SERIOUSLY...
IS MUCH MORE
OMINOUS!

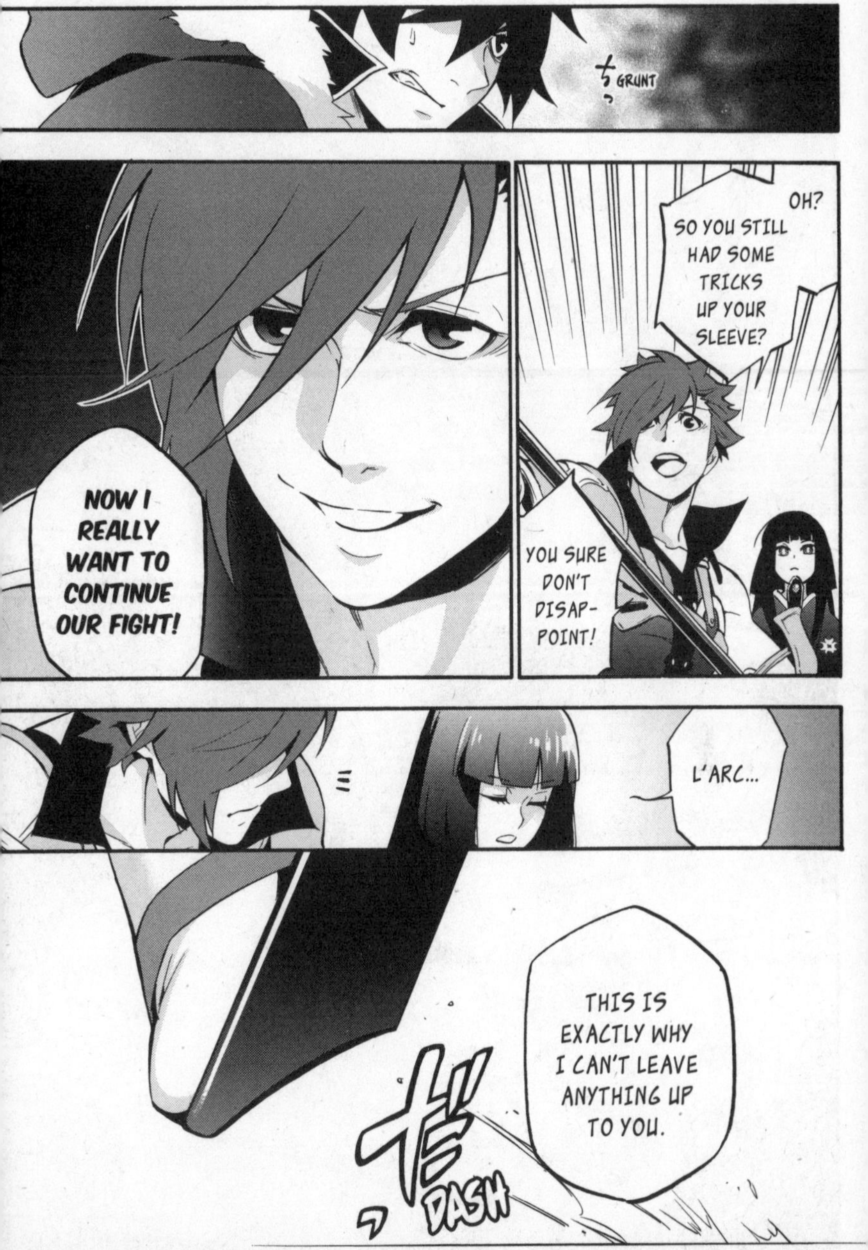
GRUNT
OH? SO YOU STILL HAD SOME TRICKS UP YOUR SLEEVE?
YOU SURE DON'T DISAP-POINT!
NOW I REALLY WANT TO CONTINUE OUR FIGHT!
L'ARC...
THIS IS EXACTLY WHY I CAN'T LEAVE ANYTHING UP TO YOU.
DASH

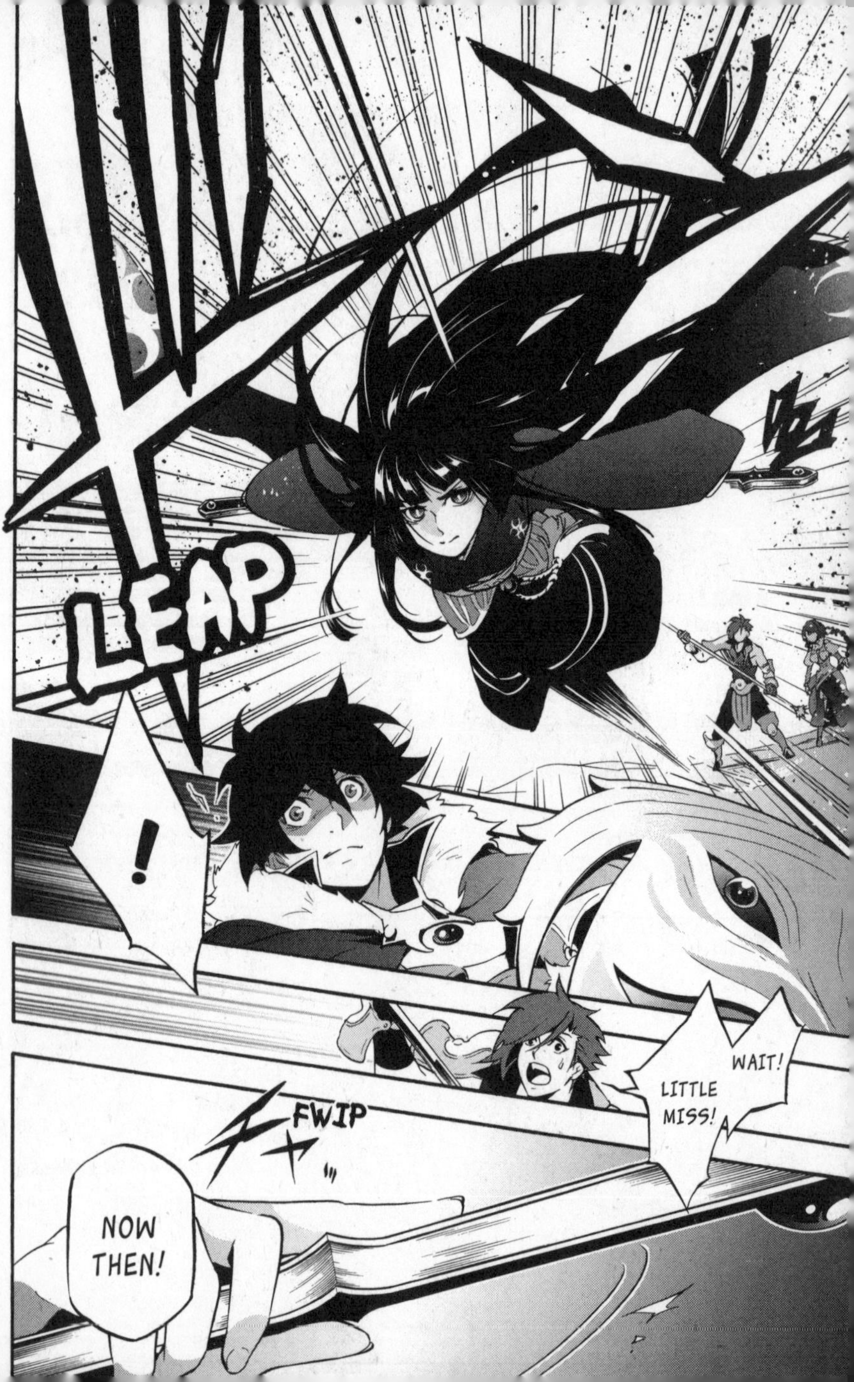
LEAP
!
WAIT! LITTLE MISS!
FWIP
NOW THEN!

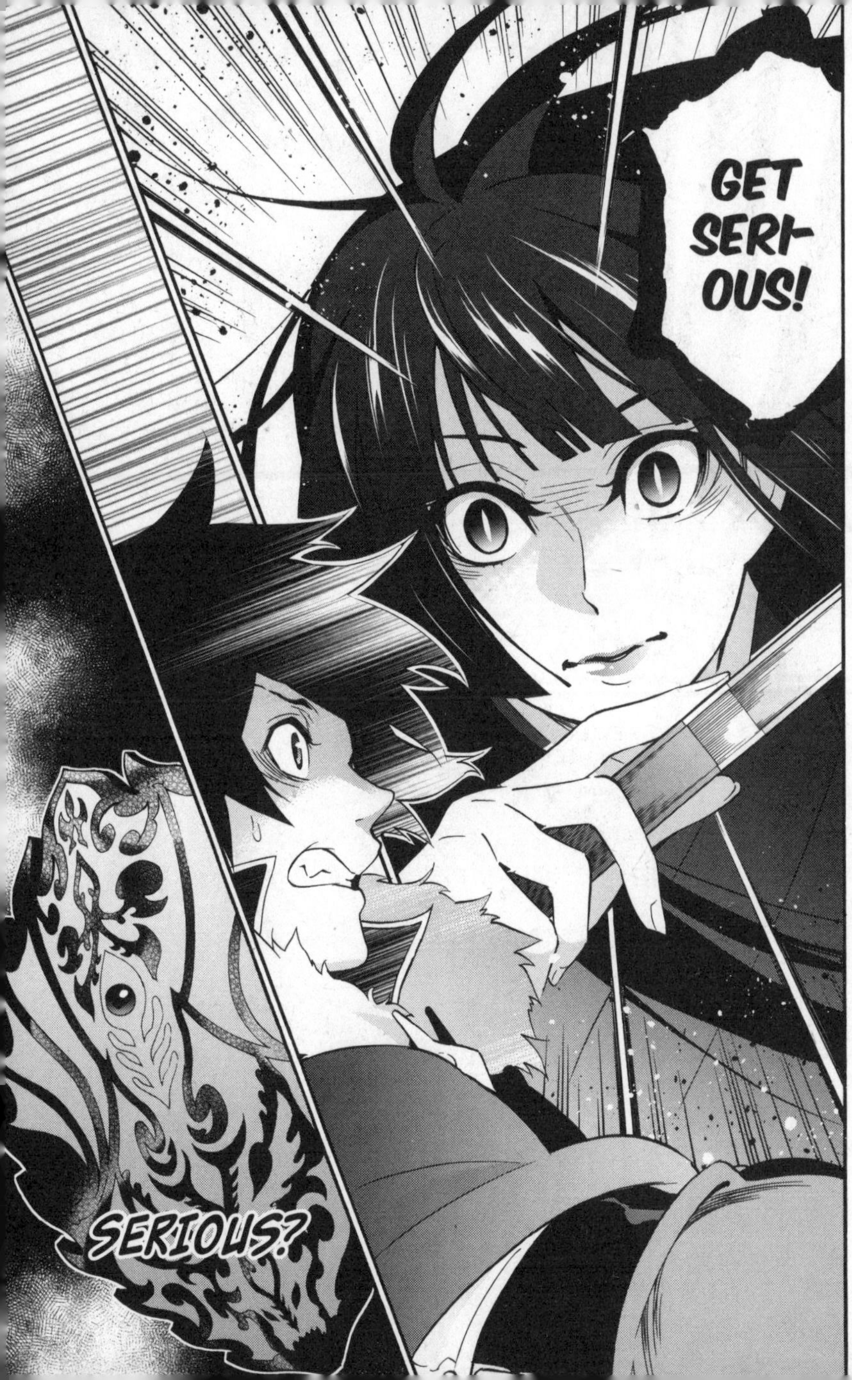
GET SERI-OUS!
SERIOUS?

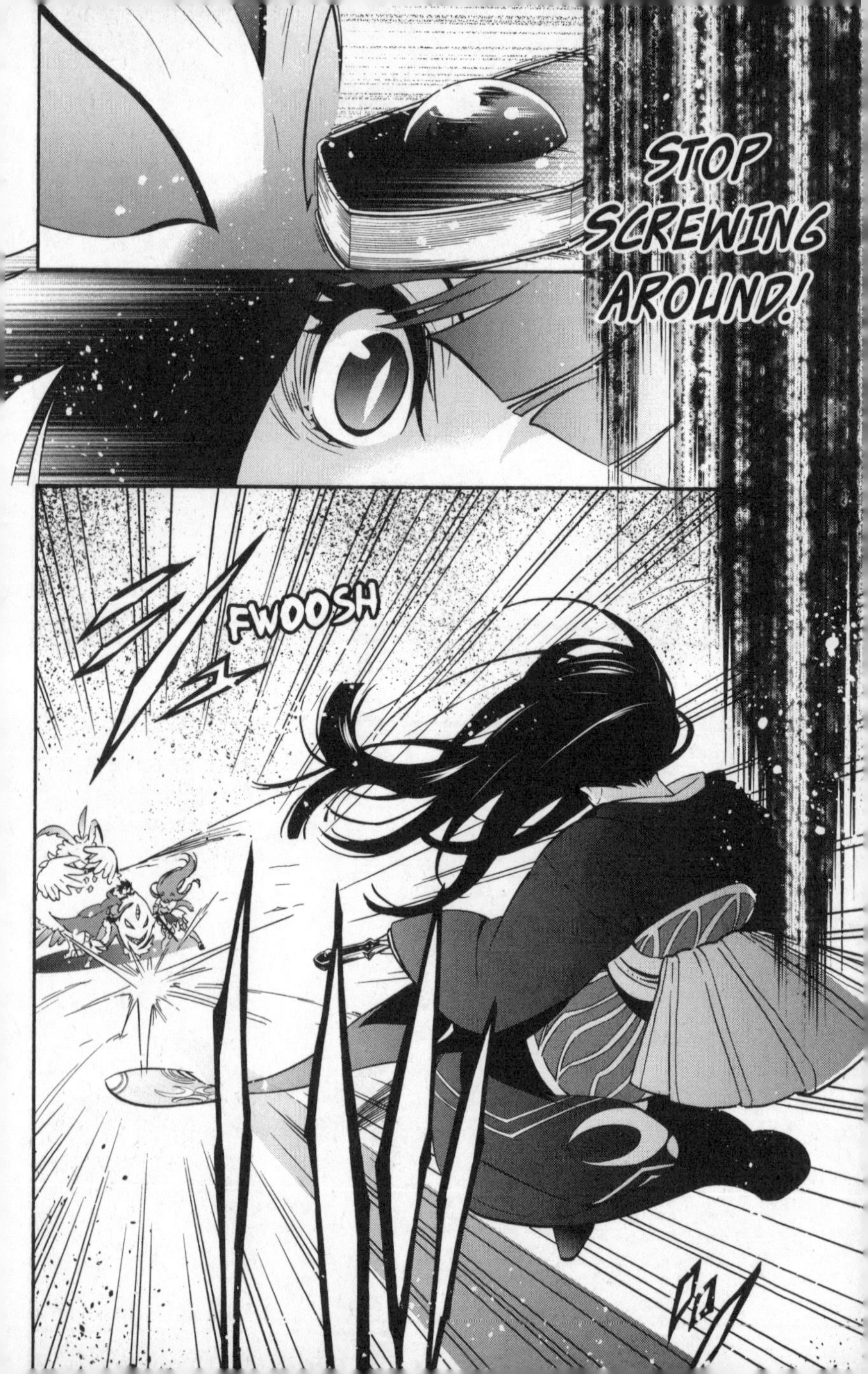
STOP SCREWING AROUND!
FWOOSH

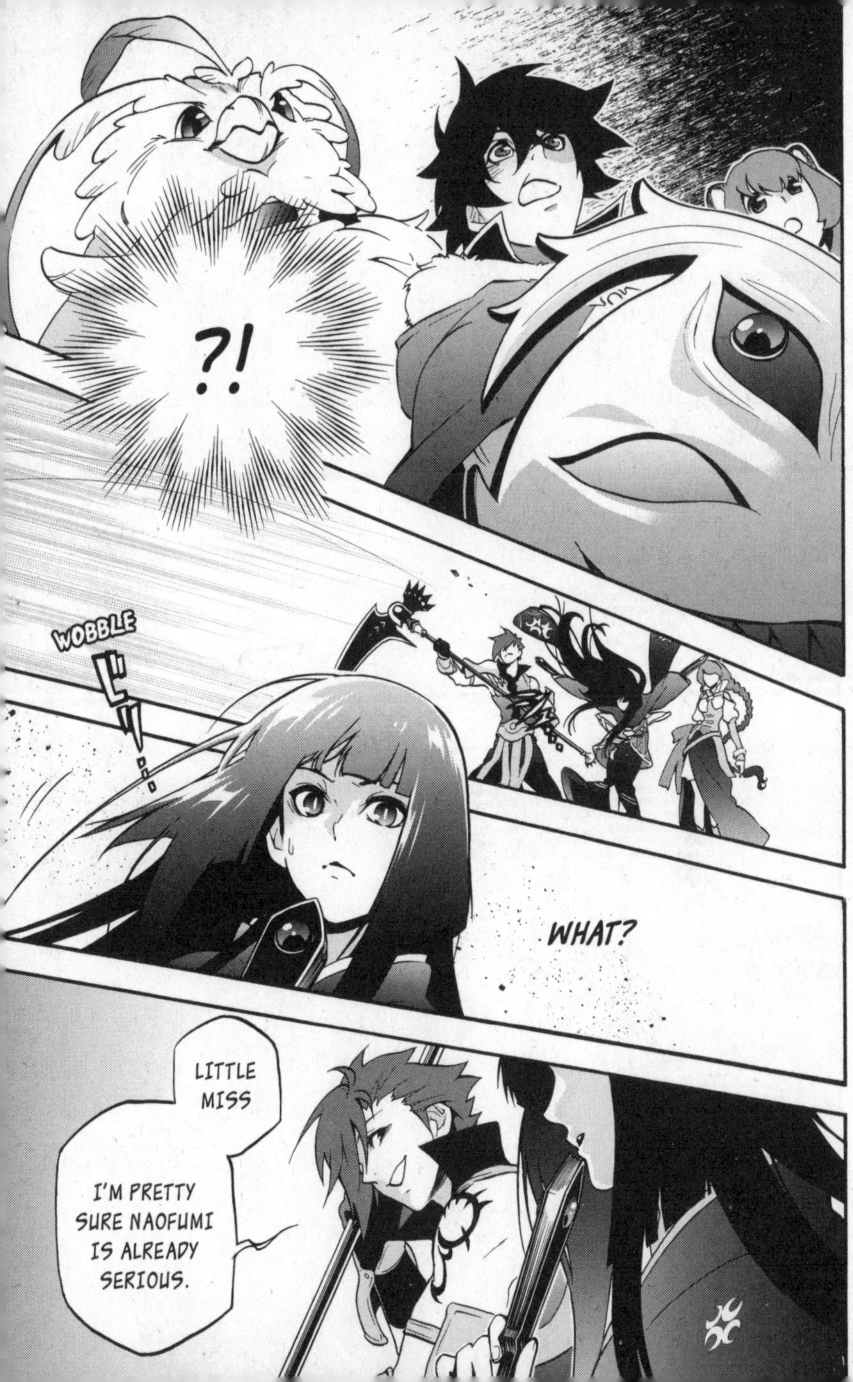
?!
WOBBLE
WHAT?
LITTLE MISS
I'M PRETTY SURE NAOFUMI IS ALREADY SERIOUS.

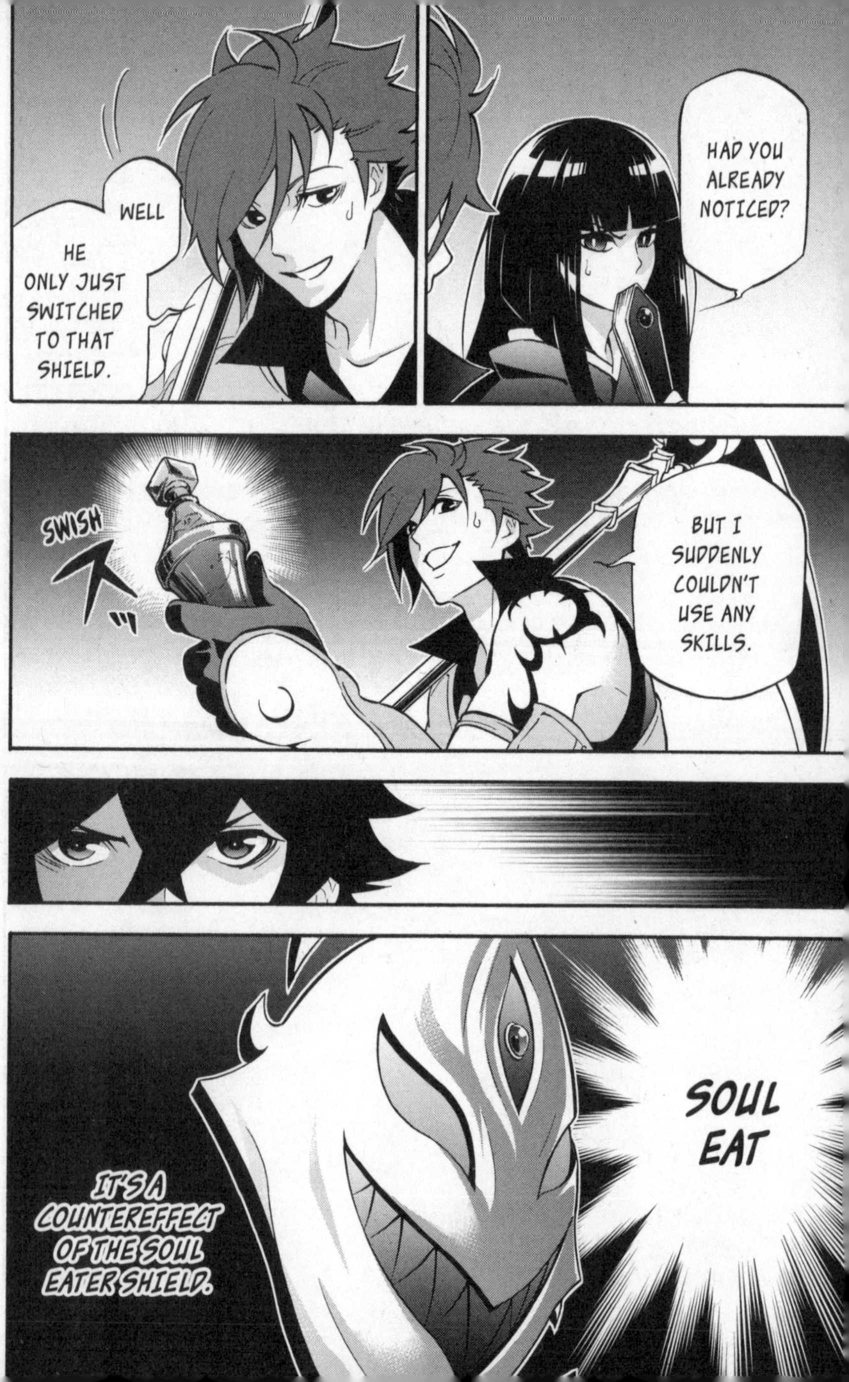
HAD YOU ALREADY NOTICED?
WELL
HE ONLY JUST SWITCHED TO THAT SHIELD.
BUT I SUDDENLY COULDN'T USE ANY SKILLS.
SWISH
SOUL EAT
IT'S A COUNTEREFFECT OF THE SOUL EATER SHIELD.

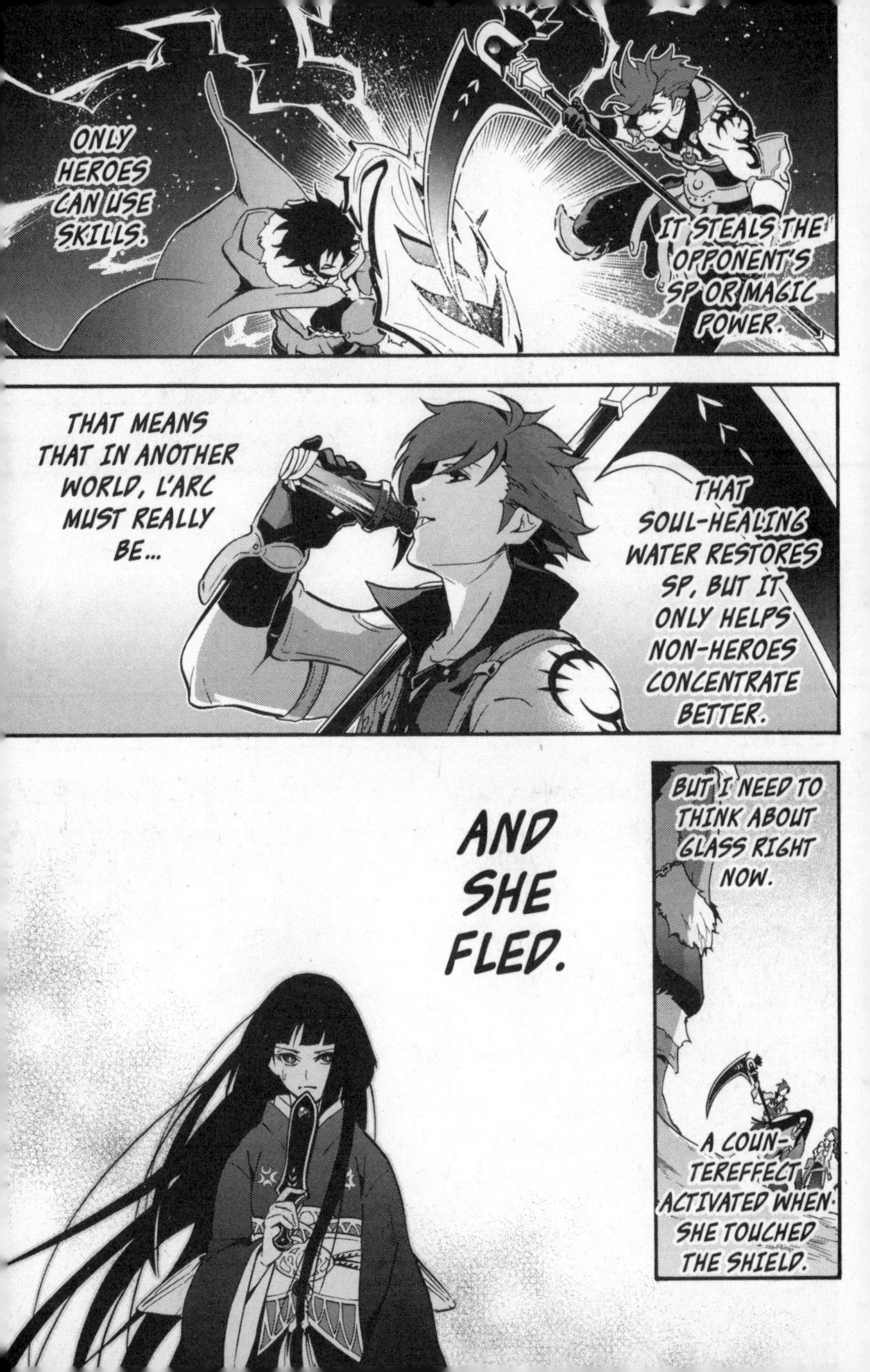
IT STEALS THE OPPONENT'S SP OR MAGIC POWER.
ONLY HEROES CAN USE SKILLS.
THAT SOUL-HEALING WATER RESTORES SP, BUT IT ONLY HELPS NON-HEROES CONCENTRATE BETTER.
THAT MEANS THAT IN ANOTHER WORLD, L'ARC MUST REALLY BE...
BUT I NEED TO THINK ABOUT GLASS RIGHT NOW.
A COUN-TEREFFECT ACTIVATED WHEN SHE TOUCHED THE SHIELD.
AND SHE FLED.

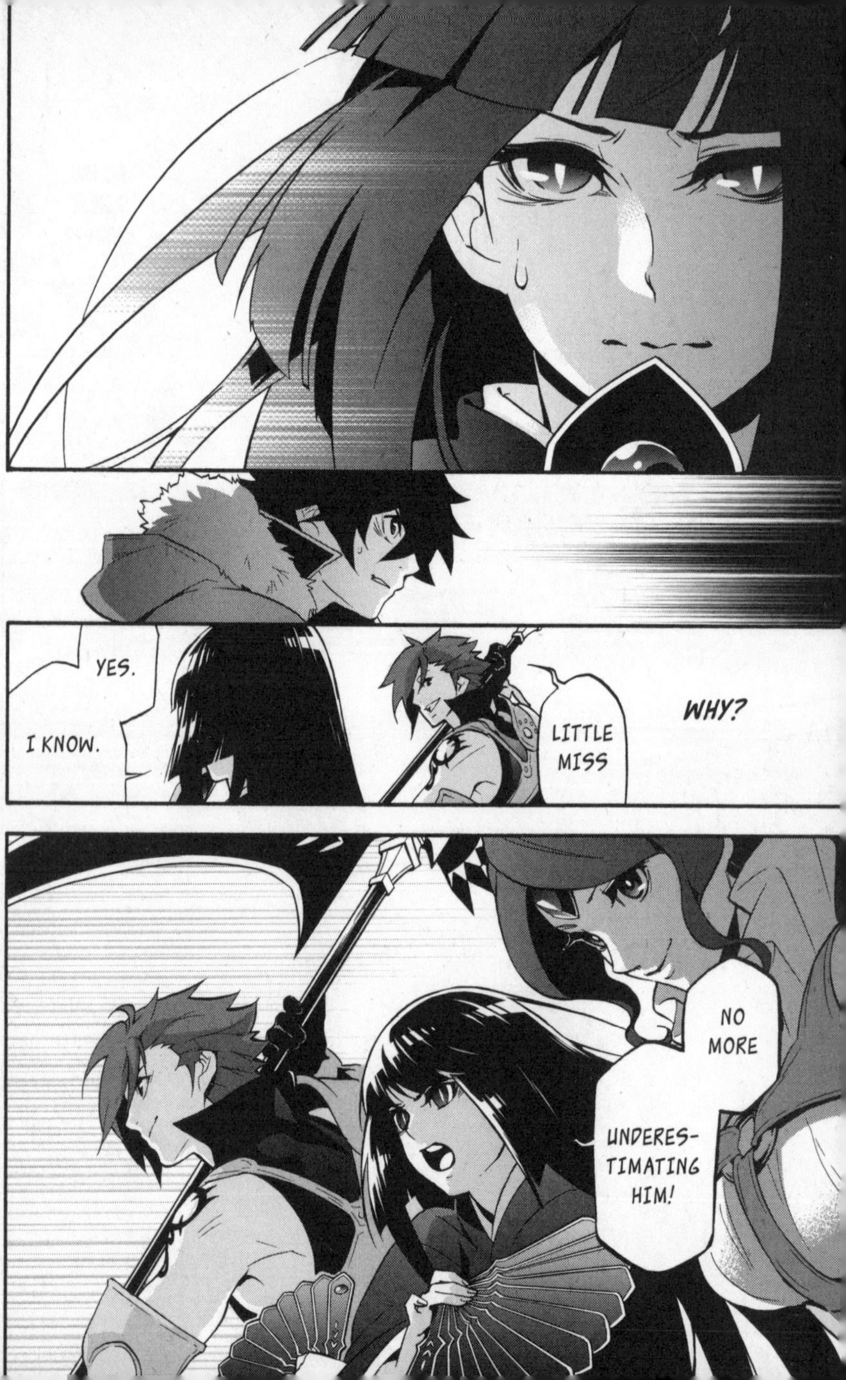
WHY?
LITTLE MISS
YES.
I KNOW.
NO MORE UNDERES-TIMATING HIM!

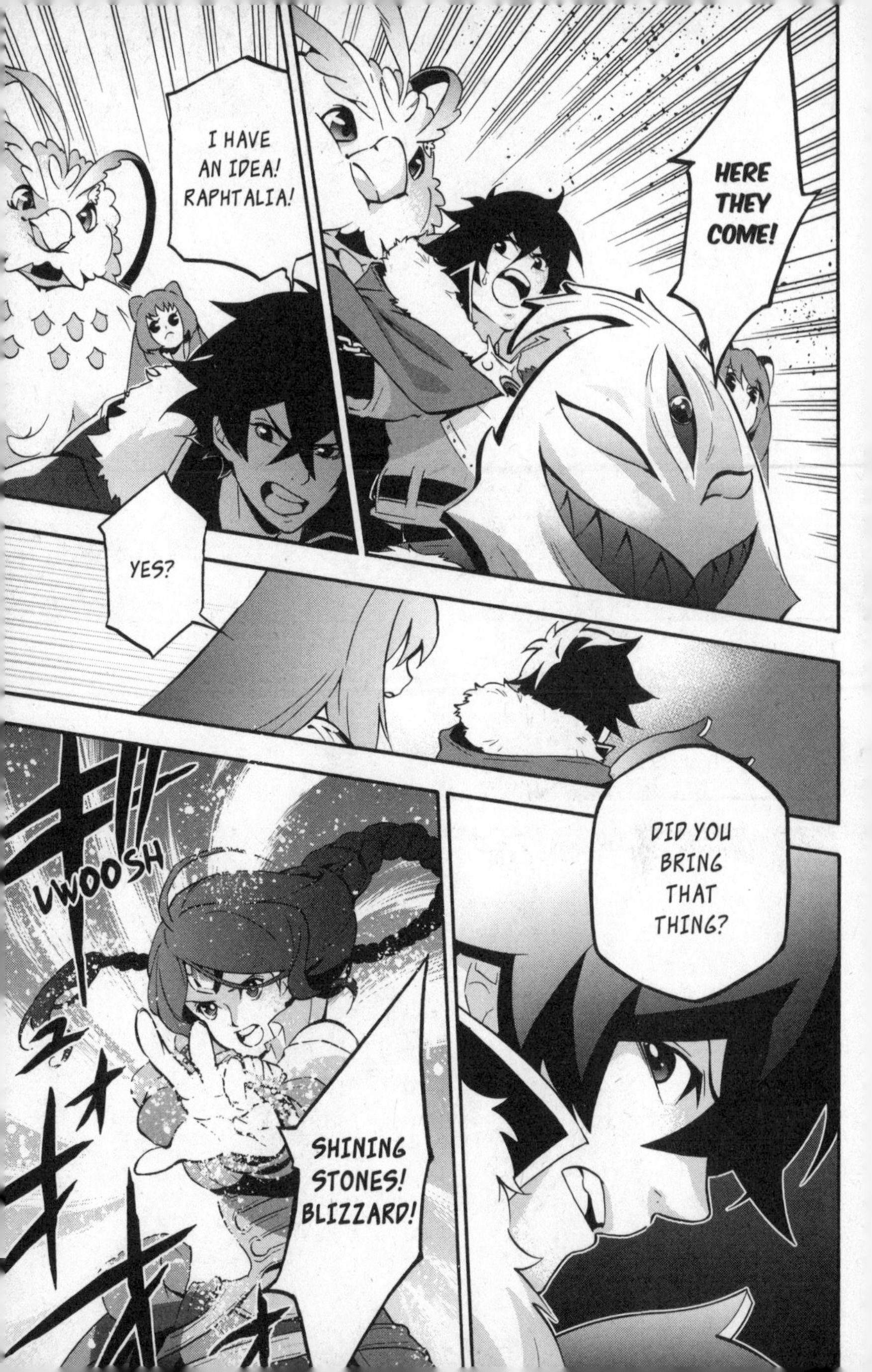
HERE THEY COME!
I HAVE AN IDEA! RAPHTALIA!
YES?
DID YOU BRING THAT THING?
WOOSH
SHINING STONES! BLIZZARD!

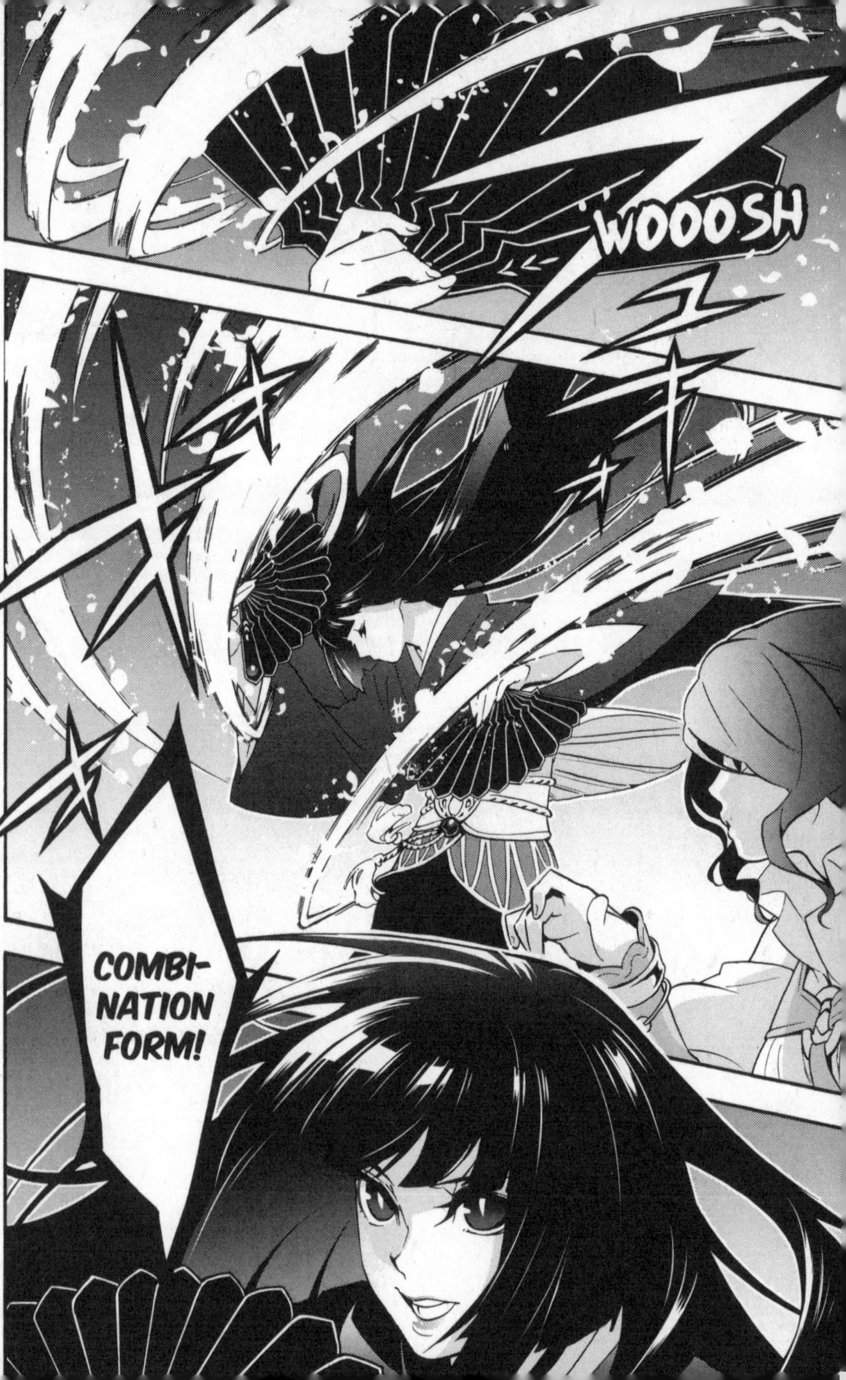
WOOOSH
COMBI-
NATION
FORM!

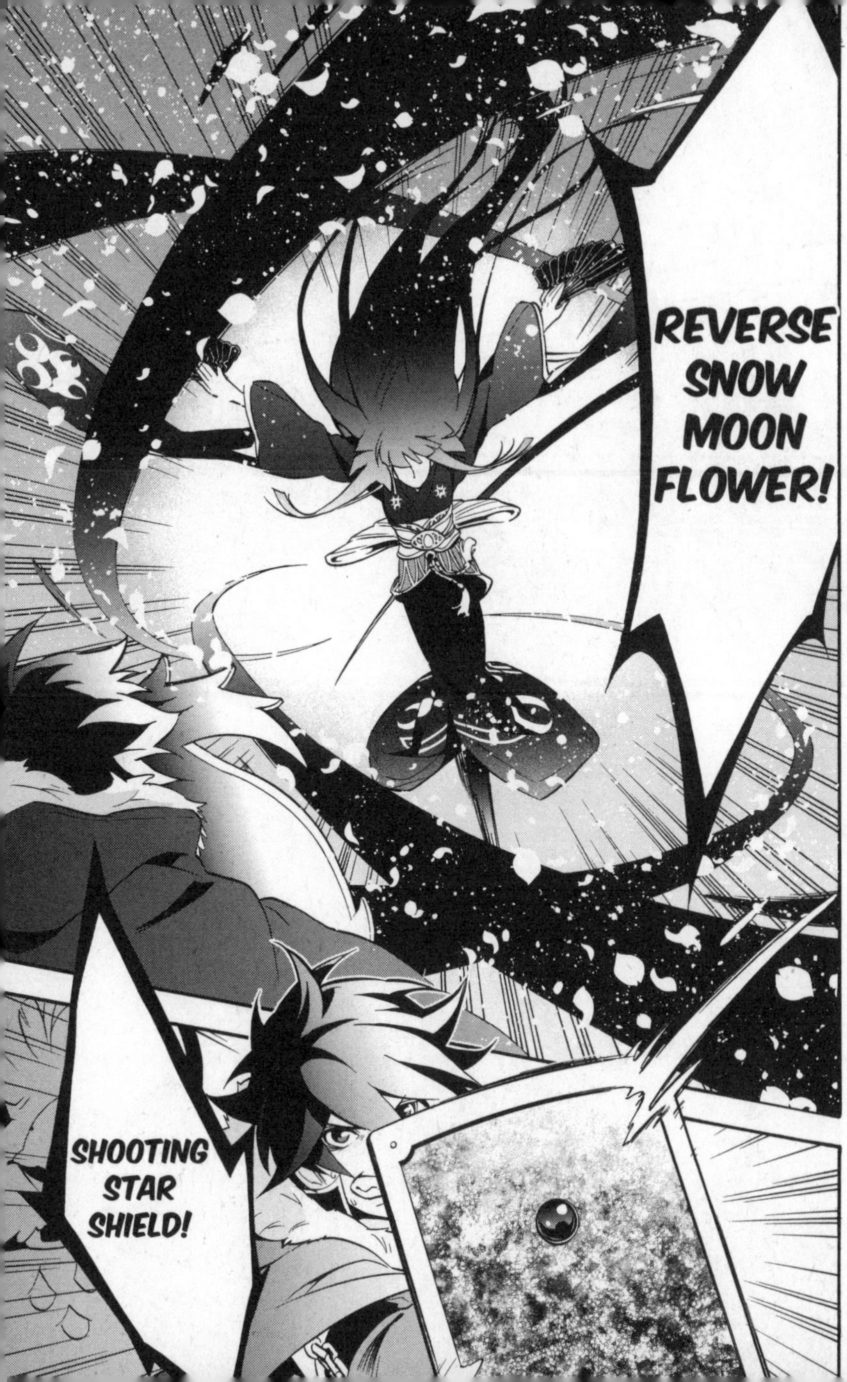
REVERSE SNOW MOON FLOWER!
SHOOTING STAR SHIELD!

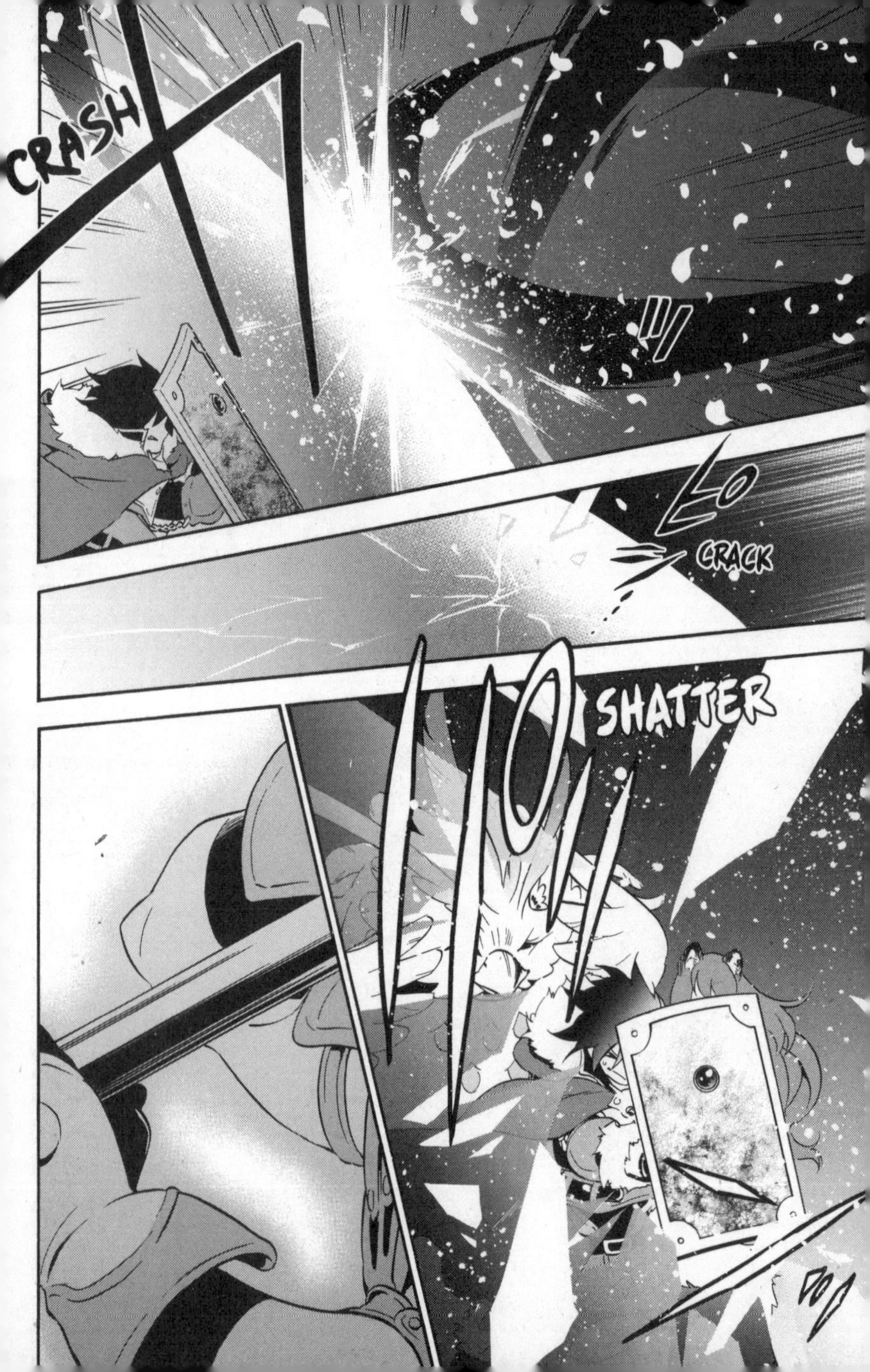
CRASH
CRACK
SHATTER

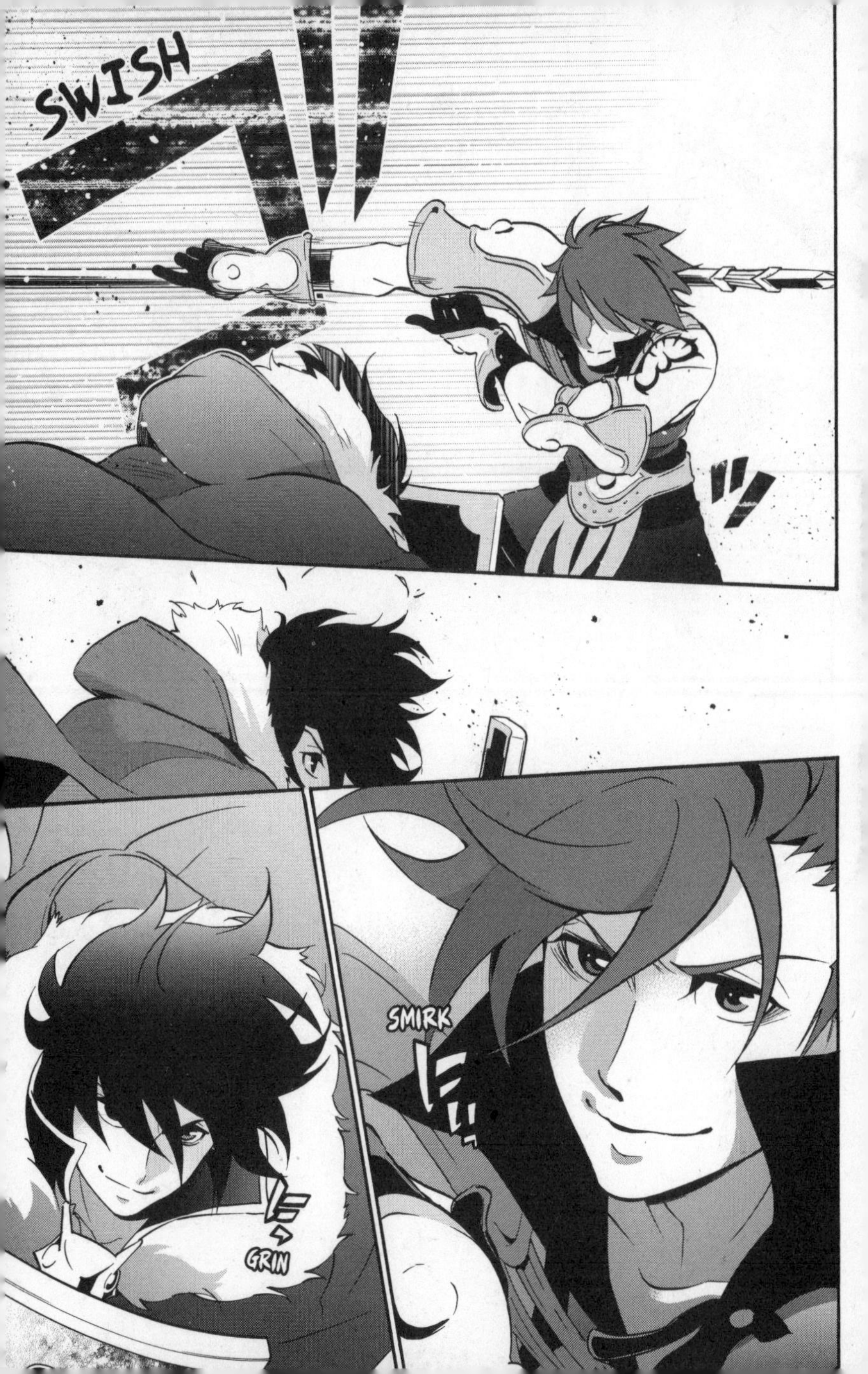
SWISH
SMIRK
GRIN

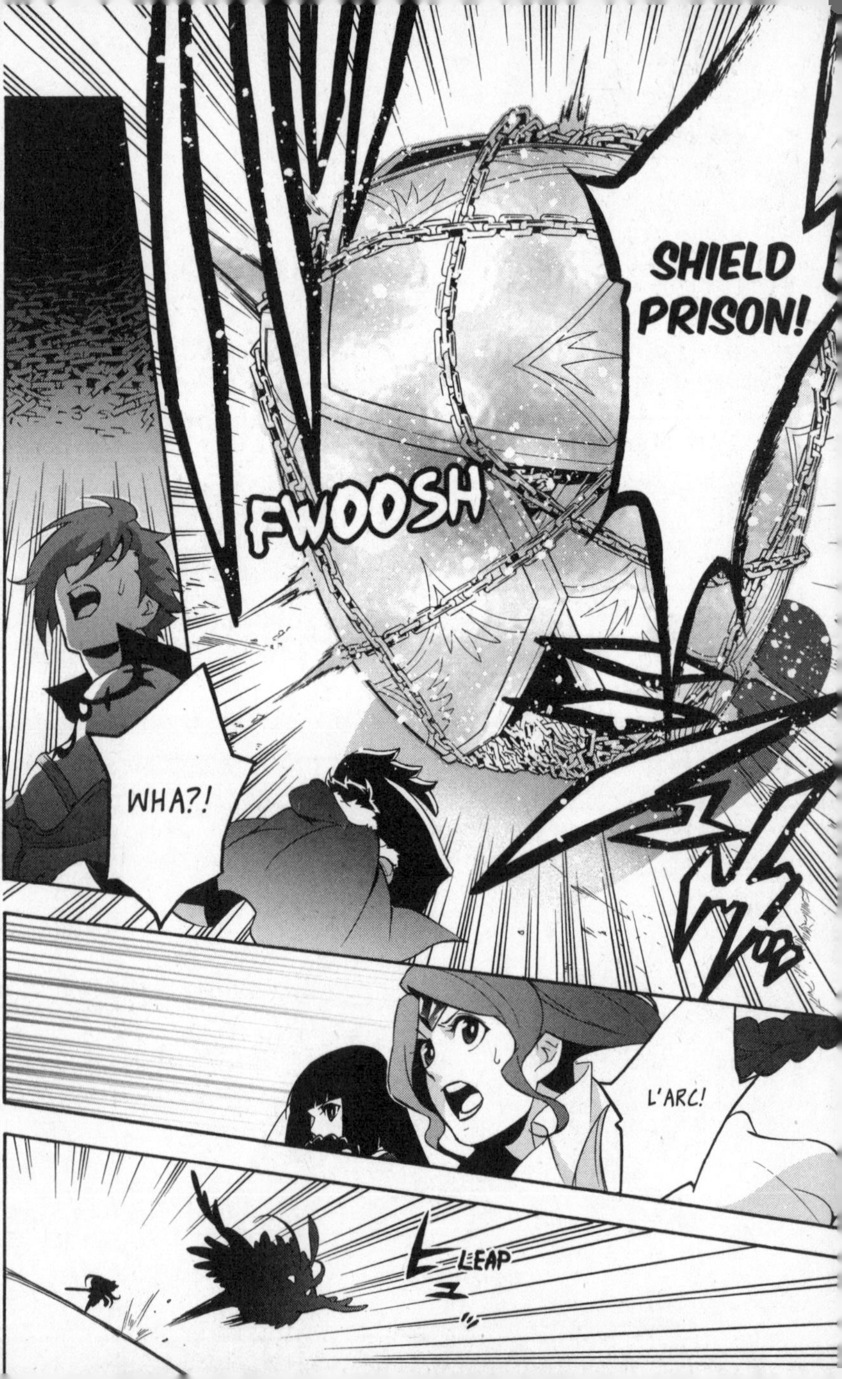
SHIELD PRISON!
FWOOSH
WHA?!
L'ARC!
LEAP

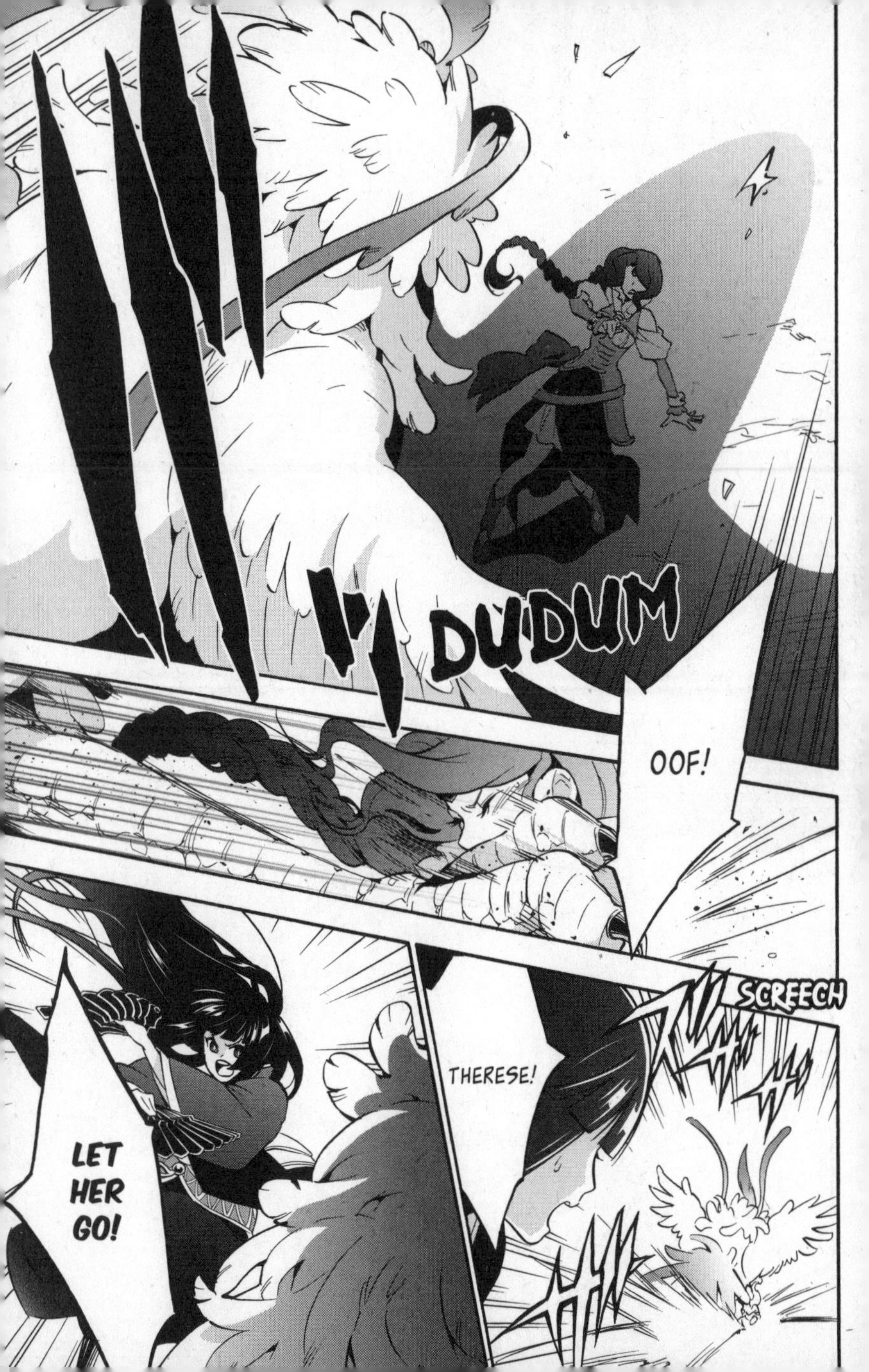
DUDUM
OOF!
SCREECH
THERESE!
LET HER GO!

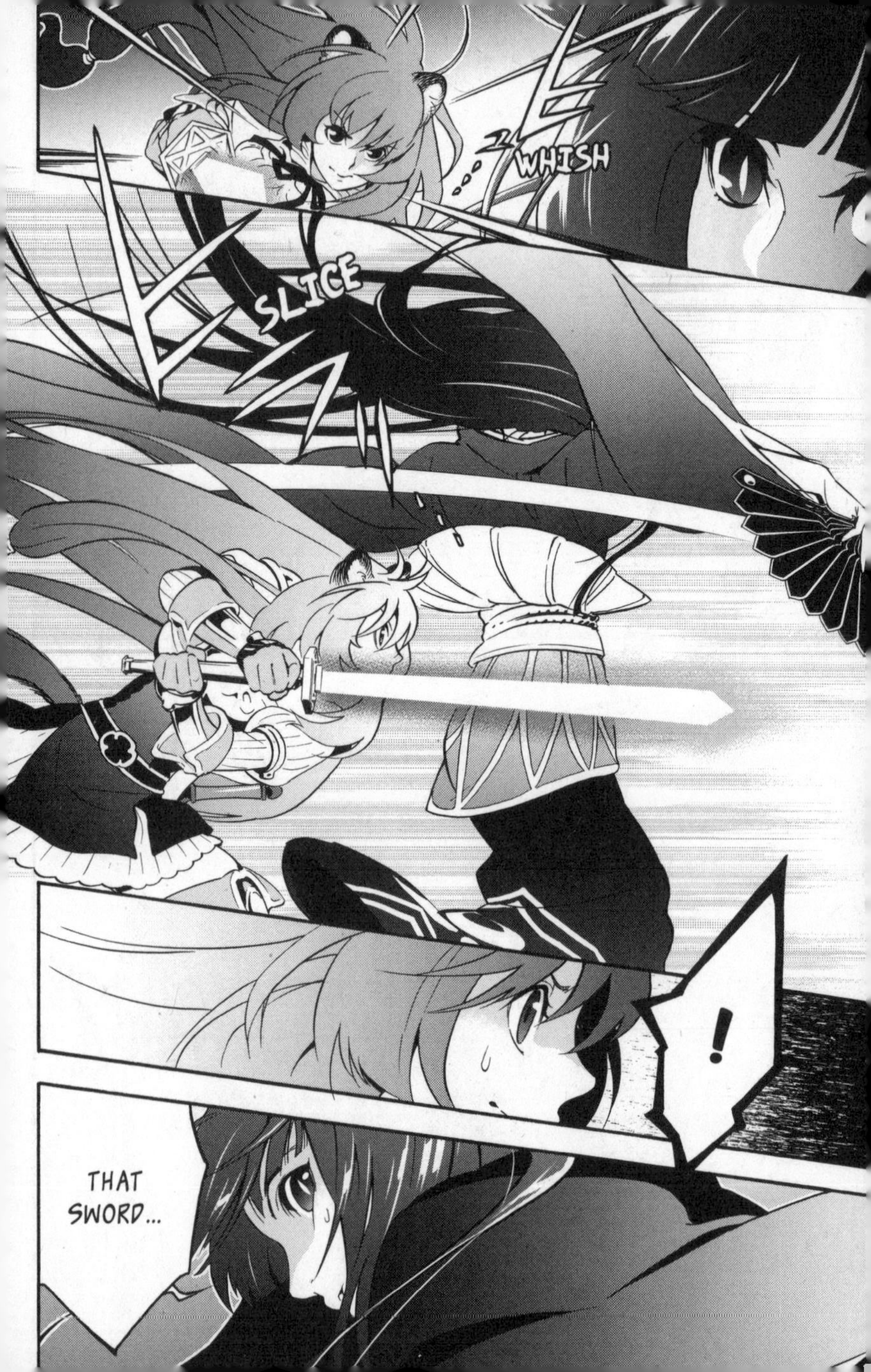
WHISH
SLICE
!
THAT SWORD...

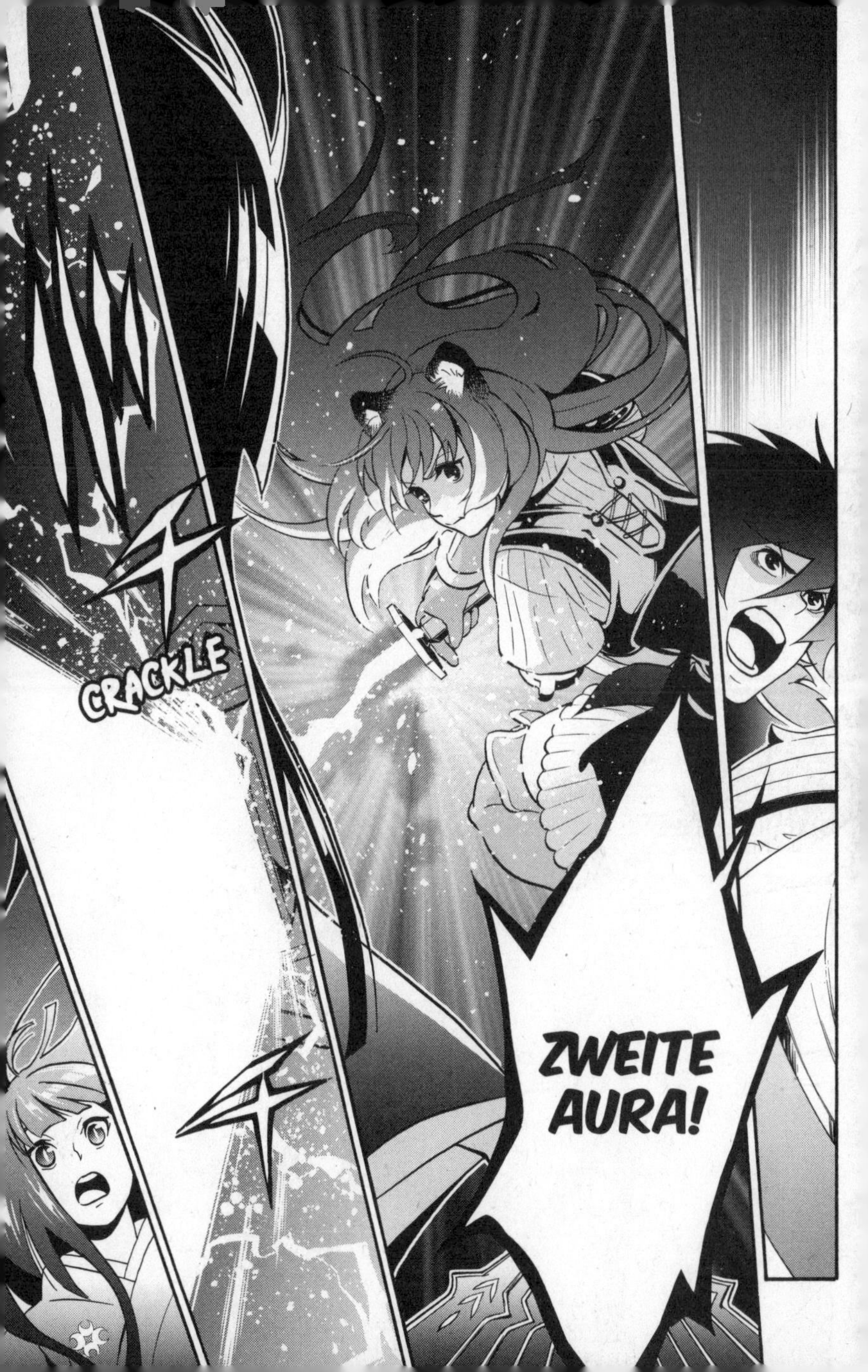
ZWEITE AURA!
CRACKLE

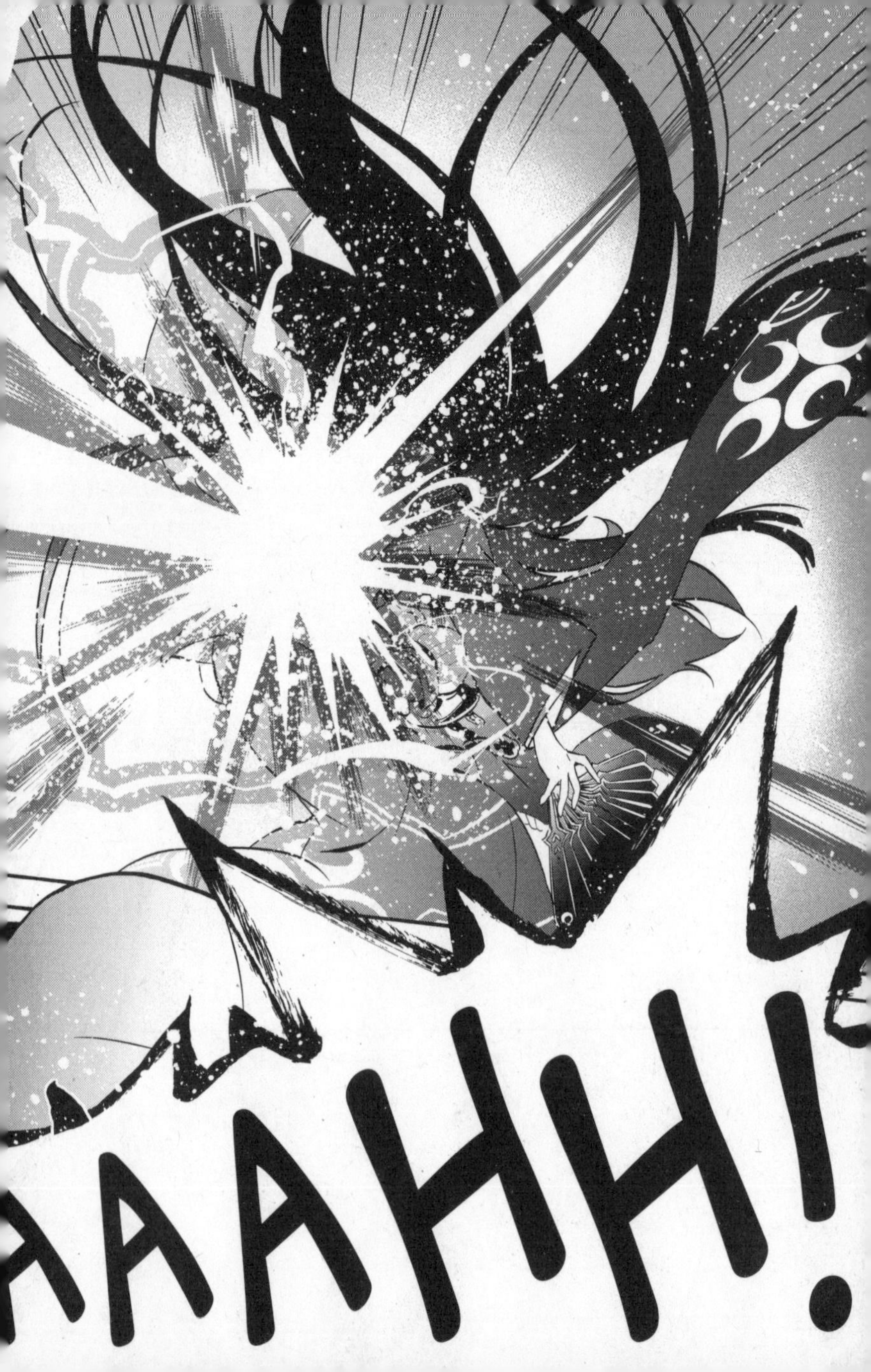
AAHH!

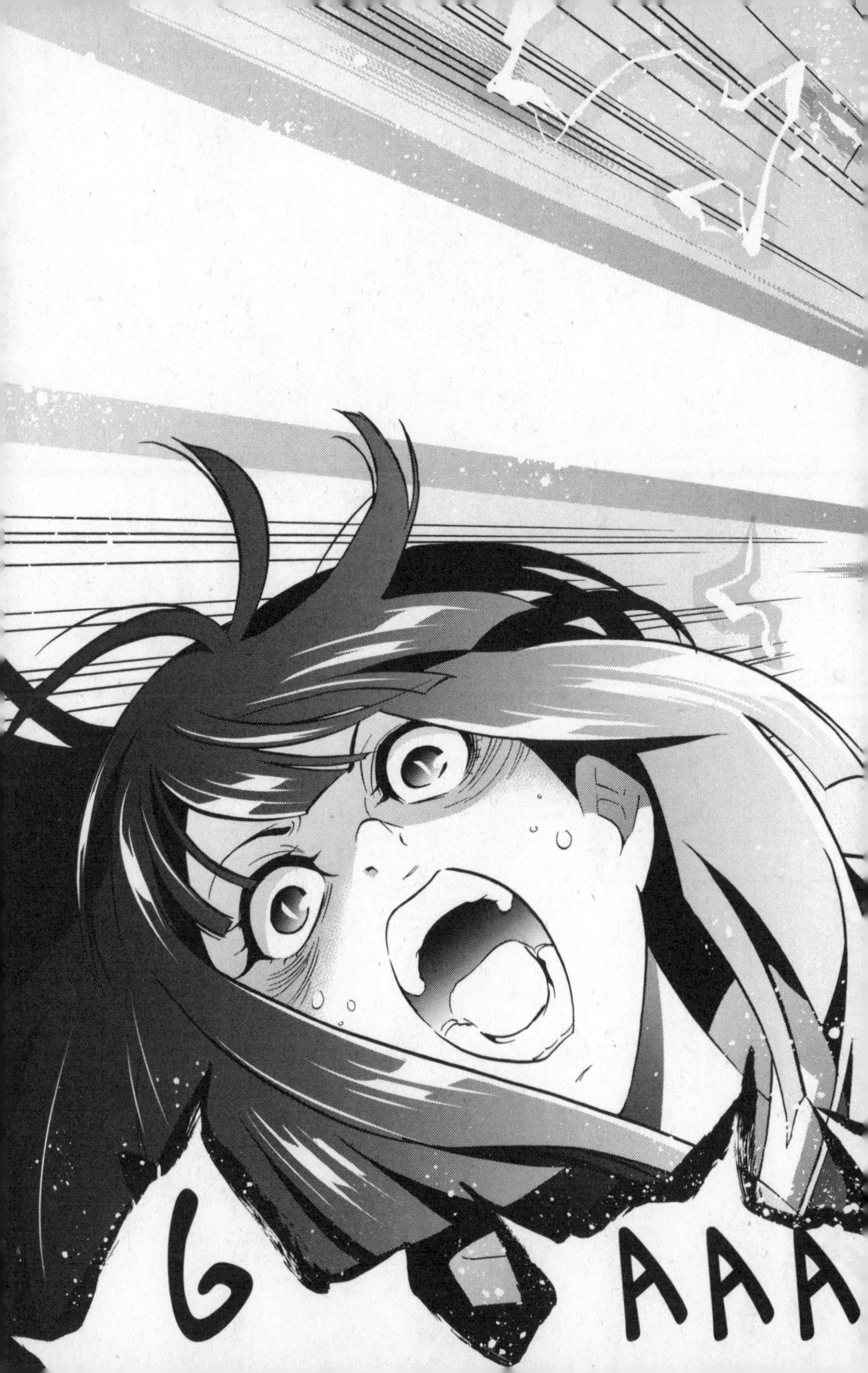
G AAA

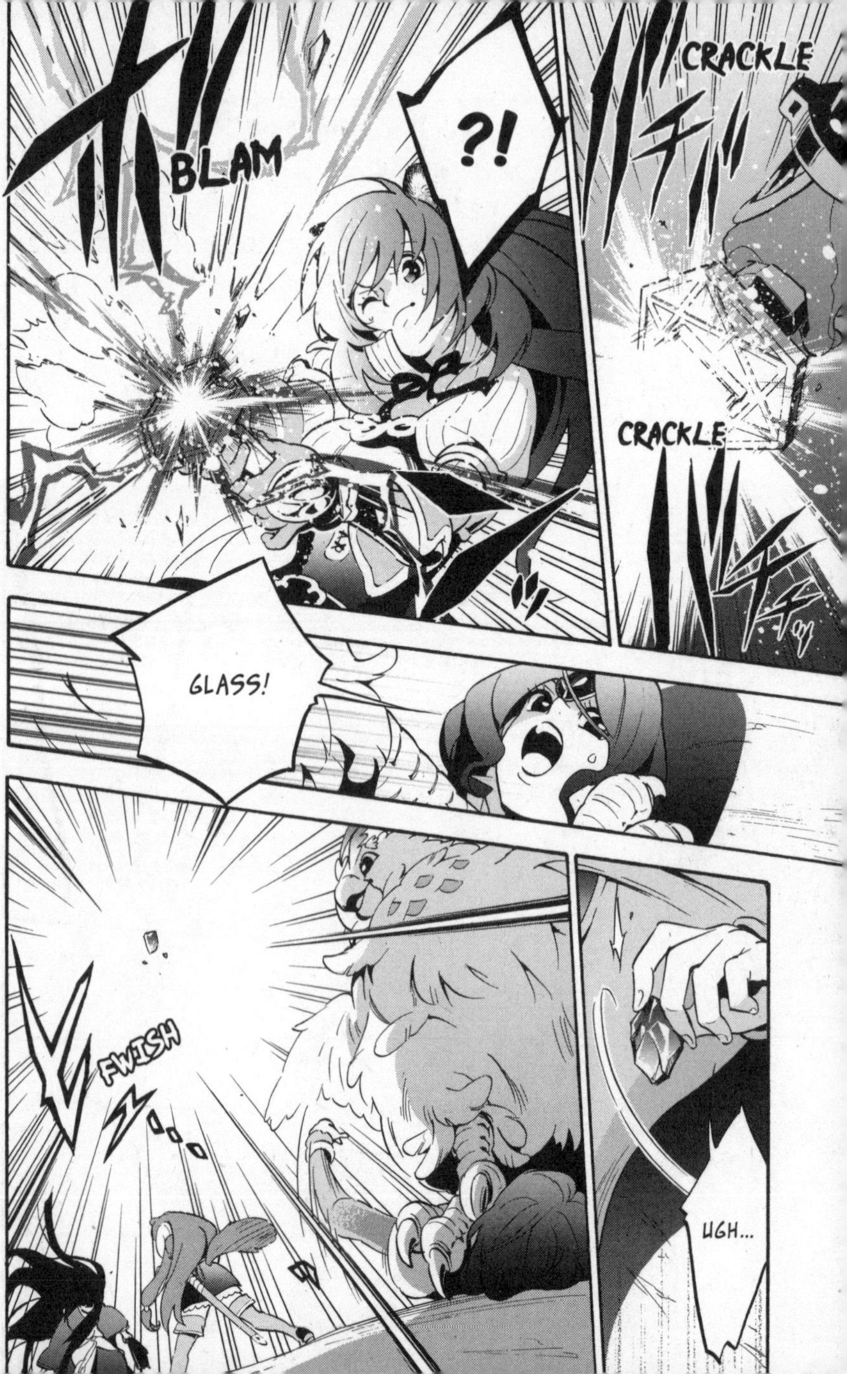
CRACKLE
CRACKLE
?!
BLAM
GLASS!
UGH...
FWISH

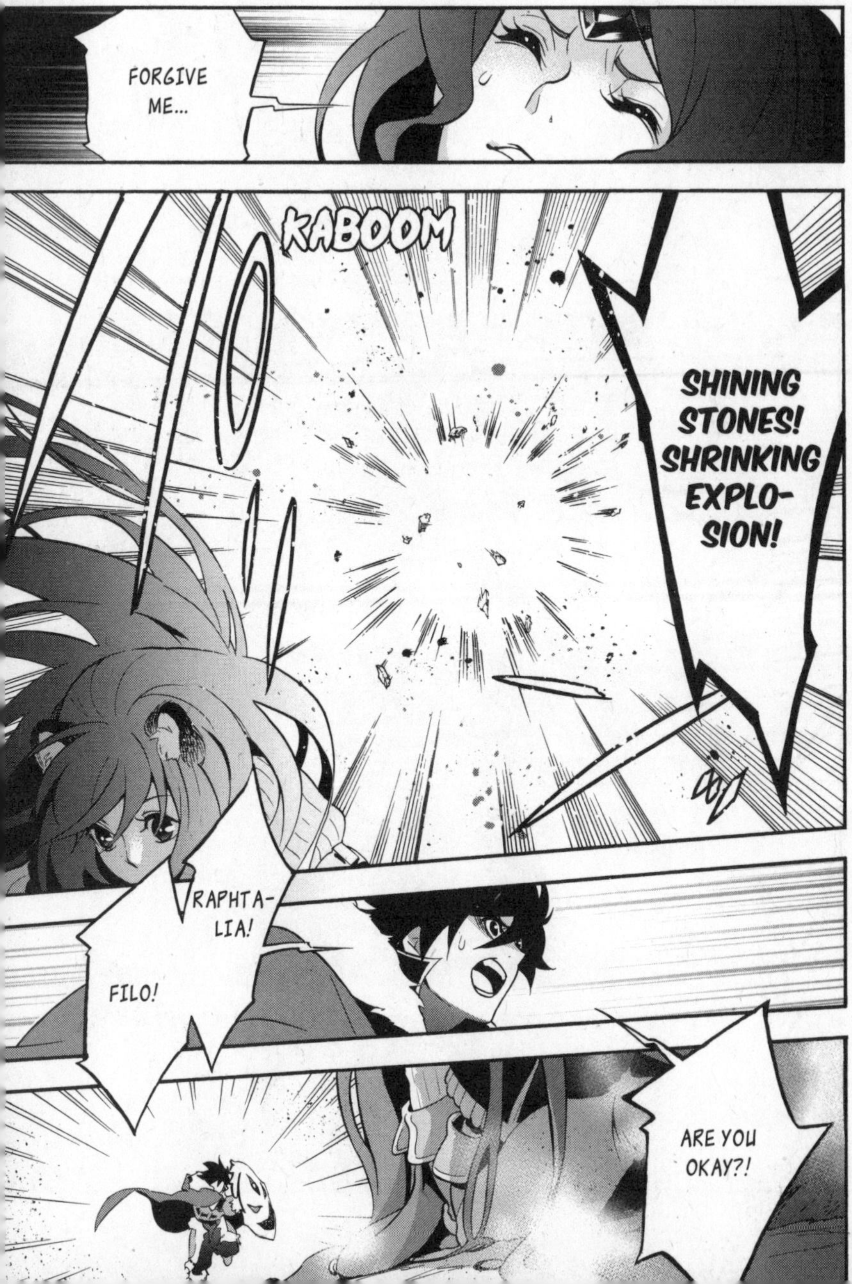
FORGIVE ME...
SHINING STONES! SHRINKING EXPLO-SION!
KABOOM
RAPHTA-LIA!
FILO!
ARE YOU OKAY?!

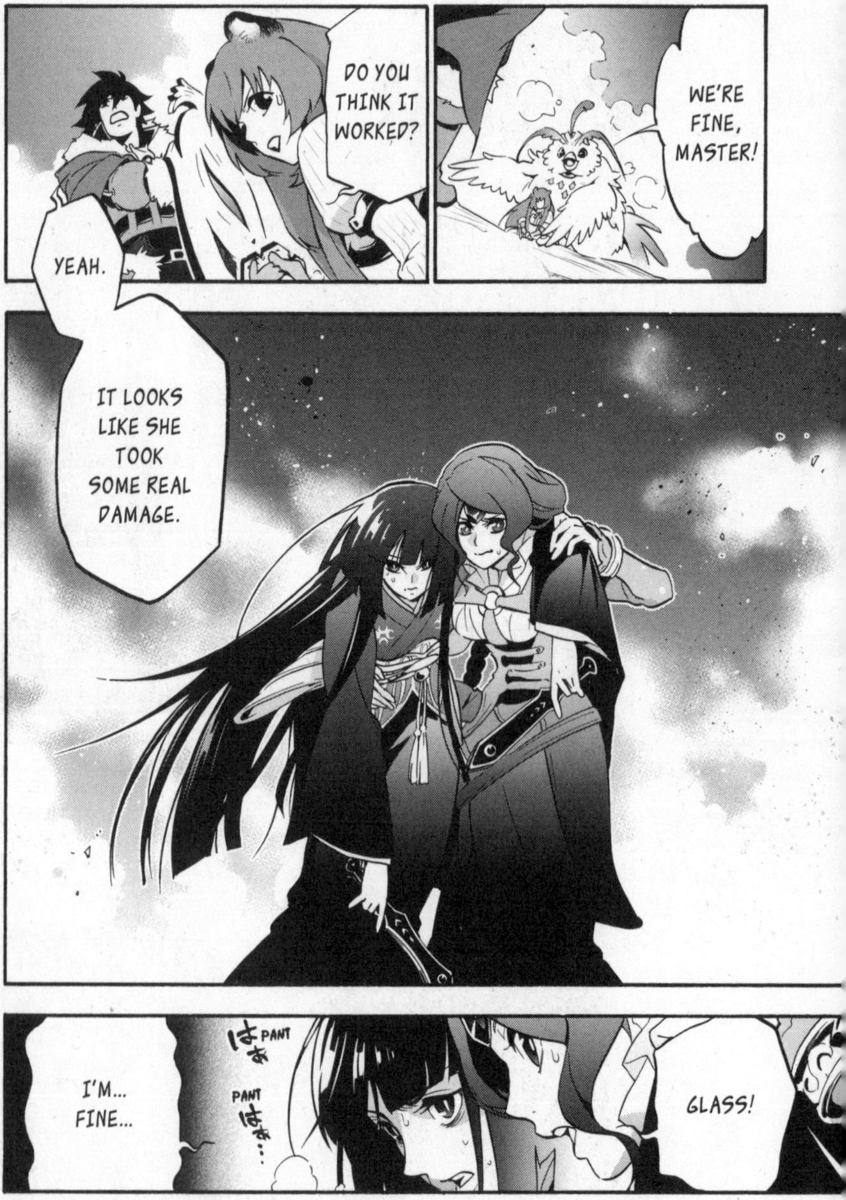
WE'RE FINE, MASTER!
DO YOU THINK IT WORKED?
YEAH.
IT LOOKS LIKE SHE TOOK SOME REAL DAMAGE.
GLASS!
はぁ PANT
はぁ… PANT
I'M... FINE...

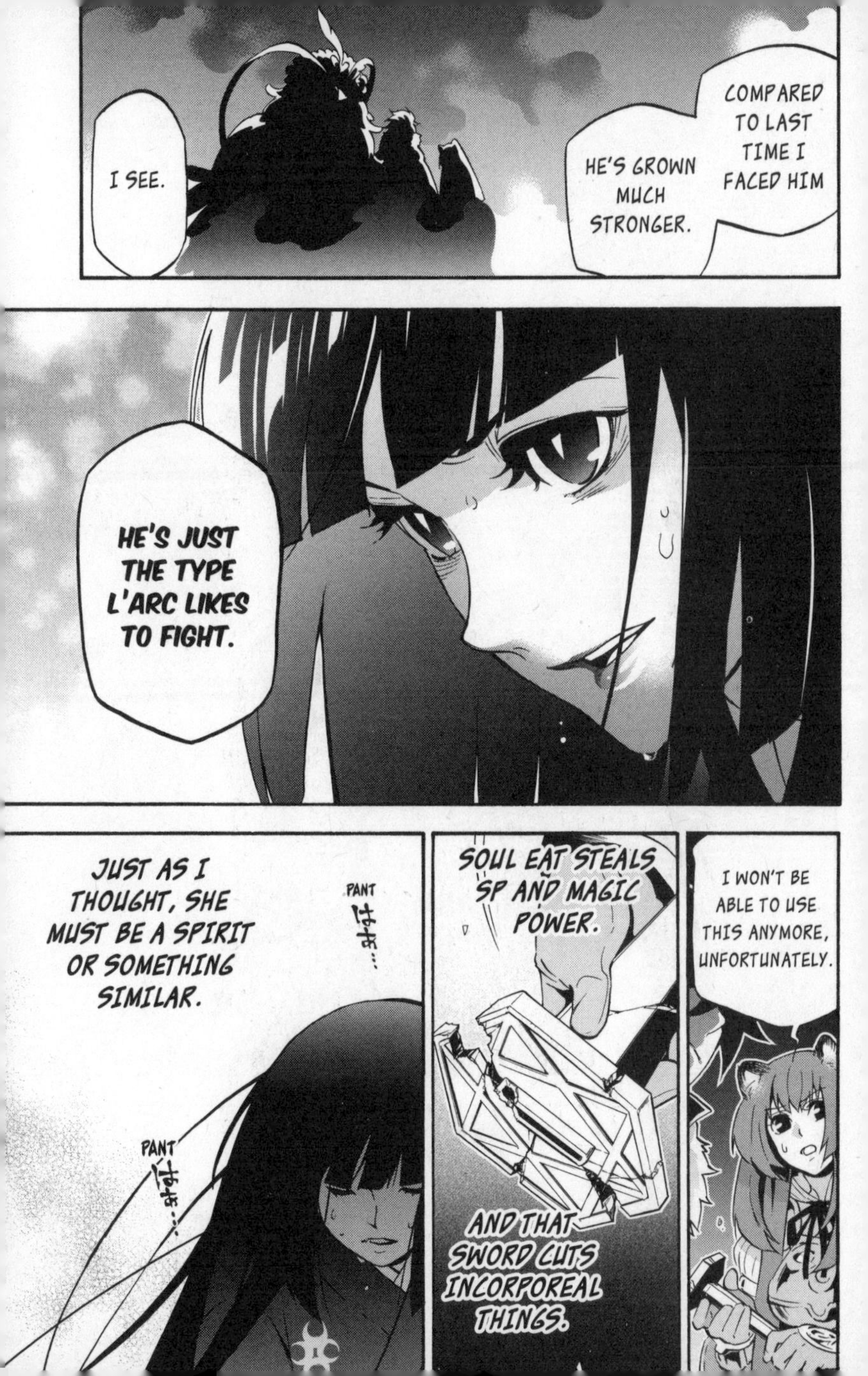
COMPARED TO LAST TIME I FACED HIM
HE'S GROWN MUCH STRONGER.
I SEE.
HE'S JUST THE TYPE L'ARC LIKES TO FIGHT.
I WON'T BE ABLE TO USE THIS ANYMORE, UNFORTUNATELY.
SOUL EAT STEALS SP AND MAGIC POWER.
AND THAT SWORD CUTS INCORPOREAL THINGS.
JUST AS I THOUGHT, SHE MUST BE A SPIRIT OR SOMETHING SIMILAR.
PANT
PANT

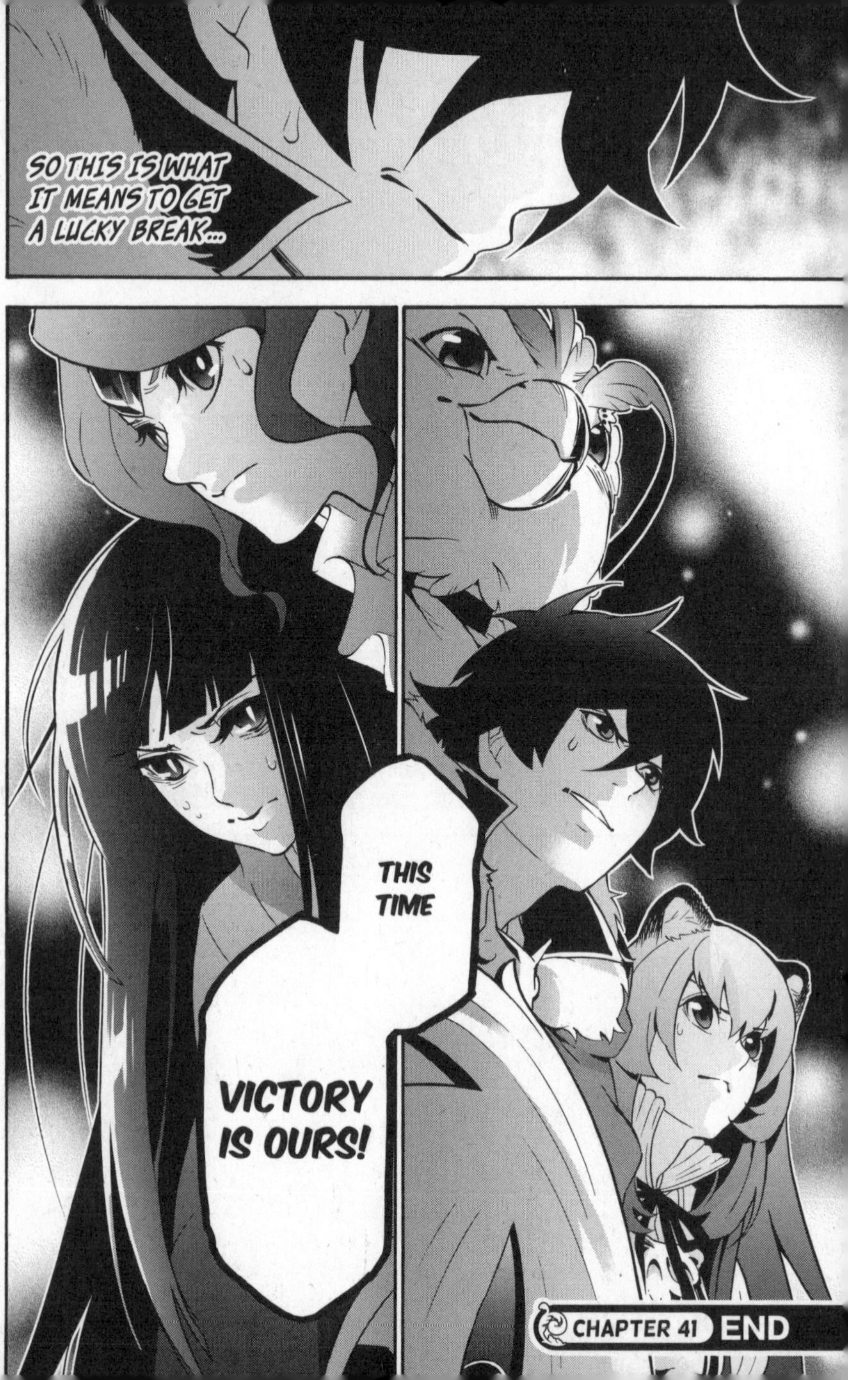
SO THIS IS WHAT IT MEANS TO GET A LUCKY BREAK...
THIS TIME
VICTORY IS OURS!
CHAPTER 41 END

# THE RISING OF THE SHIELD HERO

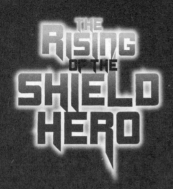

THE RISING OF THE SHIELD HERO

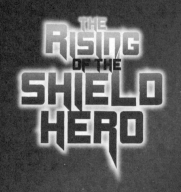

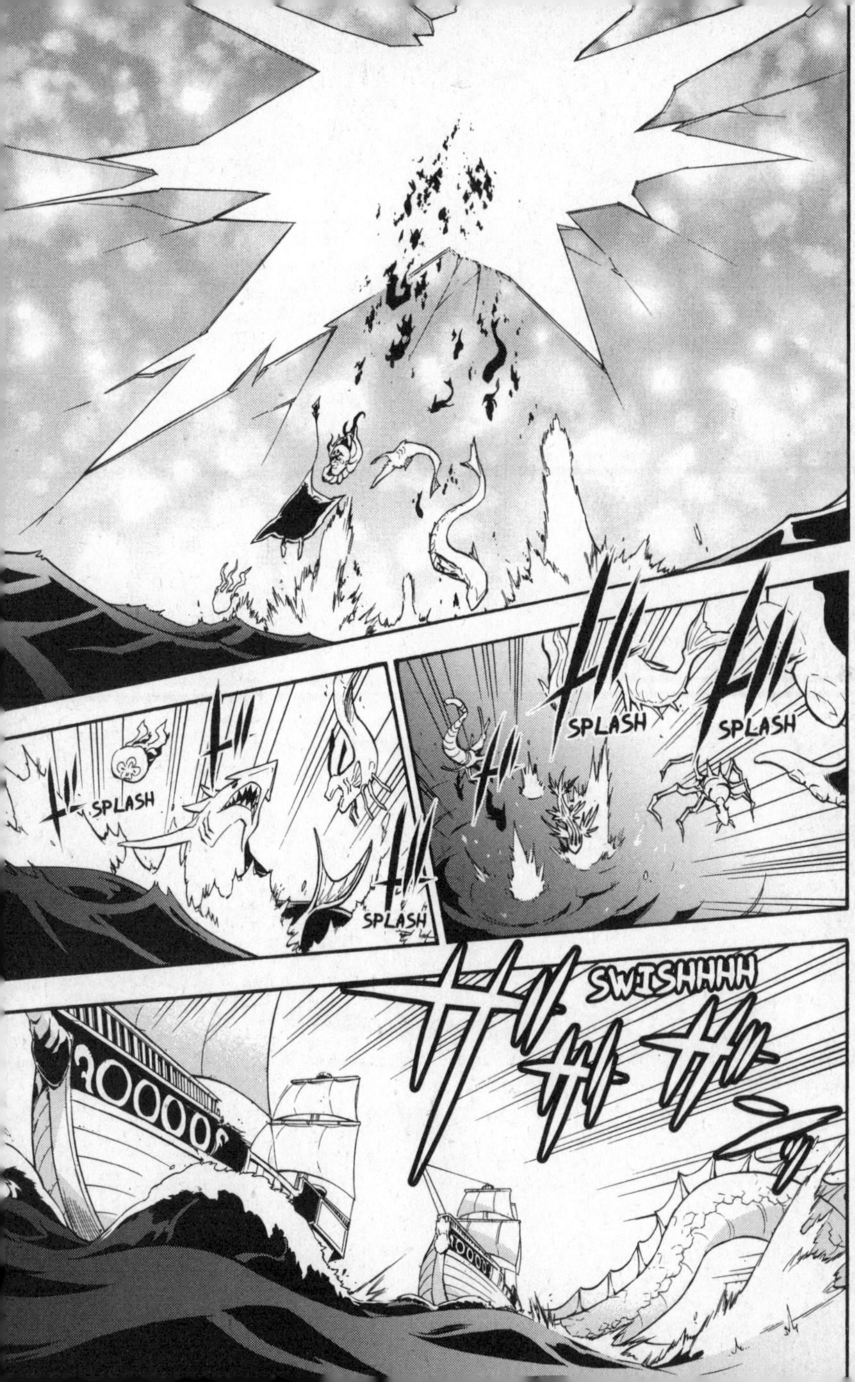
SPLASH
SPLASH
SPLASH
SPLASH
SWISHHHH

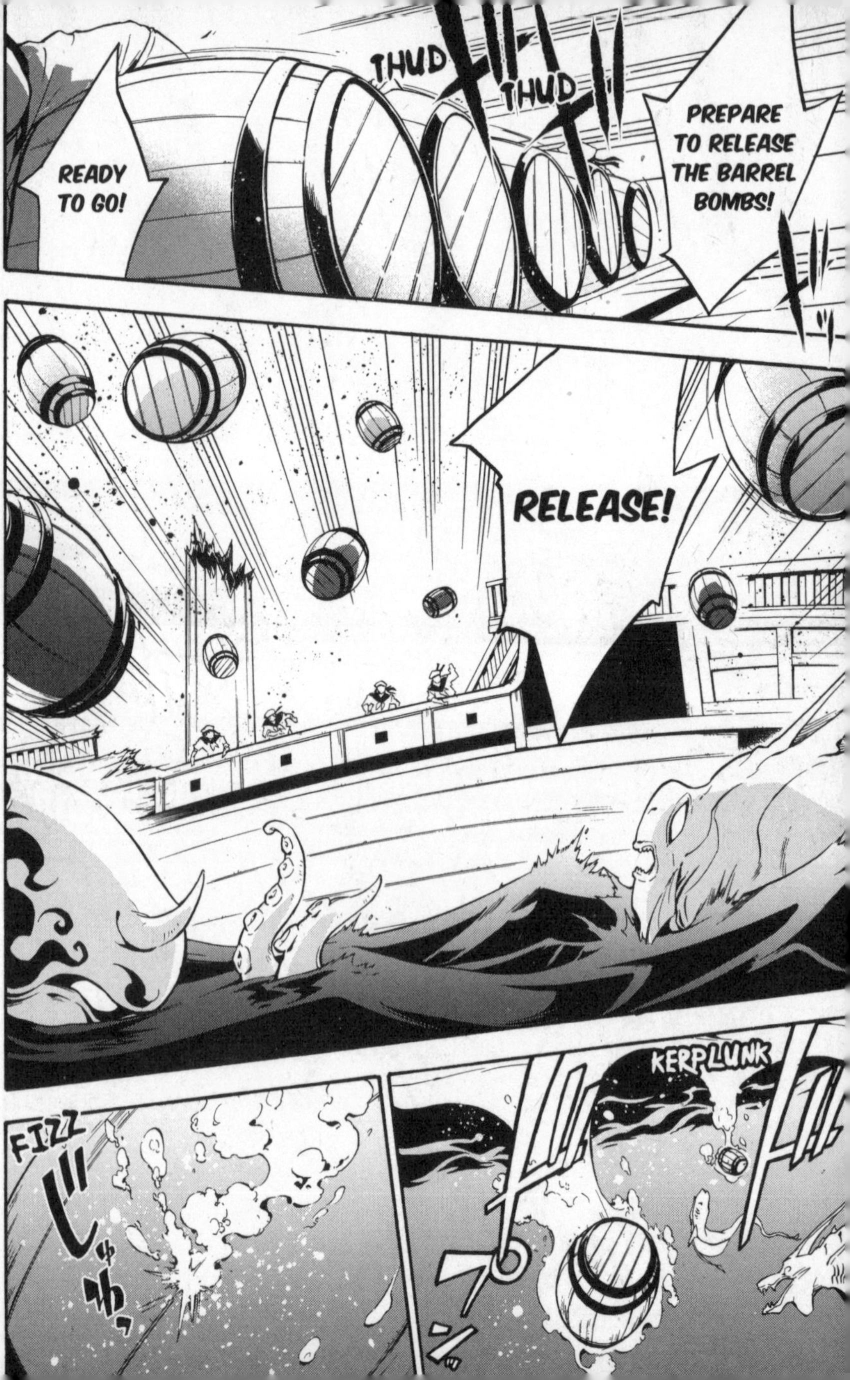
PREPARE TO RELEASE THE BARREL BOMBS!
THUD
THUD
READY TO GO!
RELEASE!
KERPLUNK
FIZZ

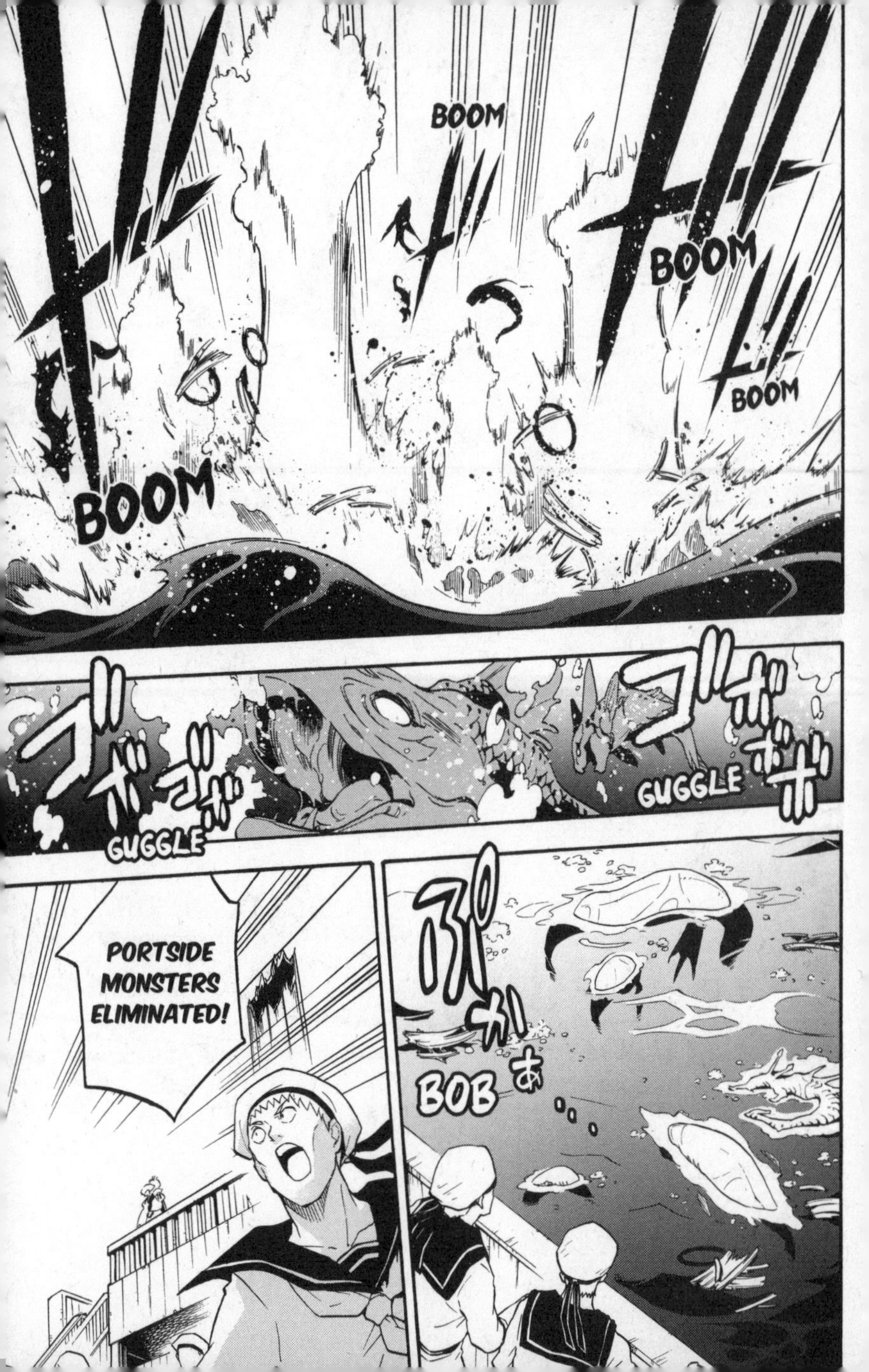
BOOM
BOOM
BOOM
BOOM
ゴボボボ
GUGGLE
ゴボゴボ
GUGGLE
ぷかあ
BOB
PORTSIDE MONSTERS ELIMINATED!

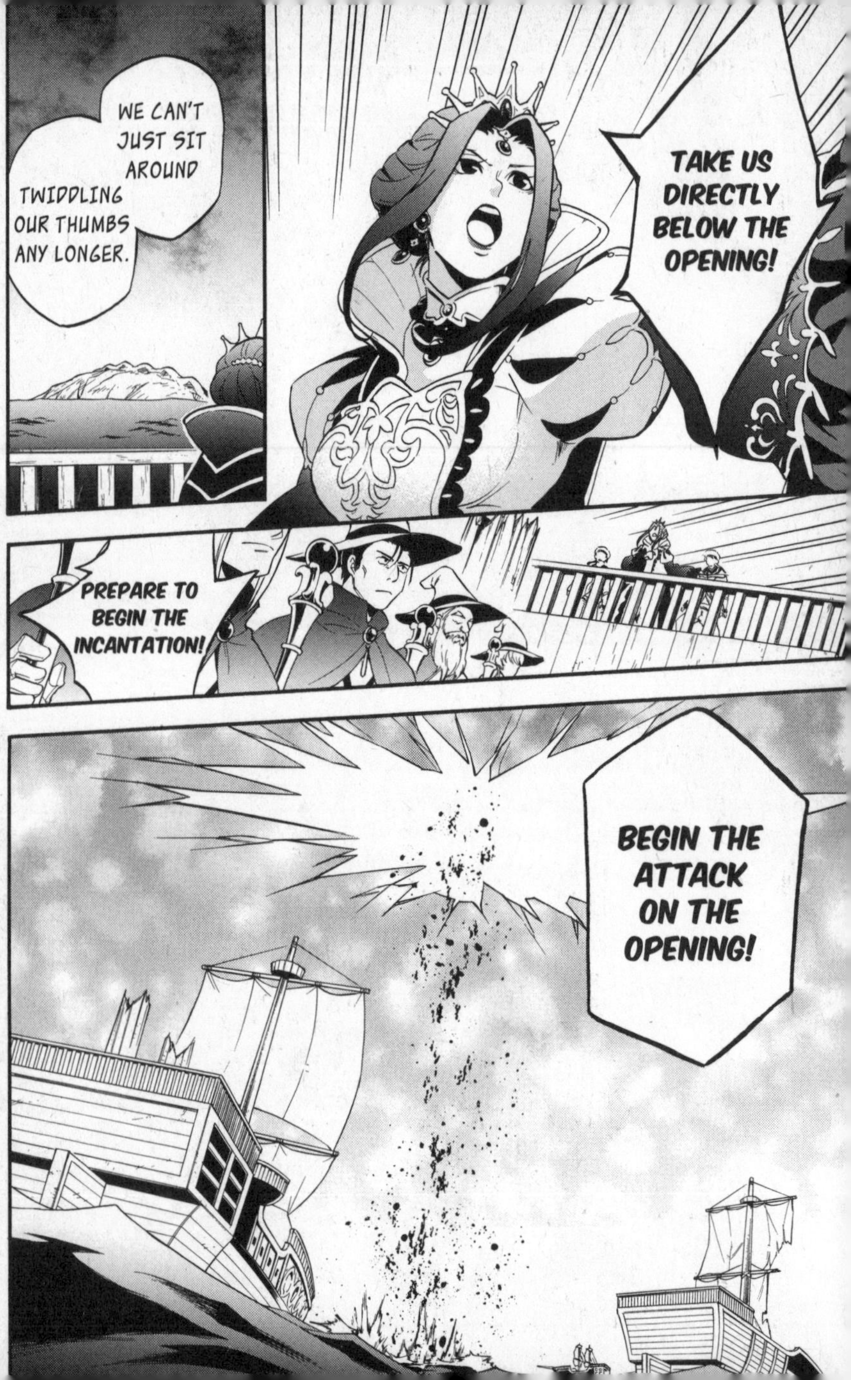
TAKE US DIRECTLY BELOW THE OPENING!
WE CAN'T JUST SIT AROUND TWIDDLING OUR THUMBS ANY LONGER.
PREPARE TO BEGIN THE INCANTATION!
BEGIN THE ATTACK ON THE OPENING!

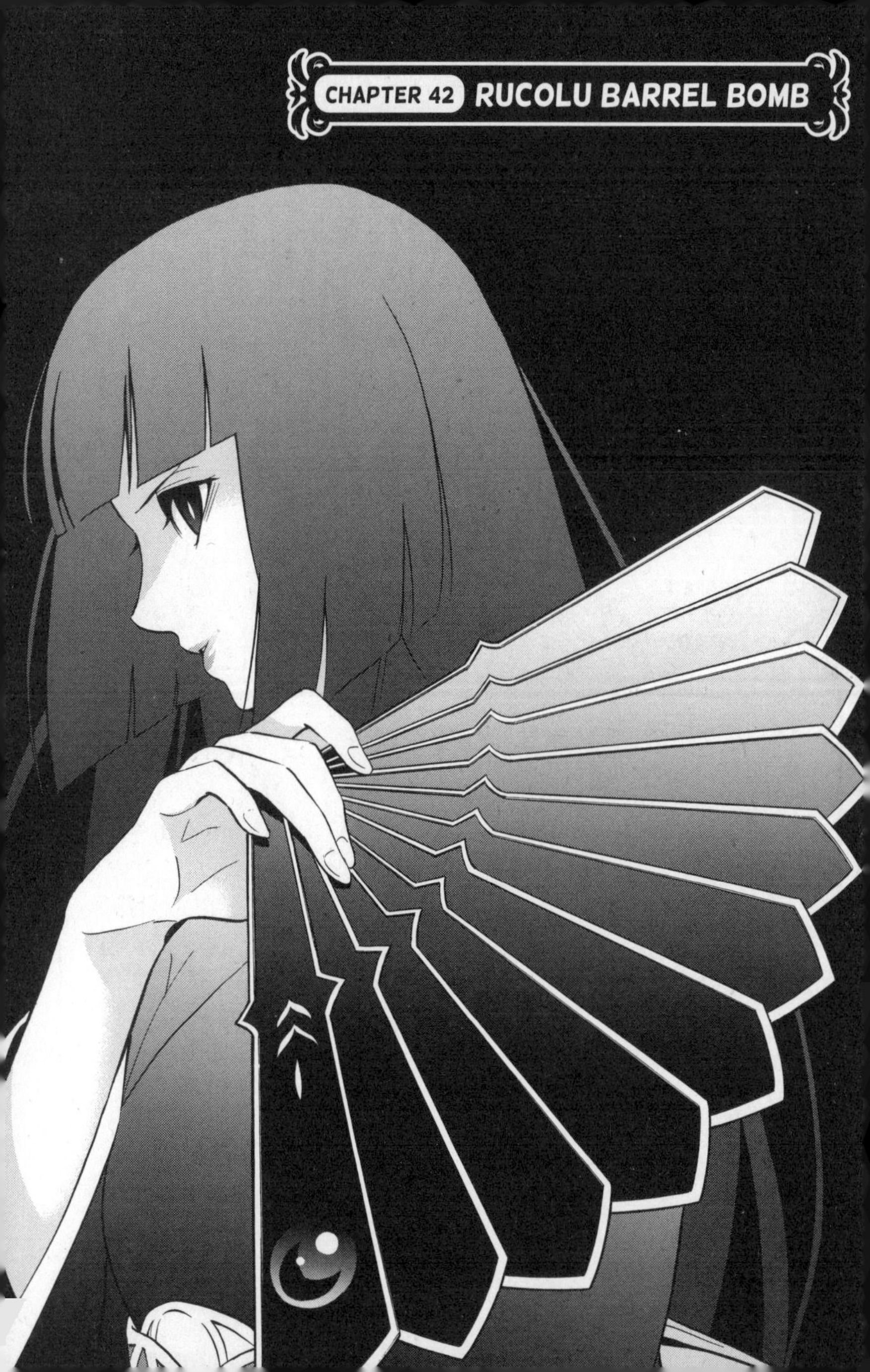
CHAPTER 42 RUCOLU BARREL BOMB

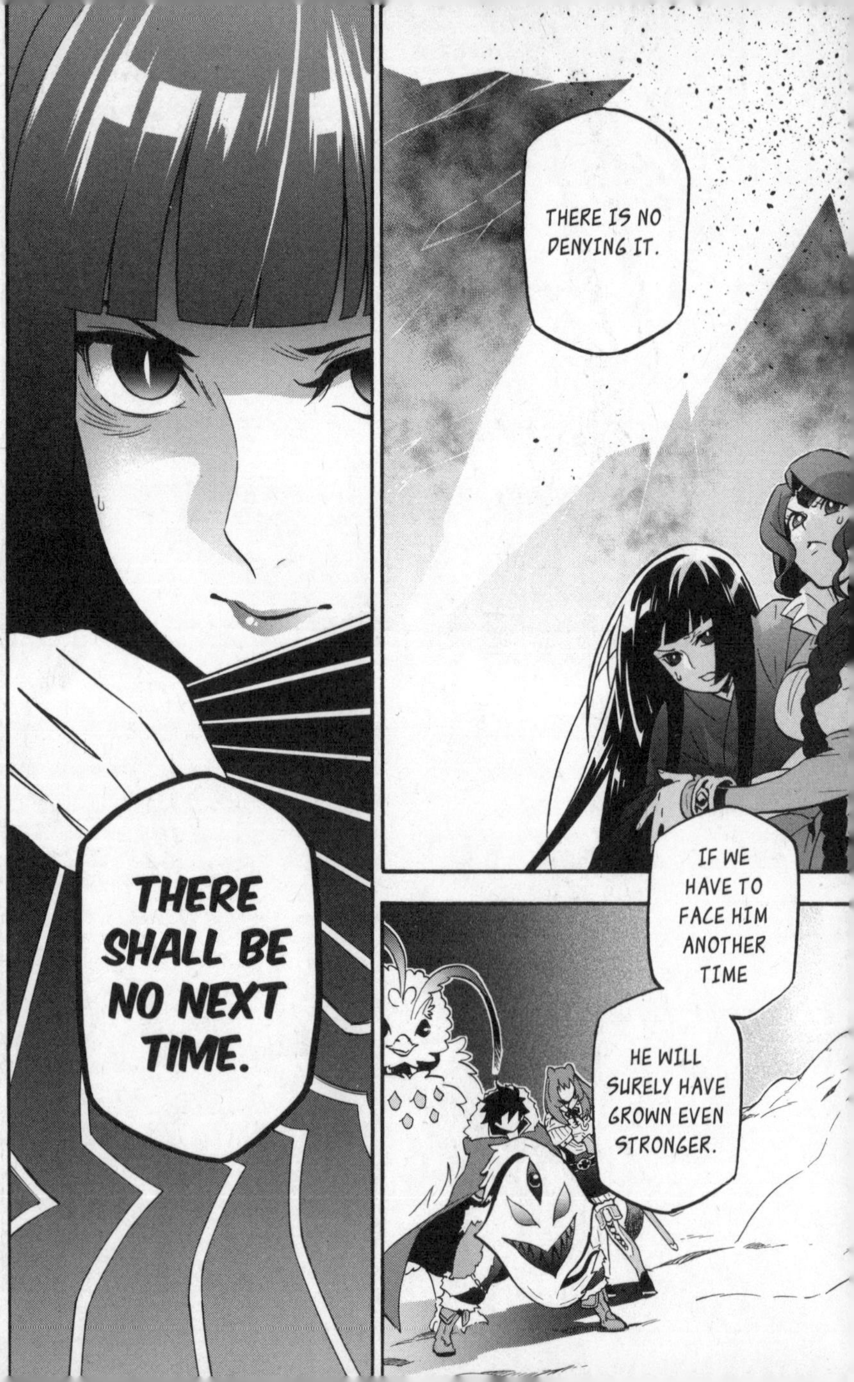
THERE IS NO DENYING IT.
IF WE HAVE TO FACE HIM ANOTHER TIME
HE WILL SURELY HAVE GROWN EVEN STRONGER.
THERE SHALL BE NO NEXT TIME.

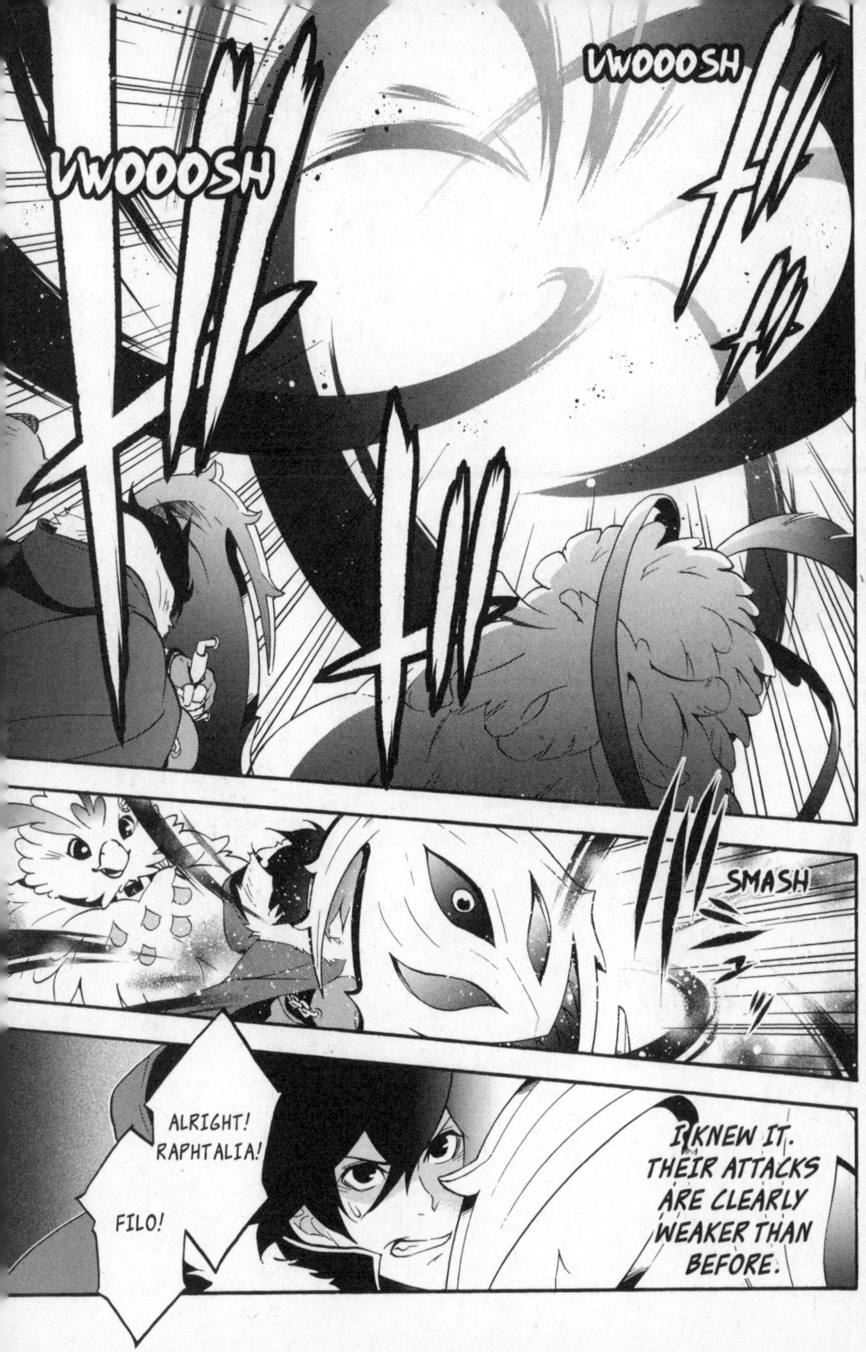
VWOOOSH
VWOOOSH
SMASH
I KNEW IT. THEIR ATTACKS ARE CLEARLY WEAKER THAN BEFORE.
ALRIGHT! RAPHTALIA!
FILO!

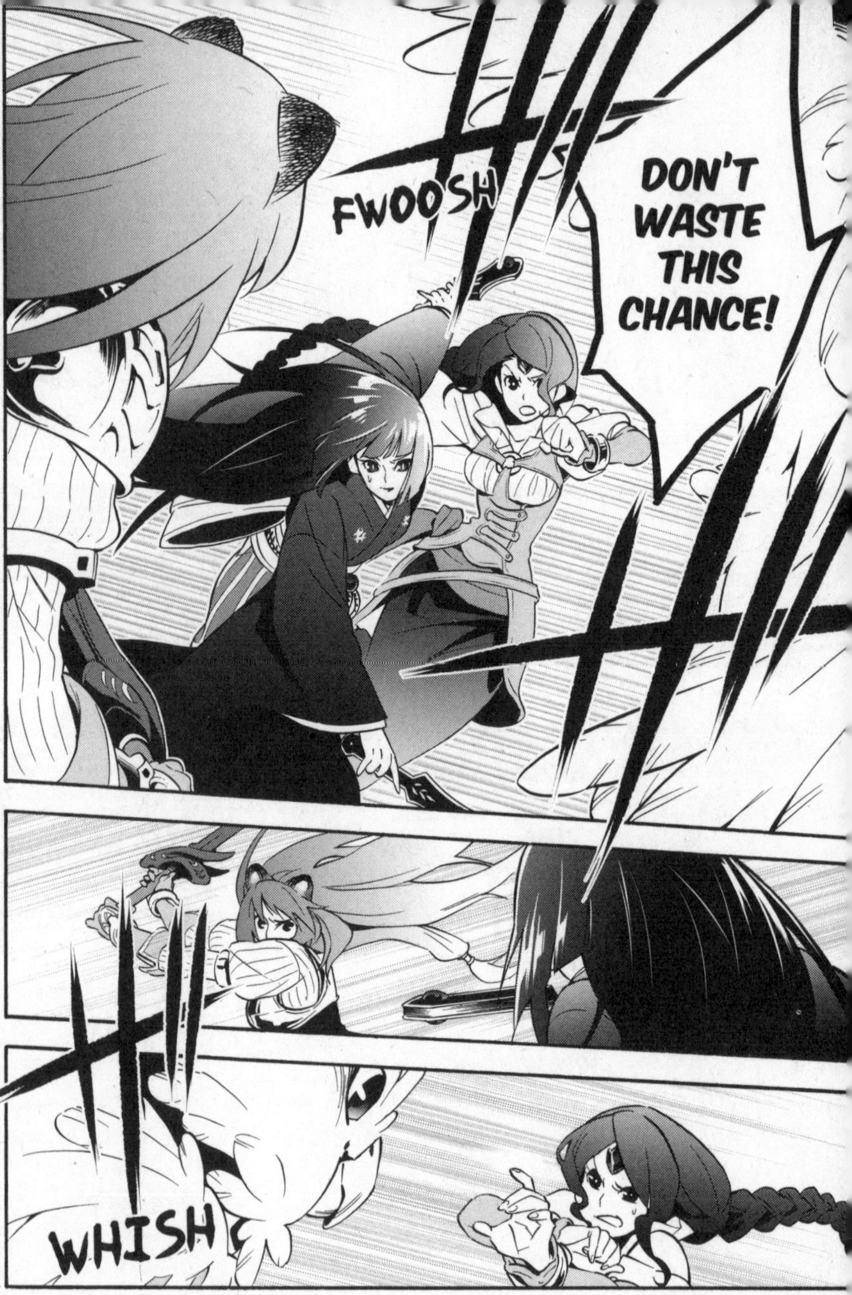
DON'T WASTE THIS CHANCE!
FWOOSH
WHISH

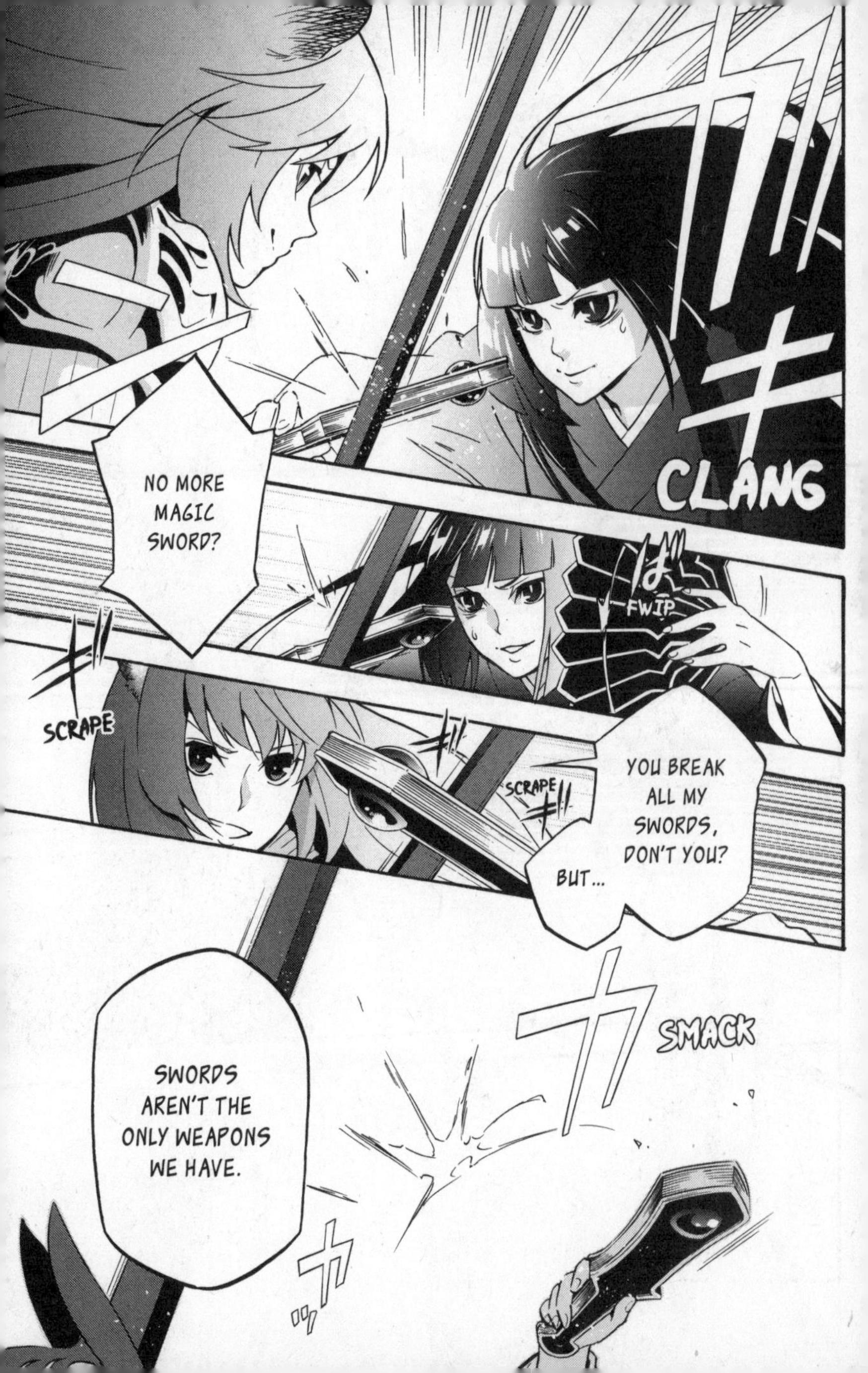
CLANG
NO MORE MAGIC SWORD?
FWIP
SCRAPE
SCRAPE
YOU BREAK ALL MY SWORDS, DON'T YOU?
BUT...
SMACK
SWORDS AREN'T THE ONLY WEAPONS WE HAVE.

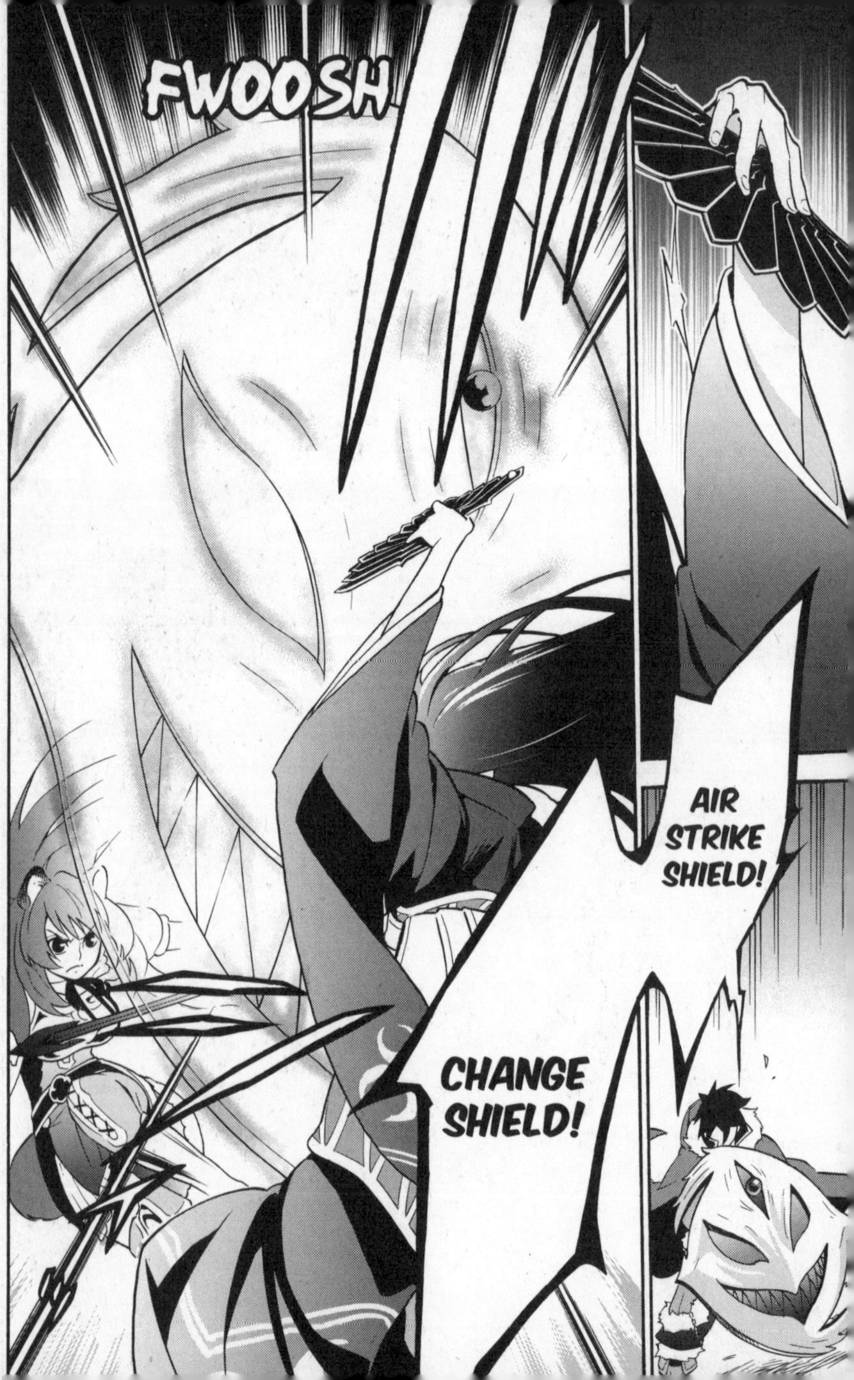
FWOOSH
AIR STRIKE SHIELD!
CHANGE SHIELD!

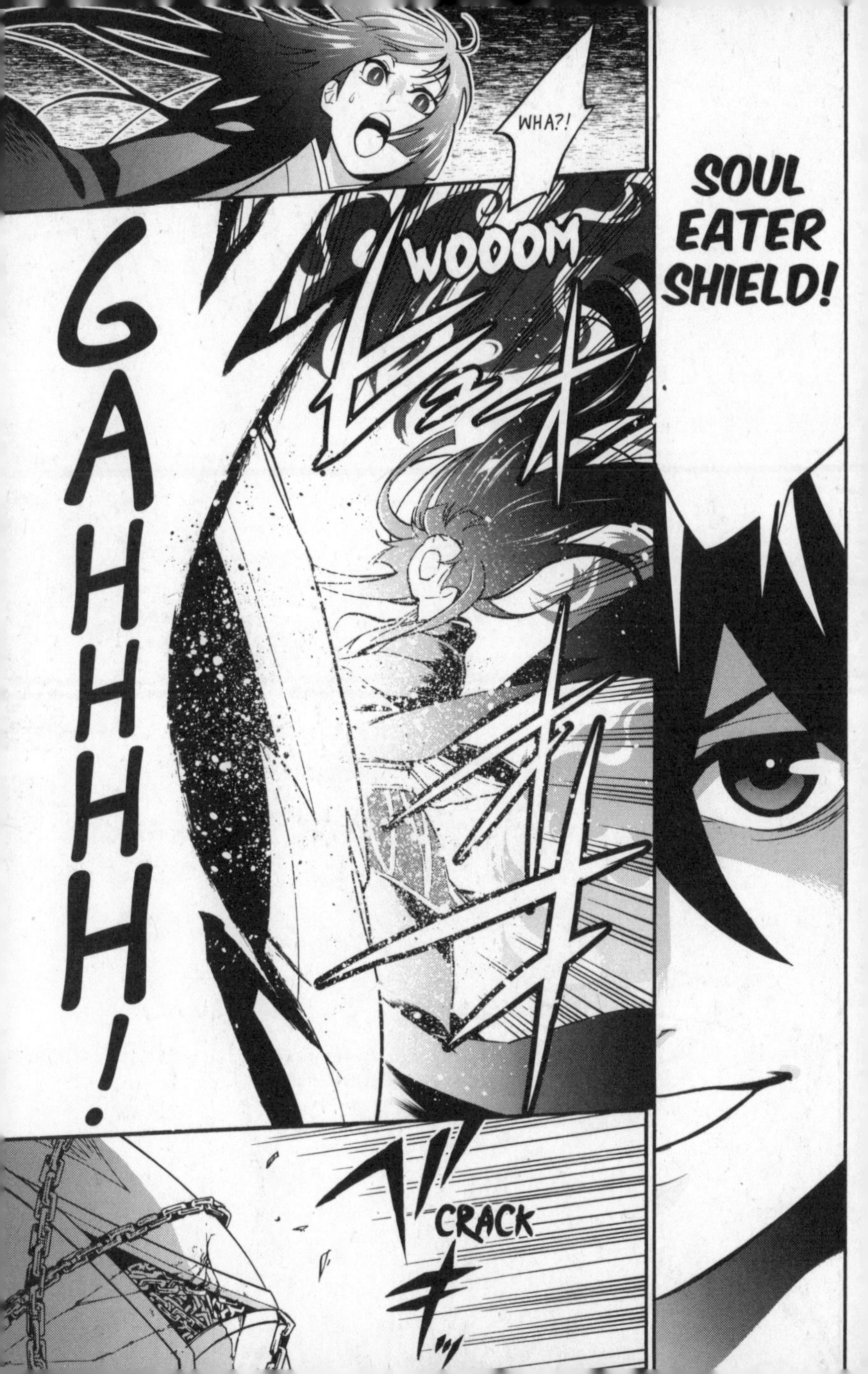
SOUL EATER SHIELD!
WHA?!
WOOOM
GAHHHH!
CRACK

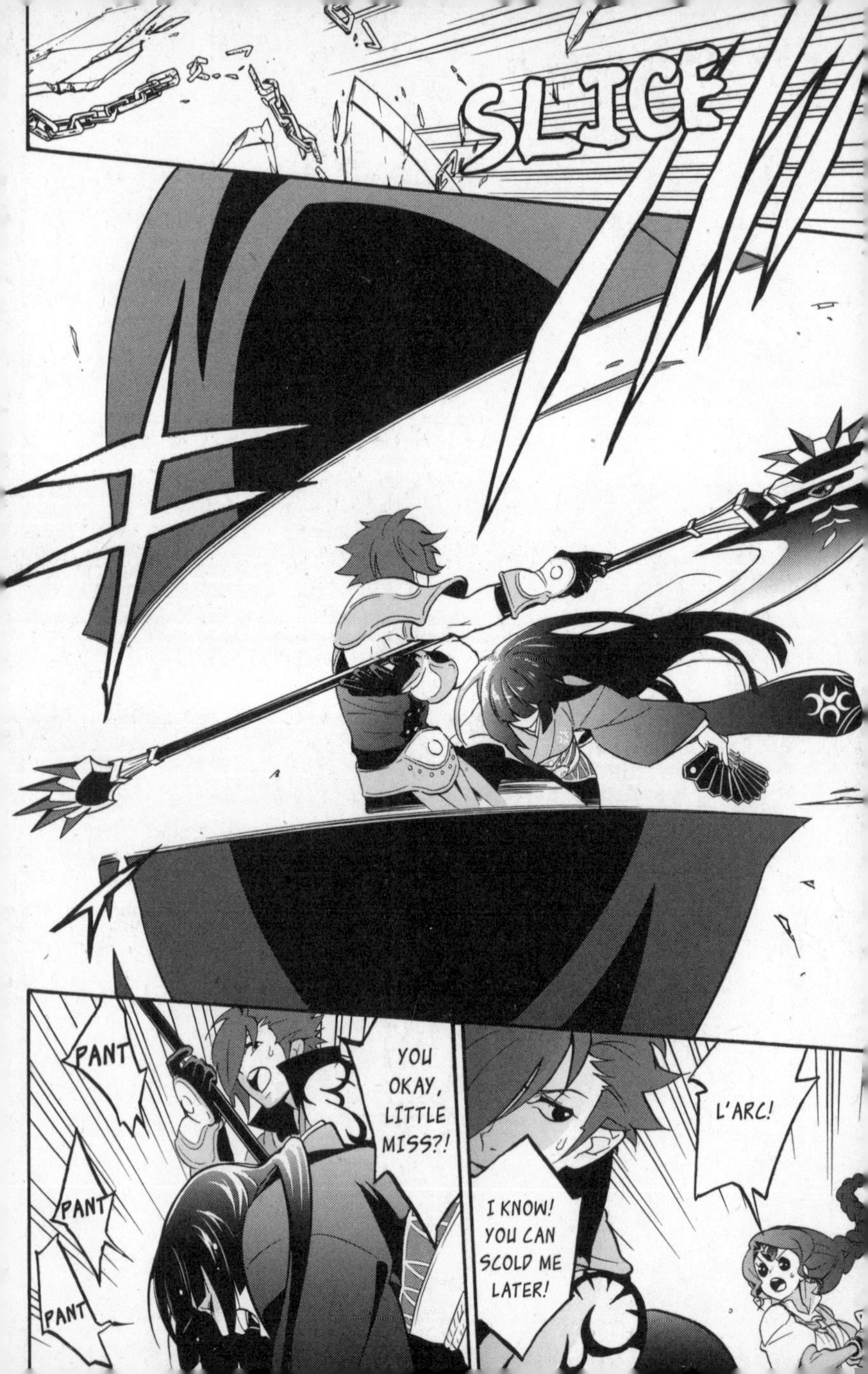
SLICE
L'ARC!
I KNOW! YOU CAN SCOLD ME LATER!
YOU OKAY, LITTLE MISS?!
PANT
PANT
PANT

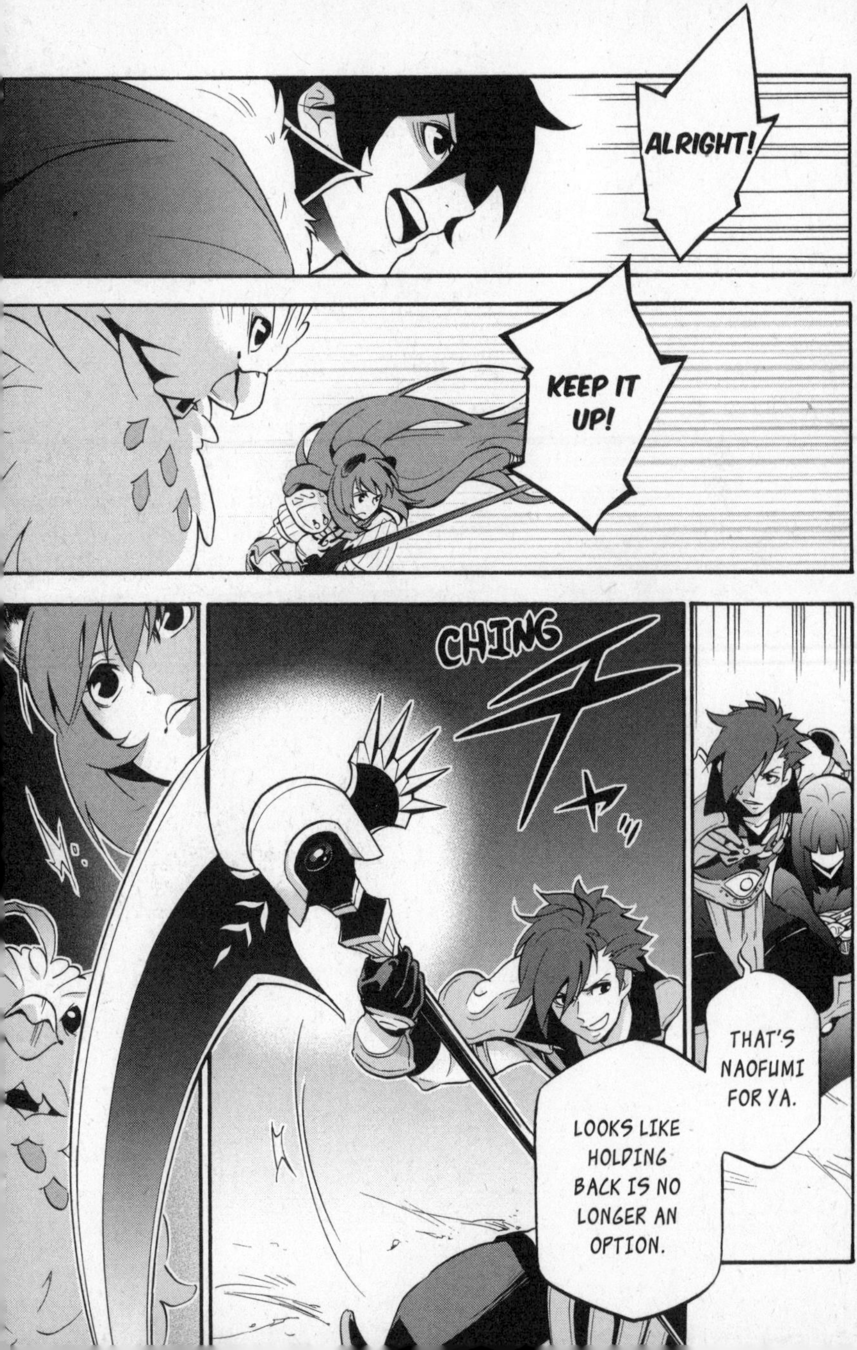
ALRIGHT!
KEEP IT UP!
THAT'S NAOFUMI FOR YA.
CHING
LOOKS LIKE HOLDING BACK IS NO LONGER AN OPTION.

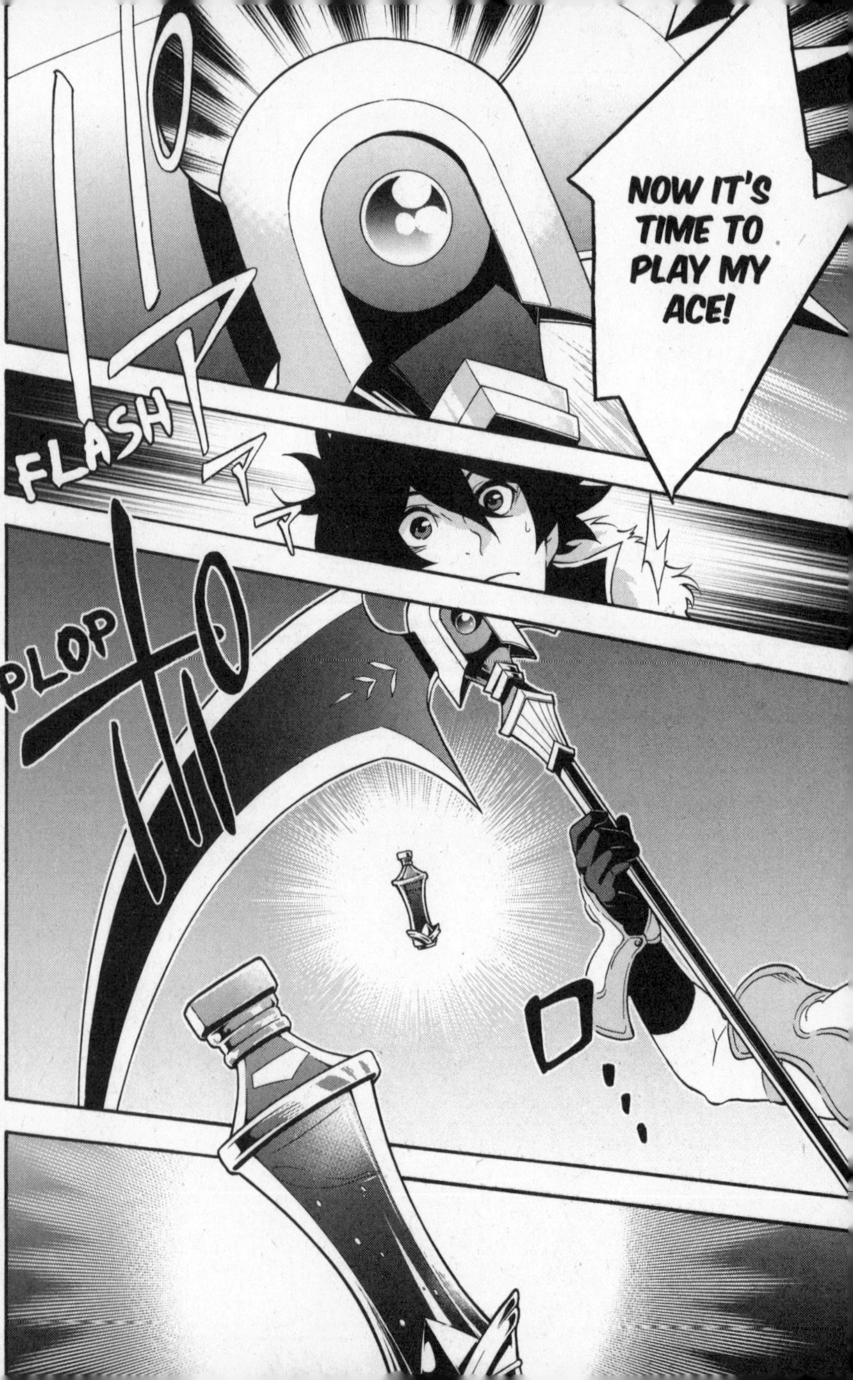
NOW IT'S TIME TO PLAY MY ACE!
FLASH
PLOP

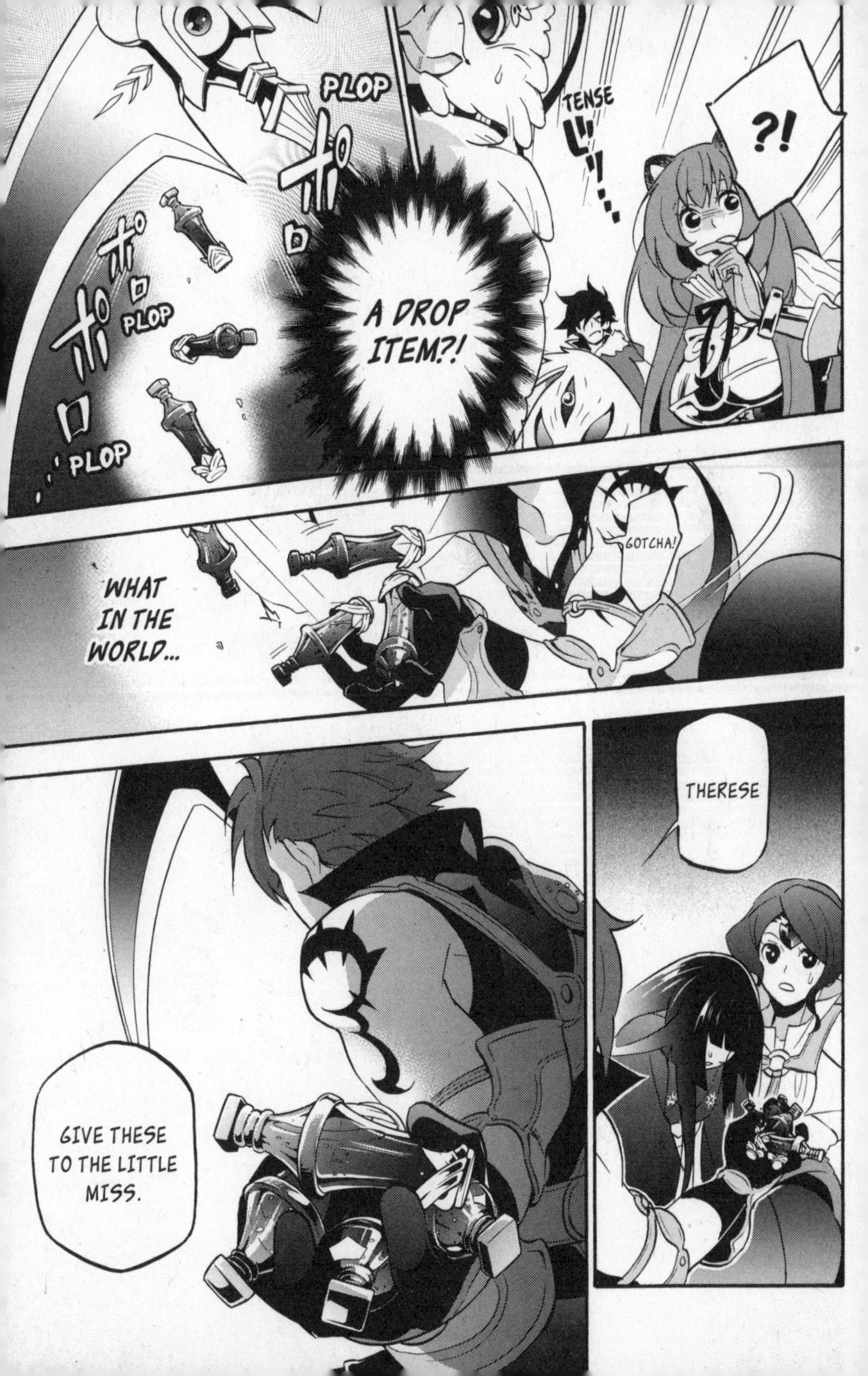
?!
TENSE
PLOP
A DROP ITEM?!
PLOP
PLOP
GOTCHA!
WHAT IN THE WORLD...
THERESE
GIVE THESE TO THE LITTLE MISS.

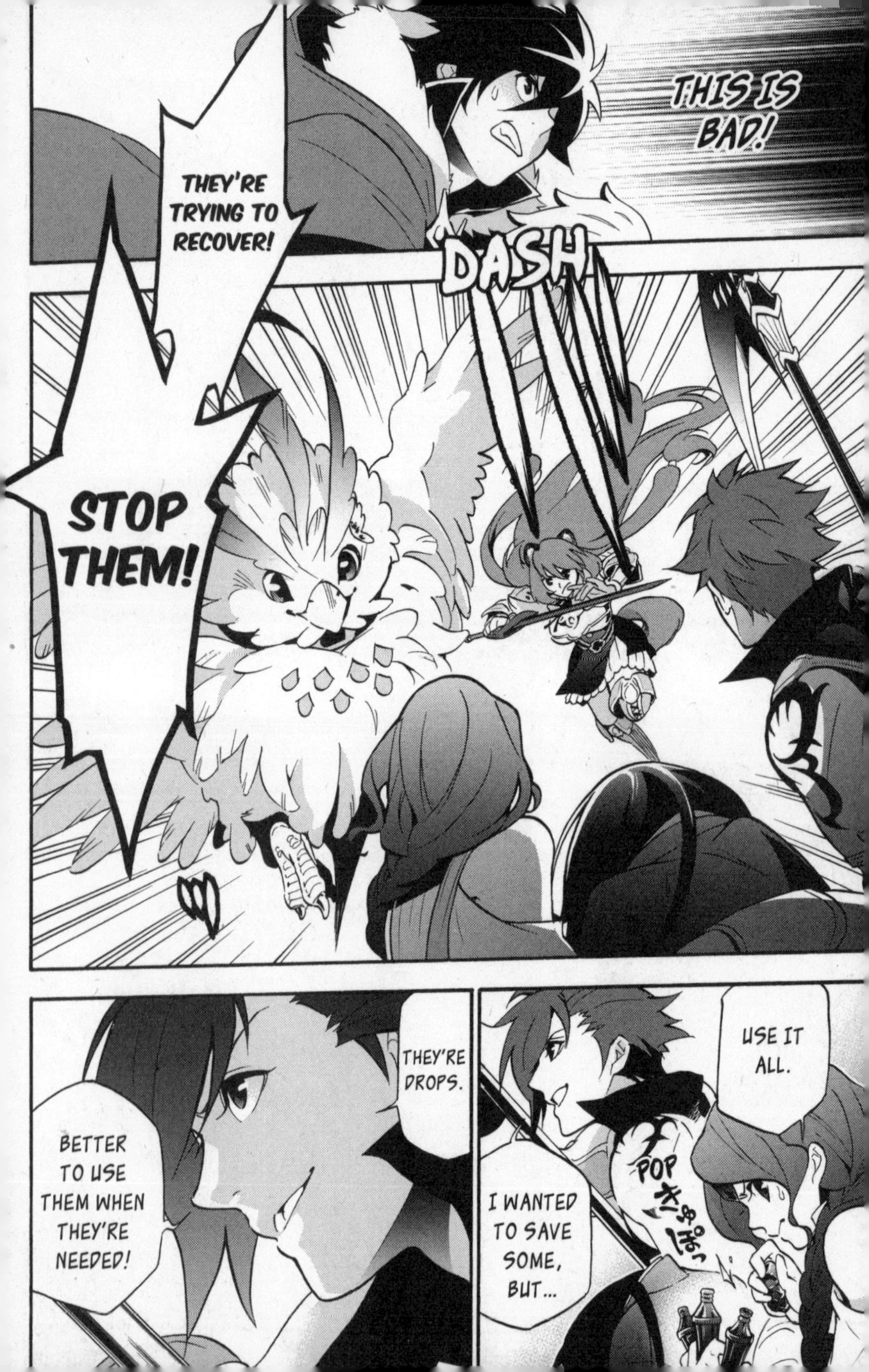
THIS IS BAD!
THEY'RE TRYING TO RECOVER!
DASH
STOP THEM!
USE IT ALL.
I WANTED TO SAVE SOME, BUT...
POP
きゅぽっ
THEY'RE DROPS.
BETTER TO USE THEM WHEN THEY'RE NEEDED!

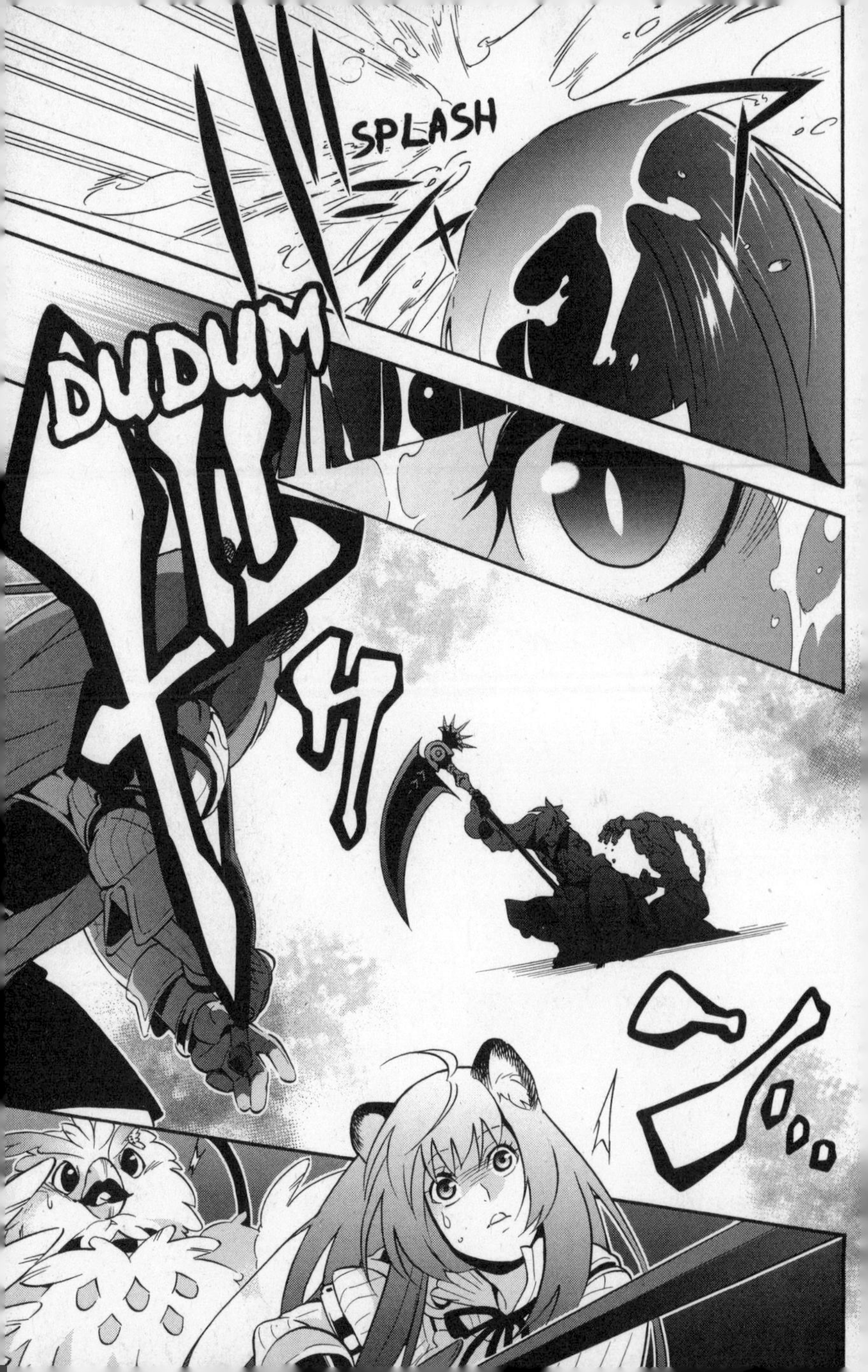
SPLASH
DUDUM

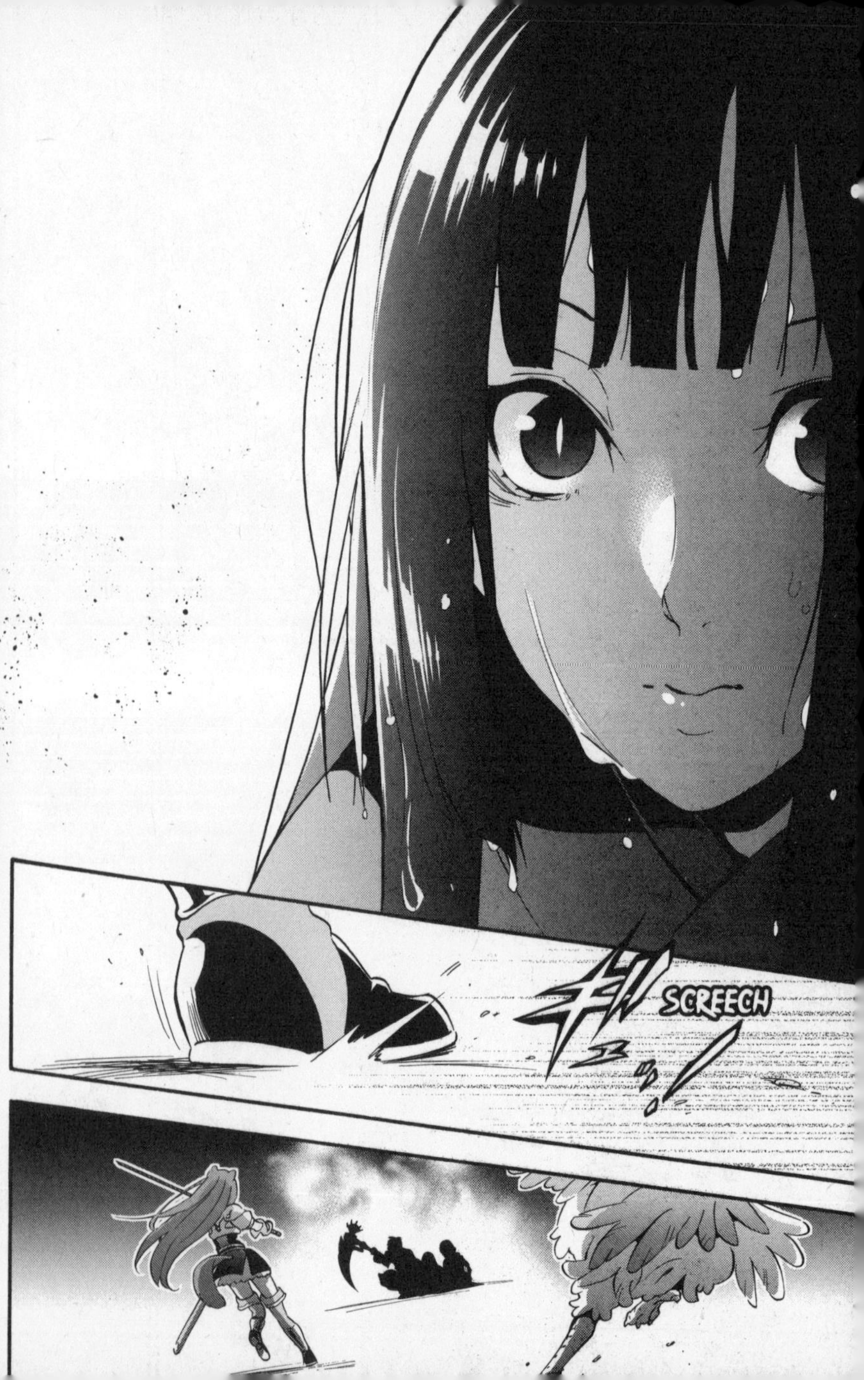
SCREECH

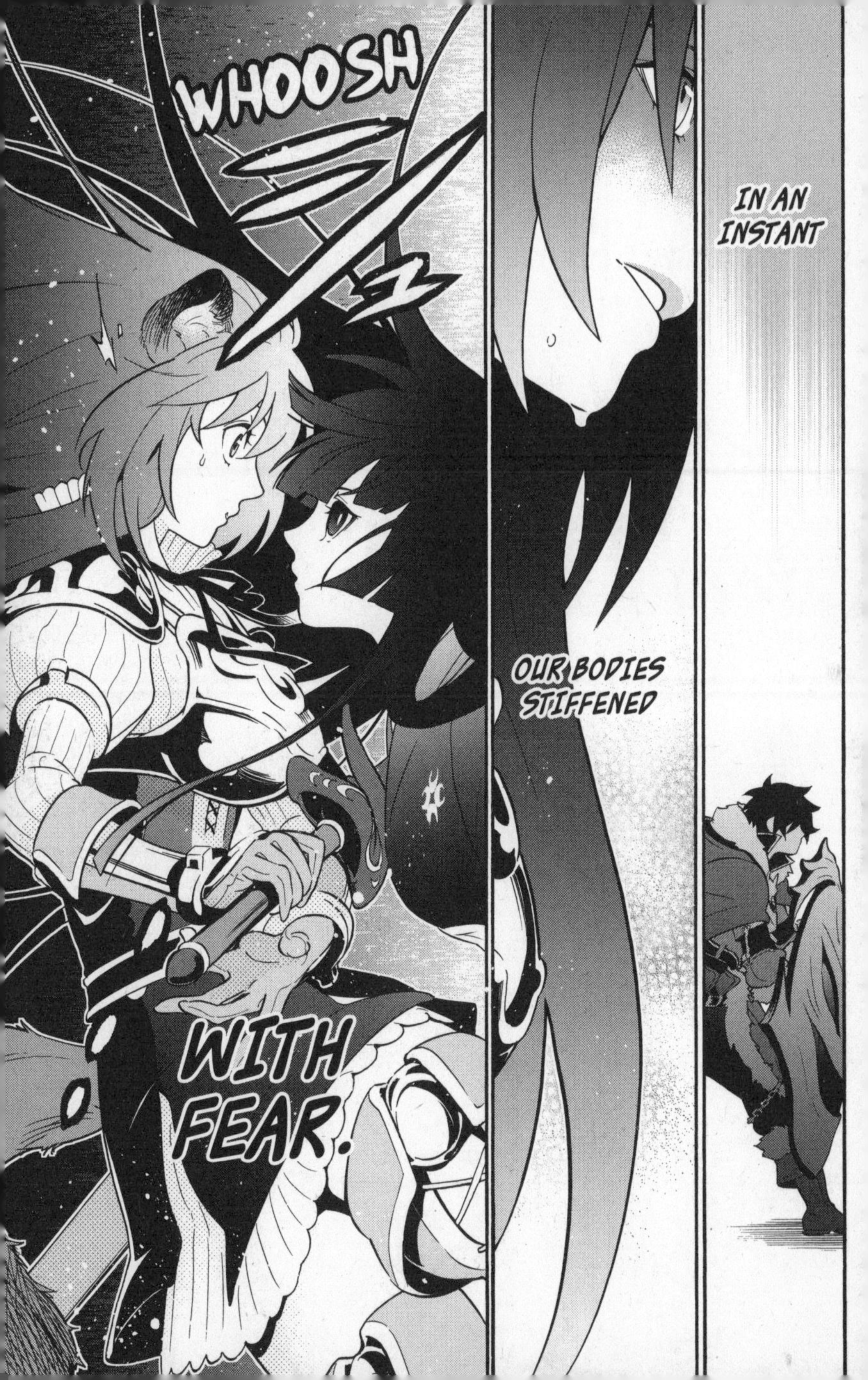
IN AN INSTANT
OUR BODIES STIFFENED
WHOOSH
WITH FEAR.

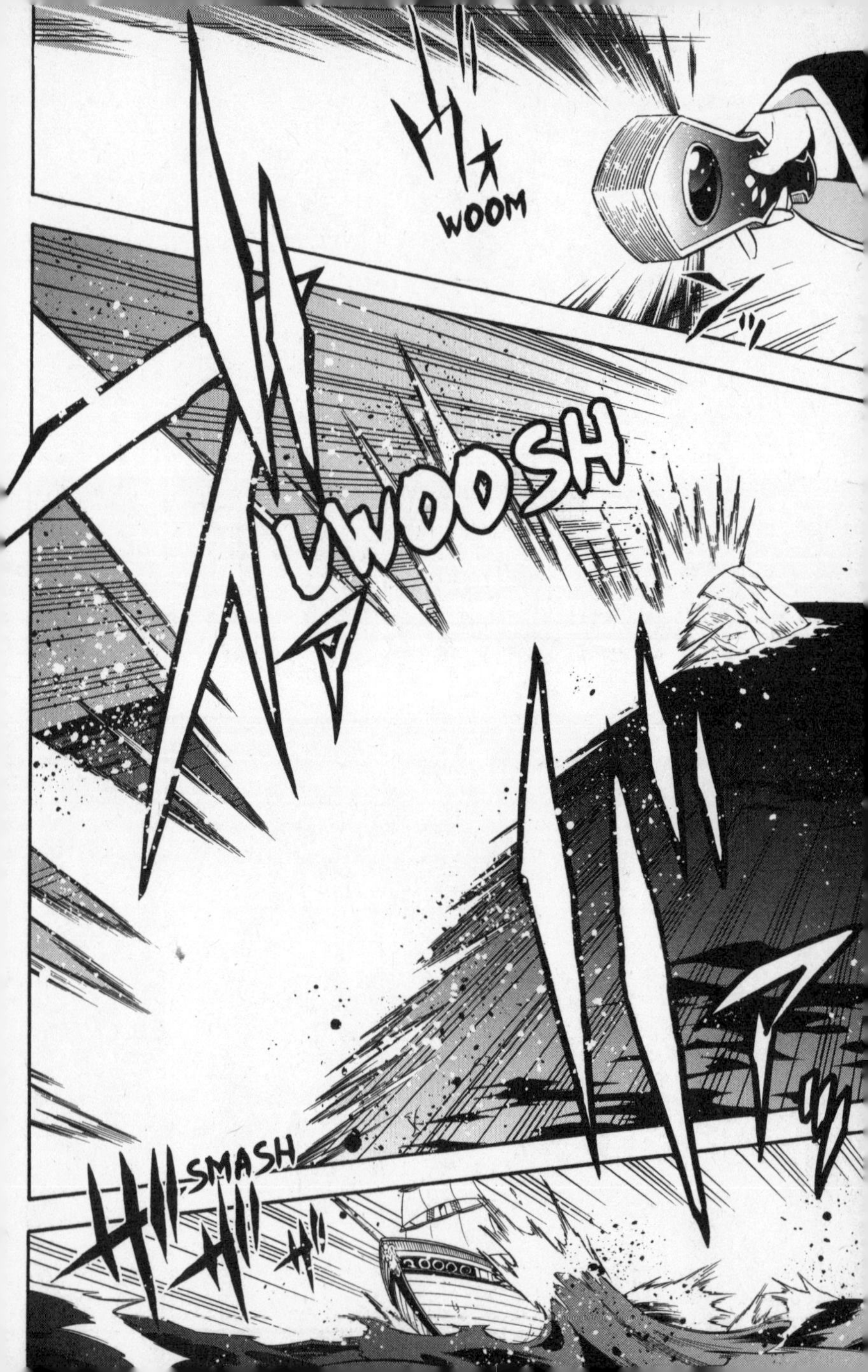
WOOM
WOOSH
SMASH

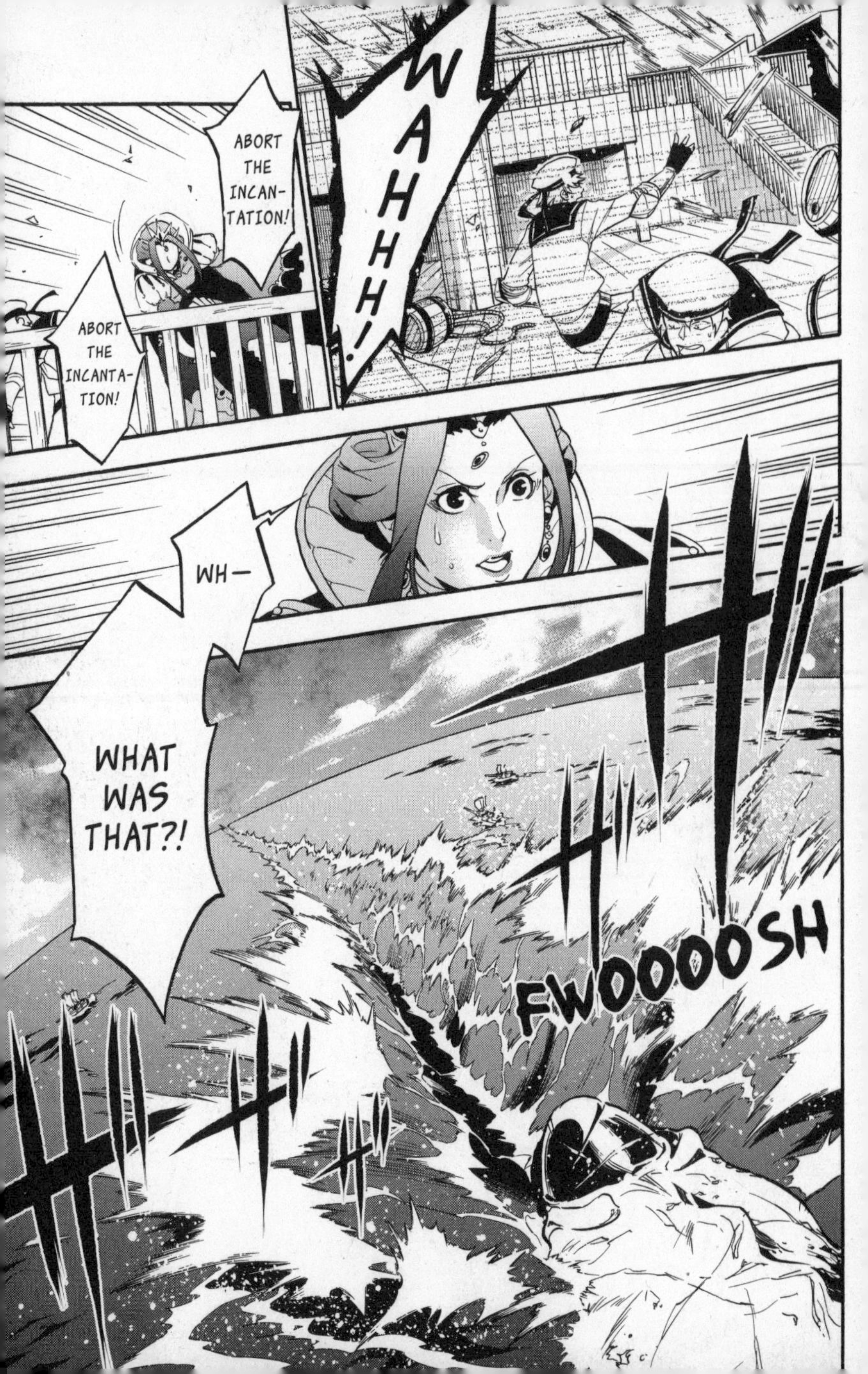
WAHHH!
ABORT THE INCAN-TATION!
ABORT THE INCANTA-TION!
WH—
WHAT WAS THAT?!
FWOOOOOSH

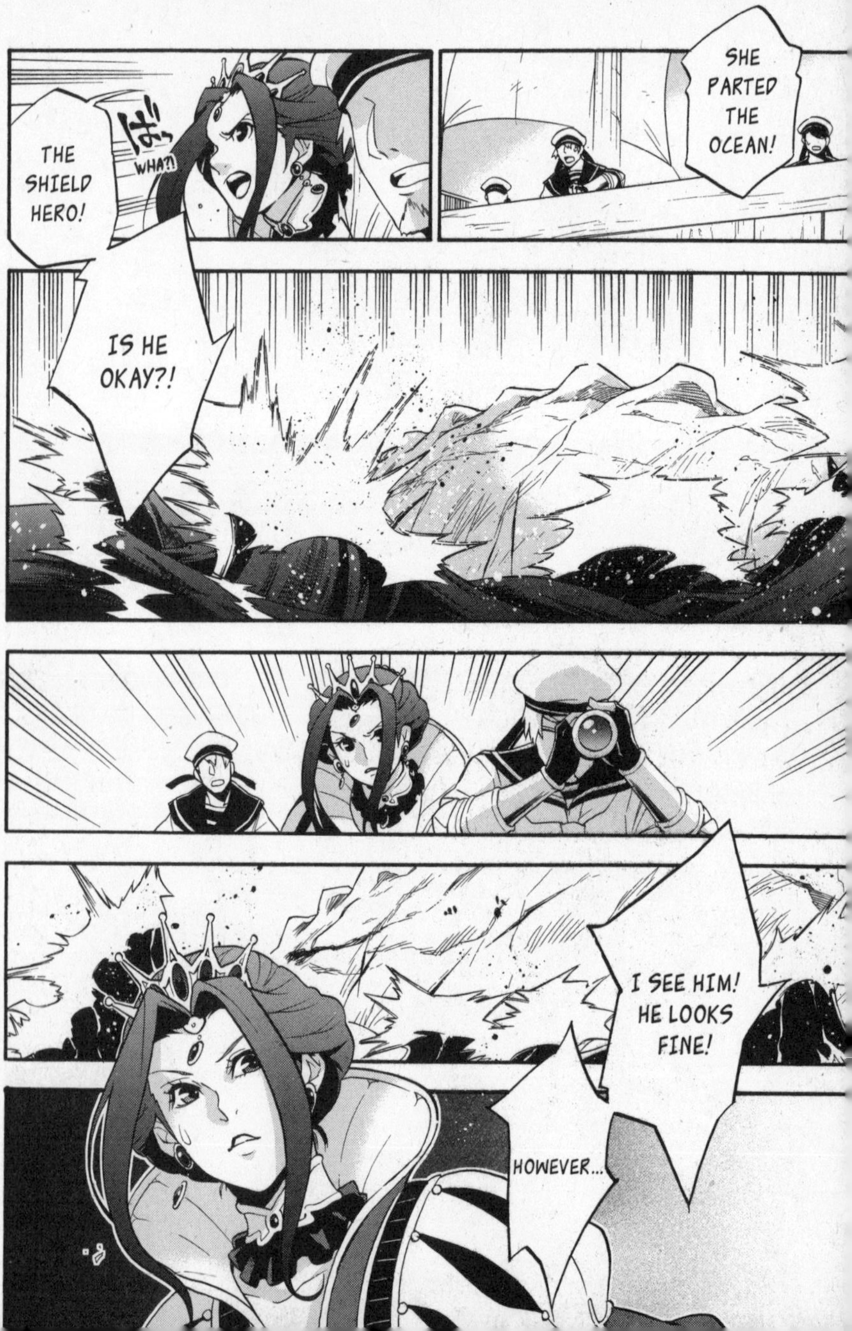
SHE PARTED THE OCEAN!
ばっ
WHA?!
THE SHIELD HERO!
IS HE OKAY?!
I SEE HIM! HE LOOKS FINE!
HOWEVER...

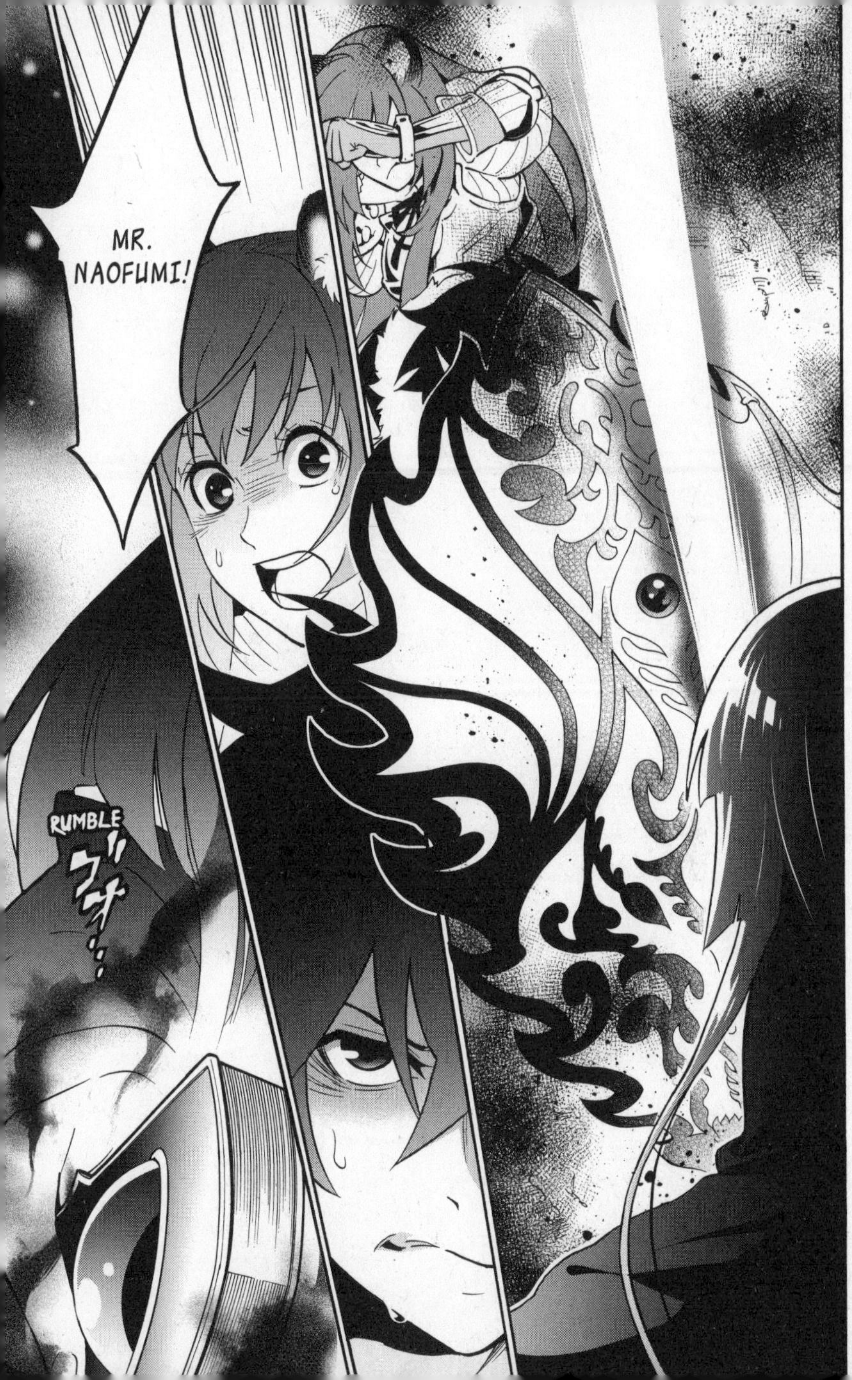
MR. NAOFUMI!
RUMBLE

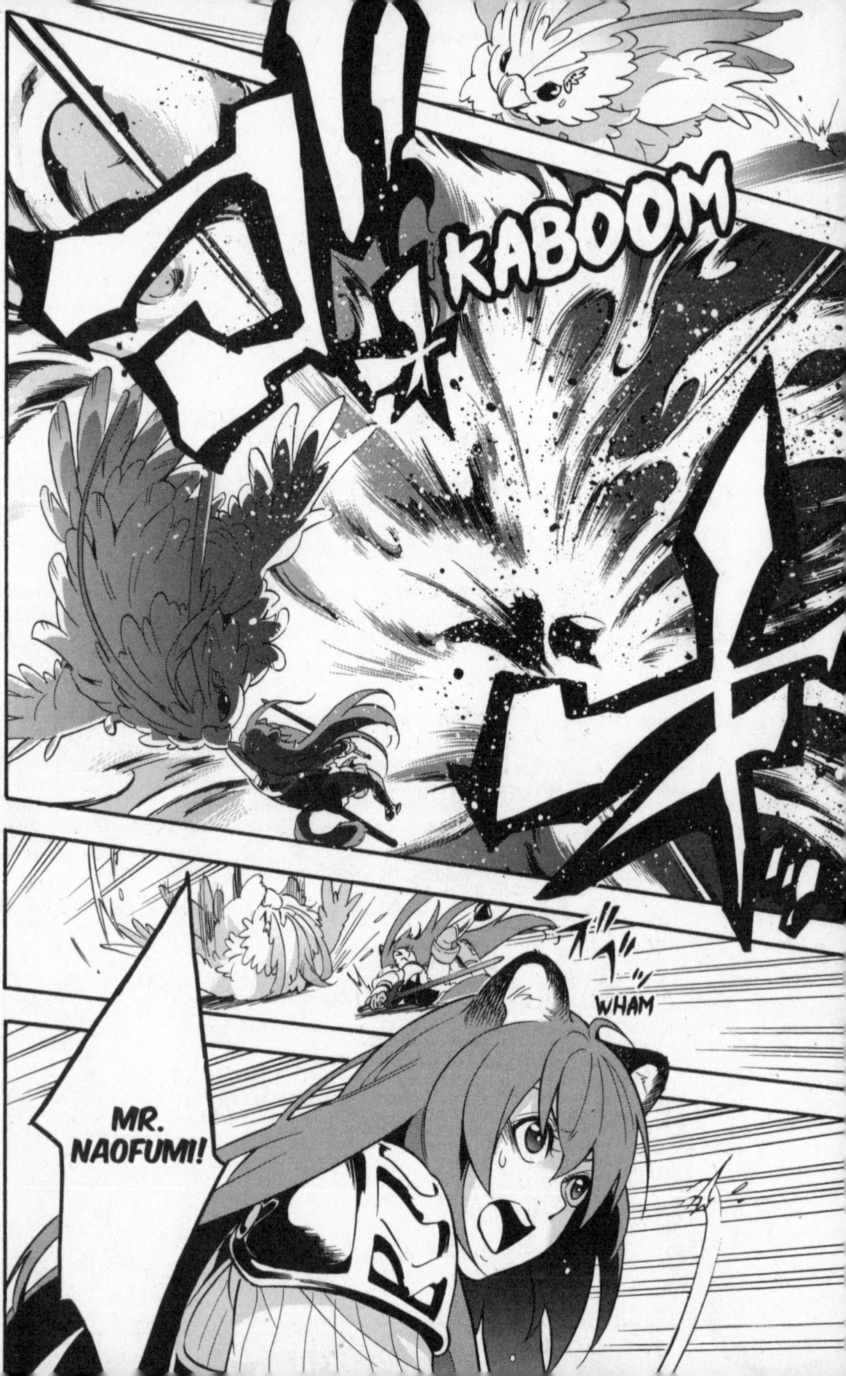
KABOOM
WHAM
MR. NAOFUMI!

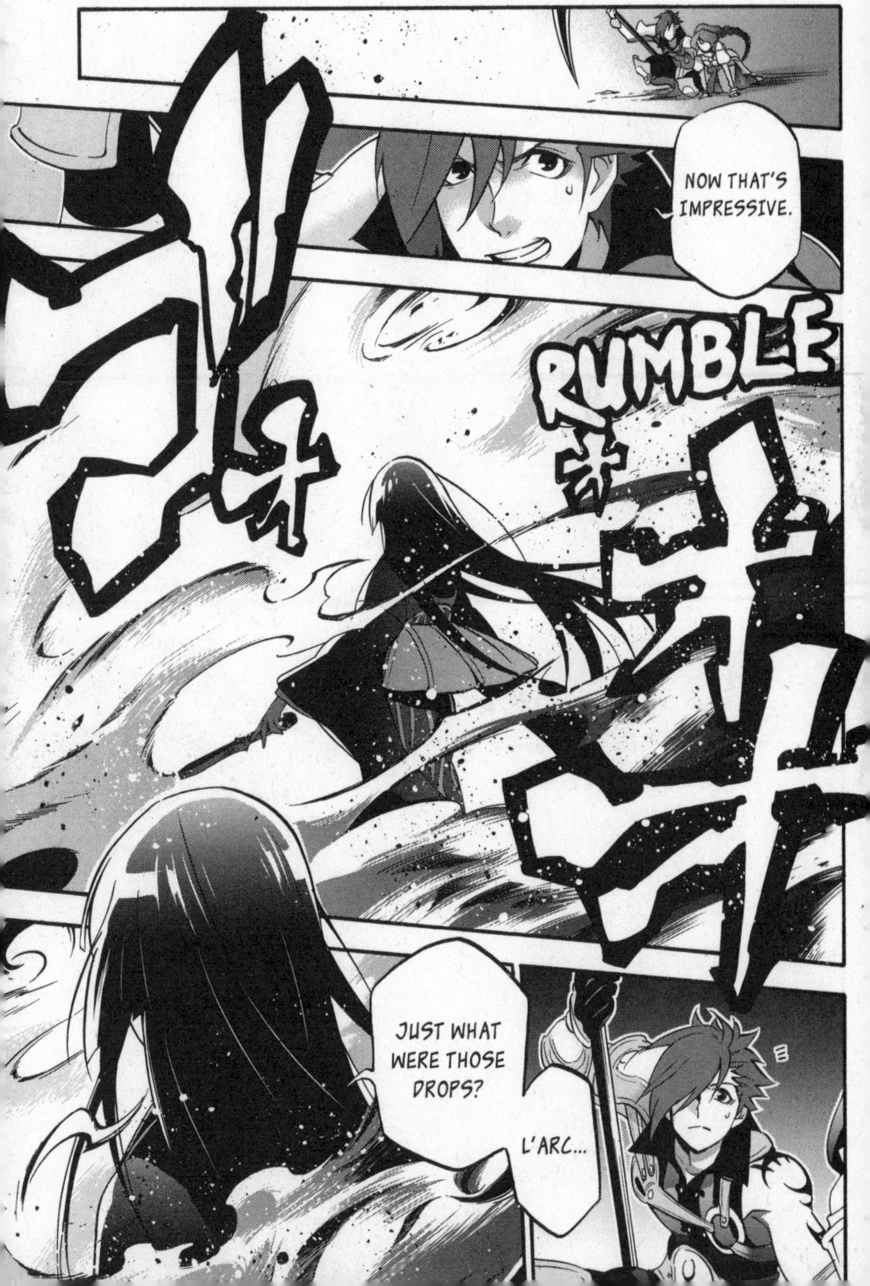
NOW THAT'S IMPRESSIVE.
RUMBLE
JUST WHAT WERE THOSE DROPS?
L'ARC...

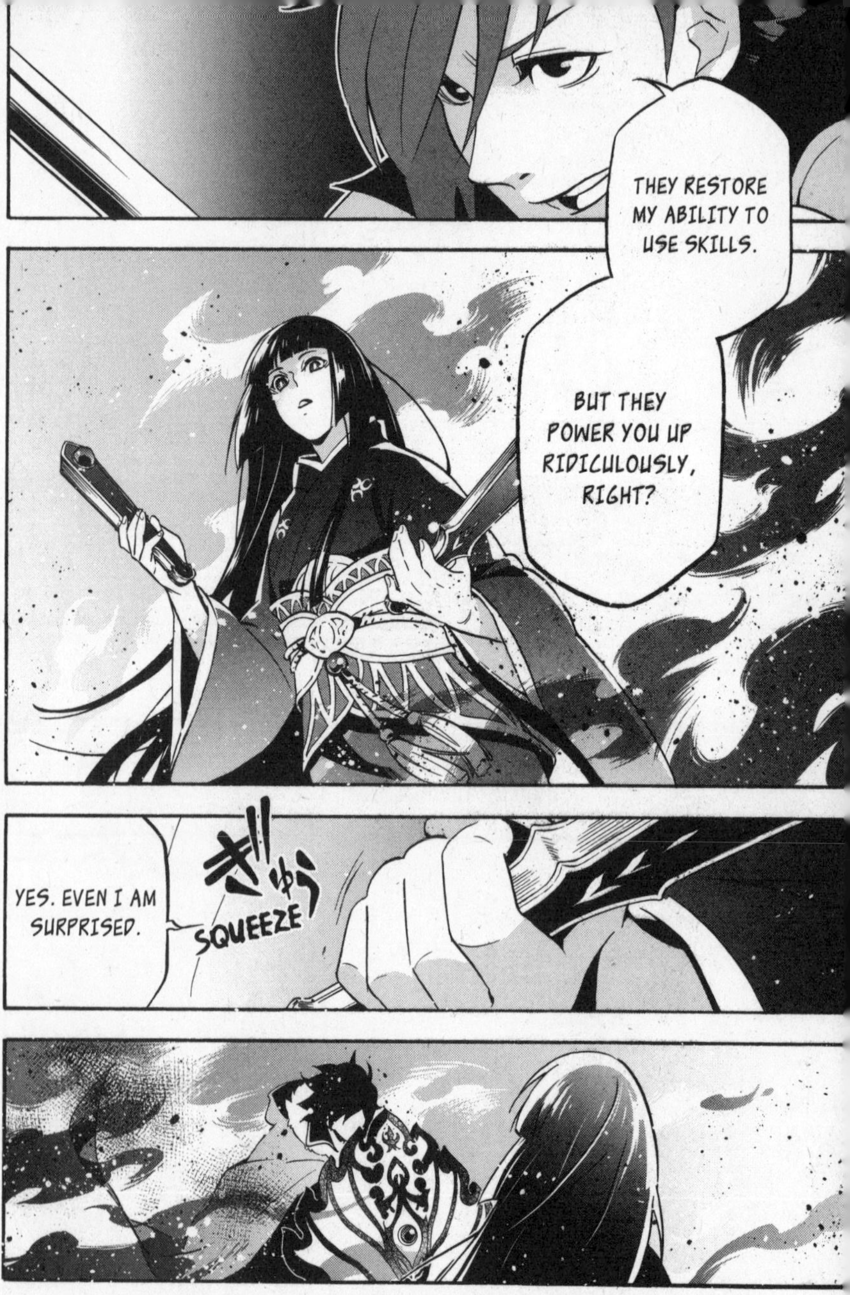
THEY RESTORE MY ABILITY TO USE SKILLS.
BUT THEY POWER YOU UP RIDICULOUSLY, RIGHT?
YES. EVEN I AM SURPRISED.
SQUEEZE

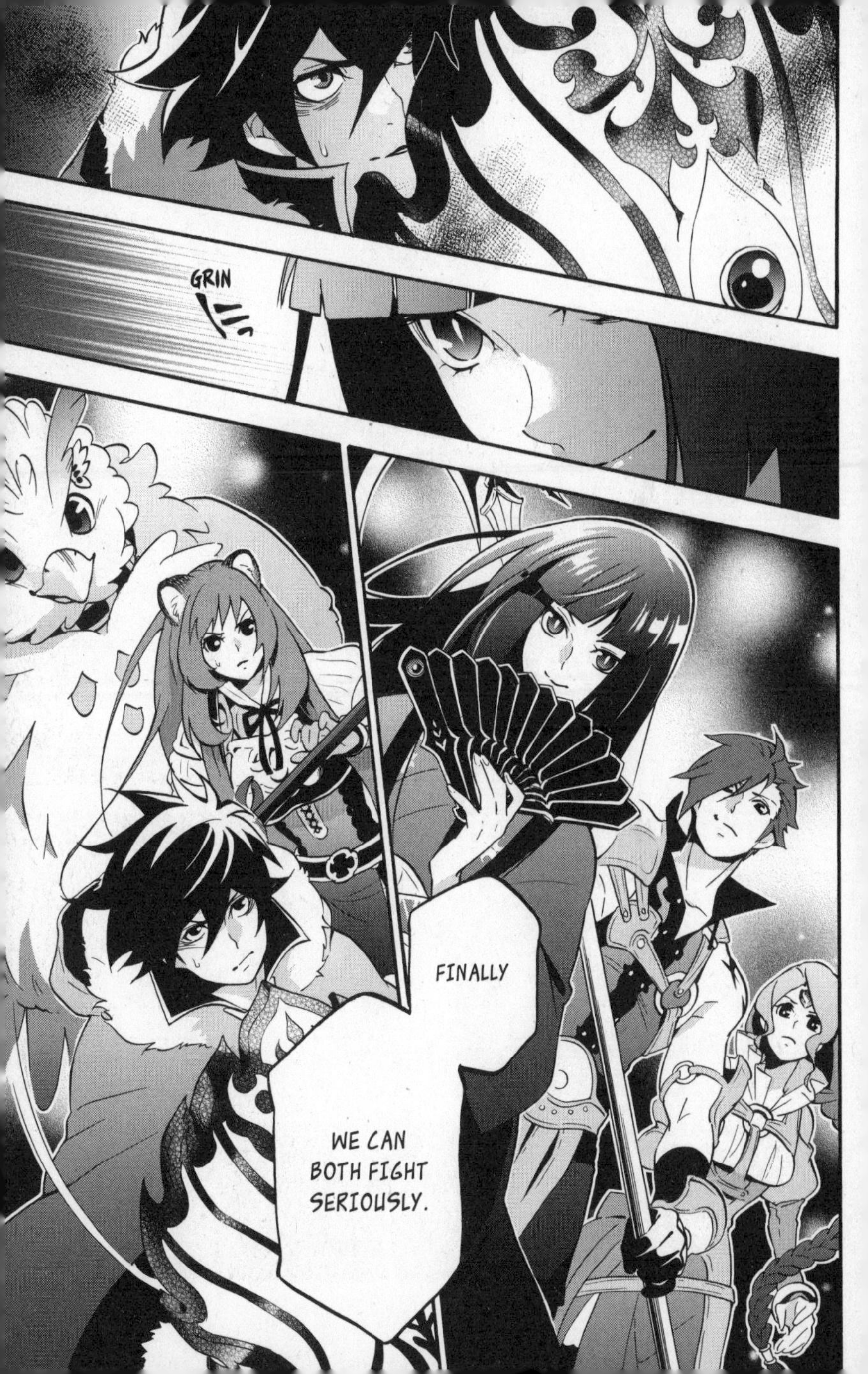
GRIN
FINALLY
WE CAN BOTH FIGHT SERIOUSLY.

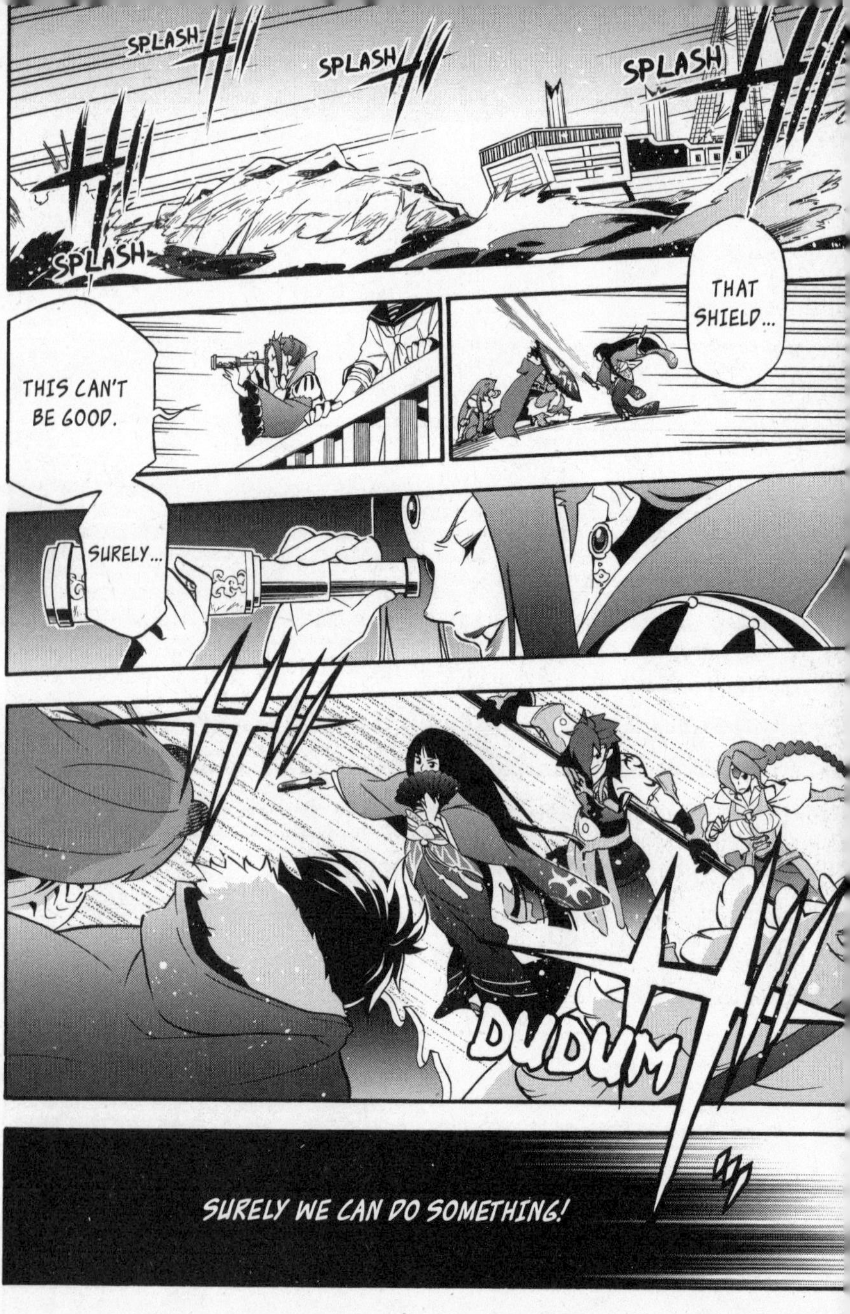
SPLASH
SPLASH
SPLASH
SPLASH
THAT SHIELD...
THIS CAN'T BE GOOD.
SURELY...
DUDUM
SURELY WE CAN DO SOMETHING!

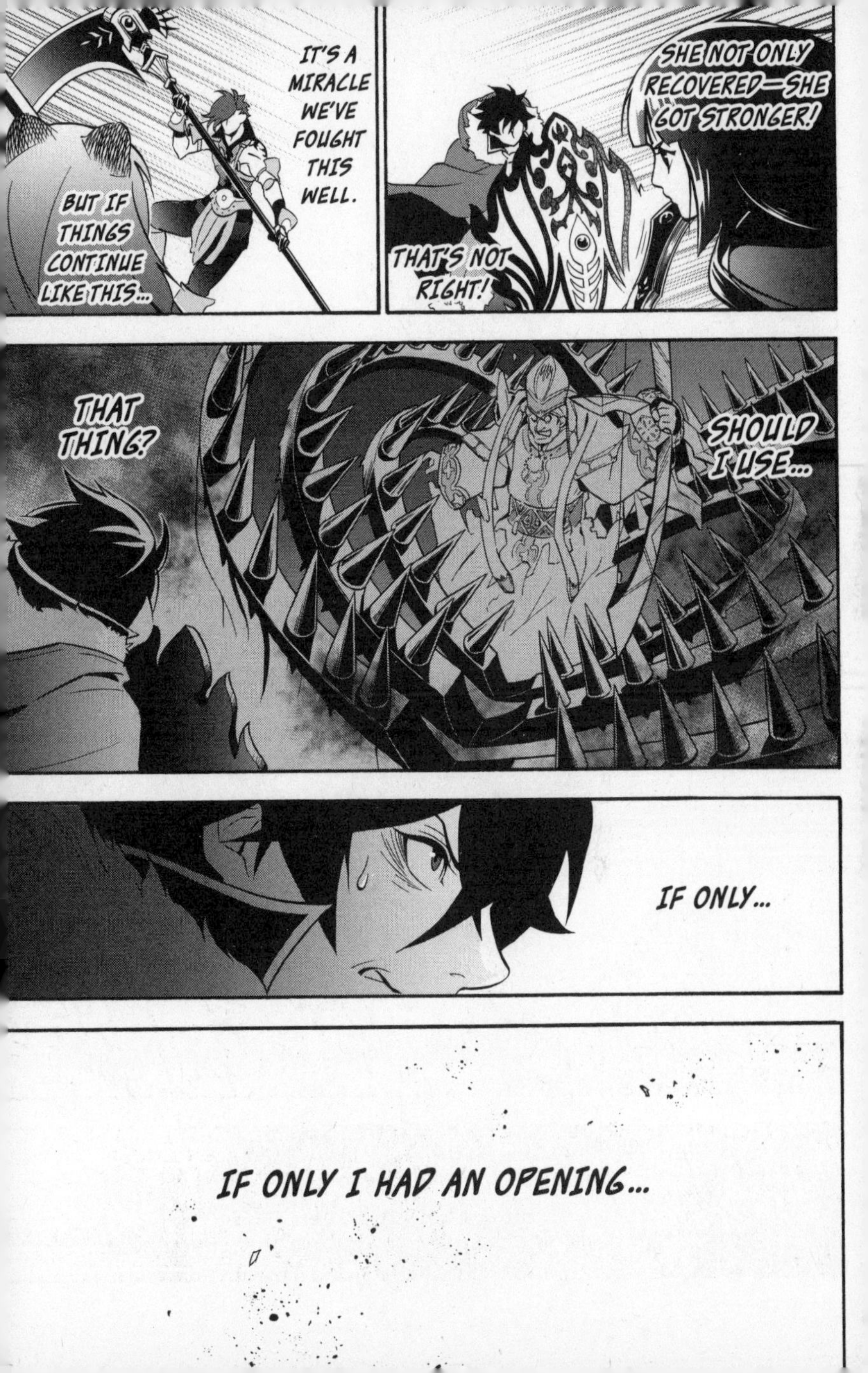
SHE NOT ONLY RECOVERED—SHE GOT STRONGER!
THAT'S NOT RIGHT!
IT'S A MIRACLE WE'VE FOUGHT THIS WELL.
BUT IF THINGS CONTINUE LIKE THIS...
SHOULD I USE...
THAT THING?
IF ONLY...
IF ONLY I HAD AN OPENING...

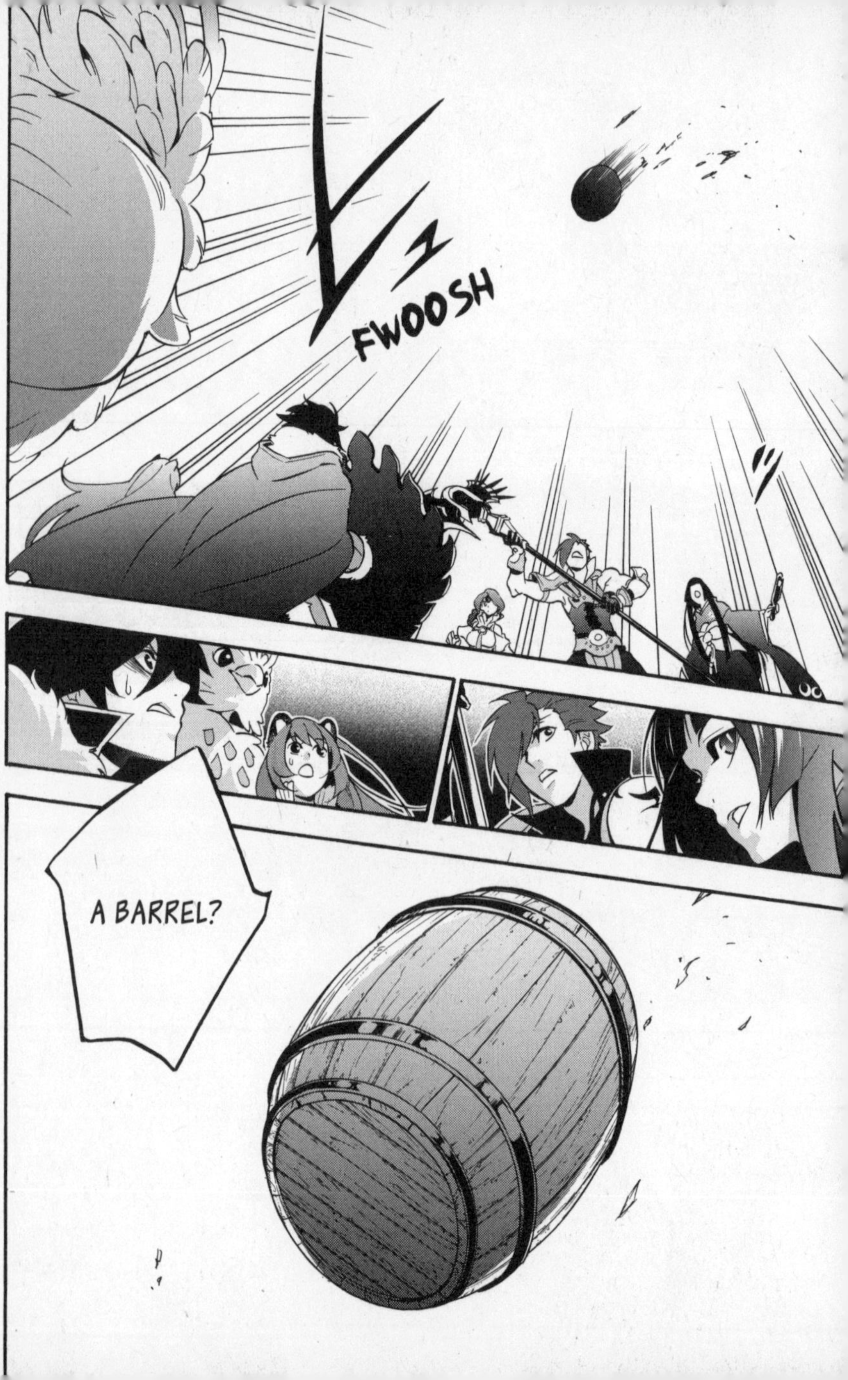
FWOOSH
A BARREL?

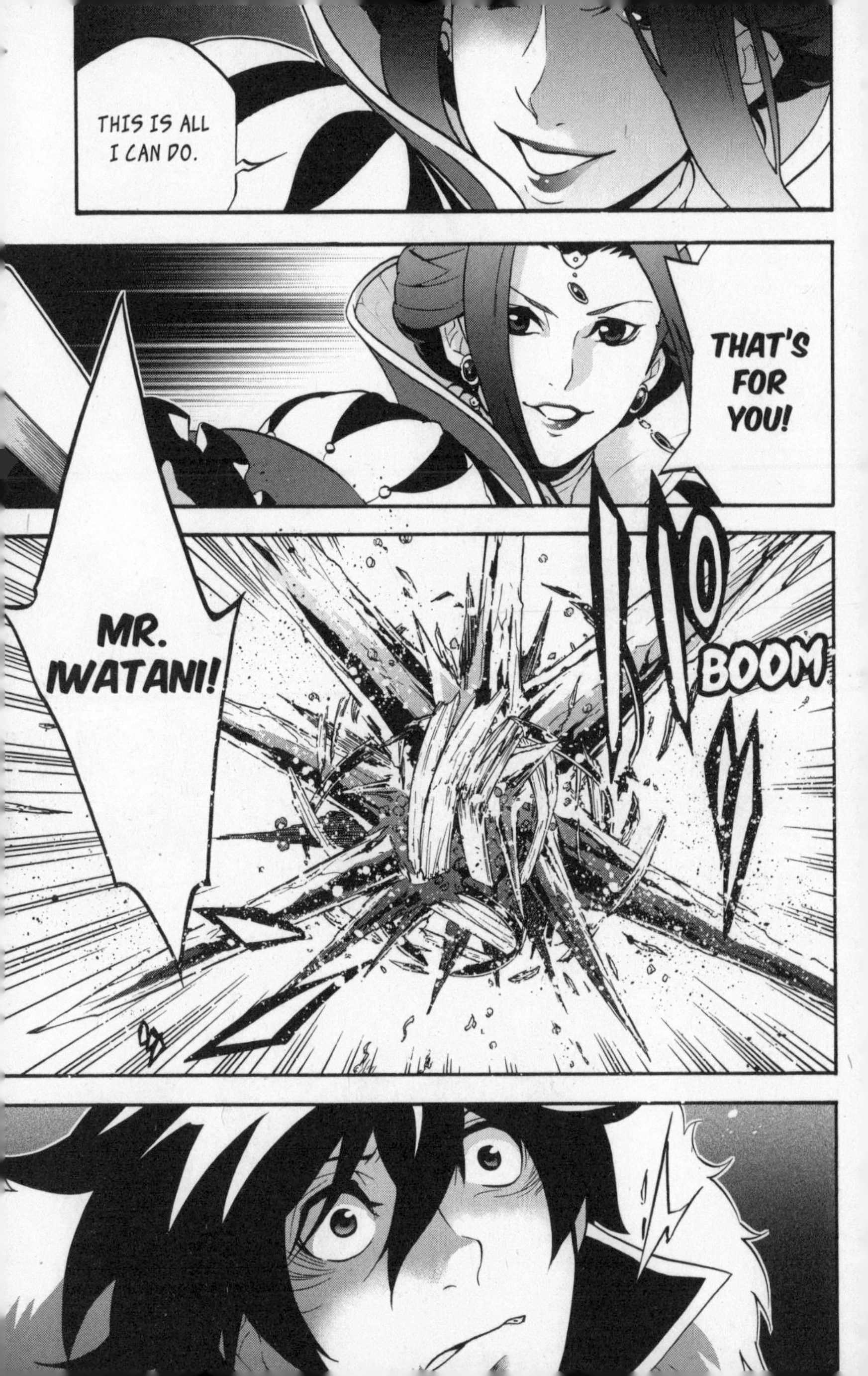
THIS IS ALL I CAN DO.
THAT'S FOR YOU!
BOOM
MR. IWATANI!

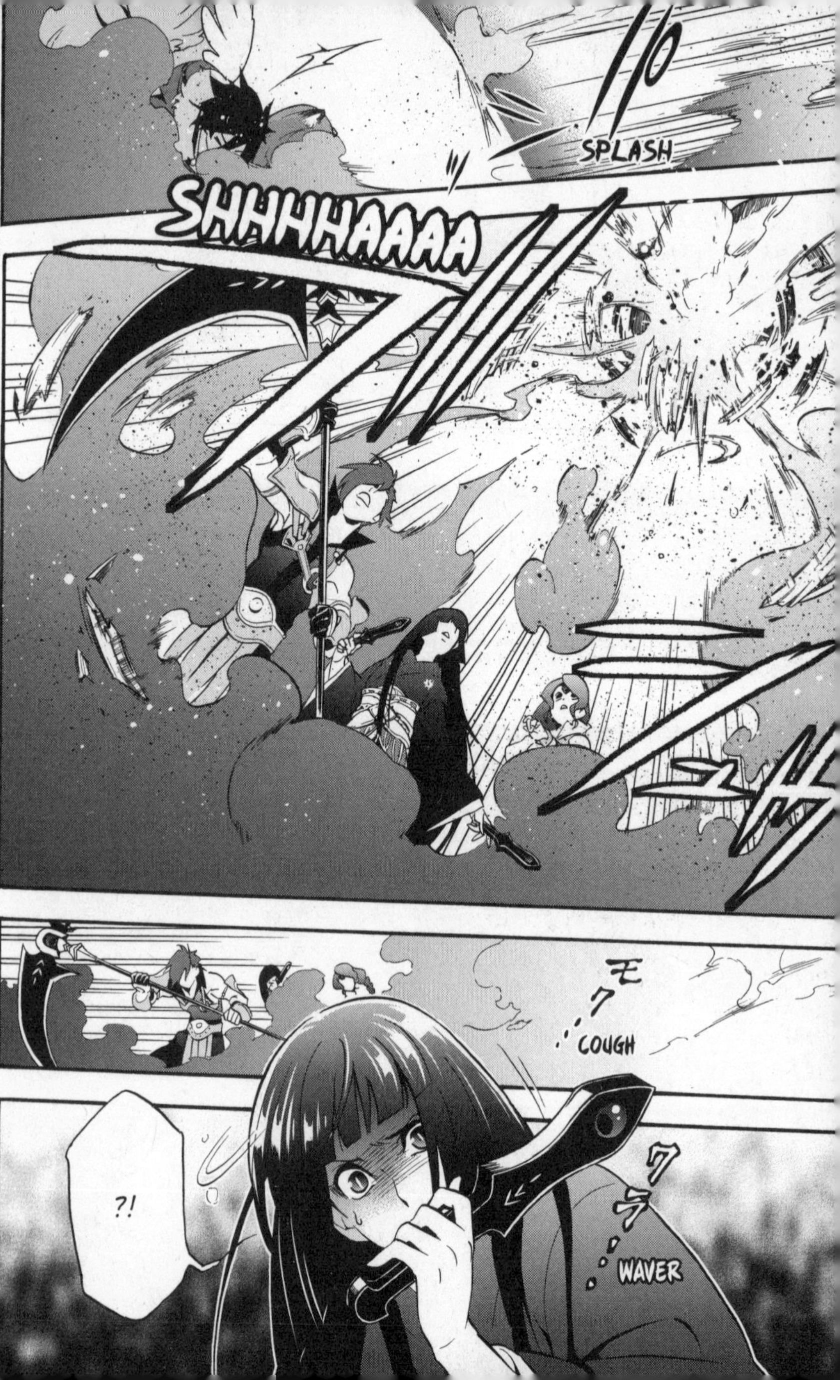
SPLASH
SHHHHAAAA
COUGH
WAVER
?!

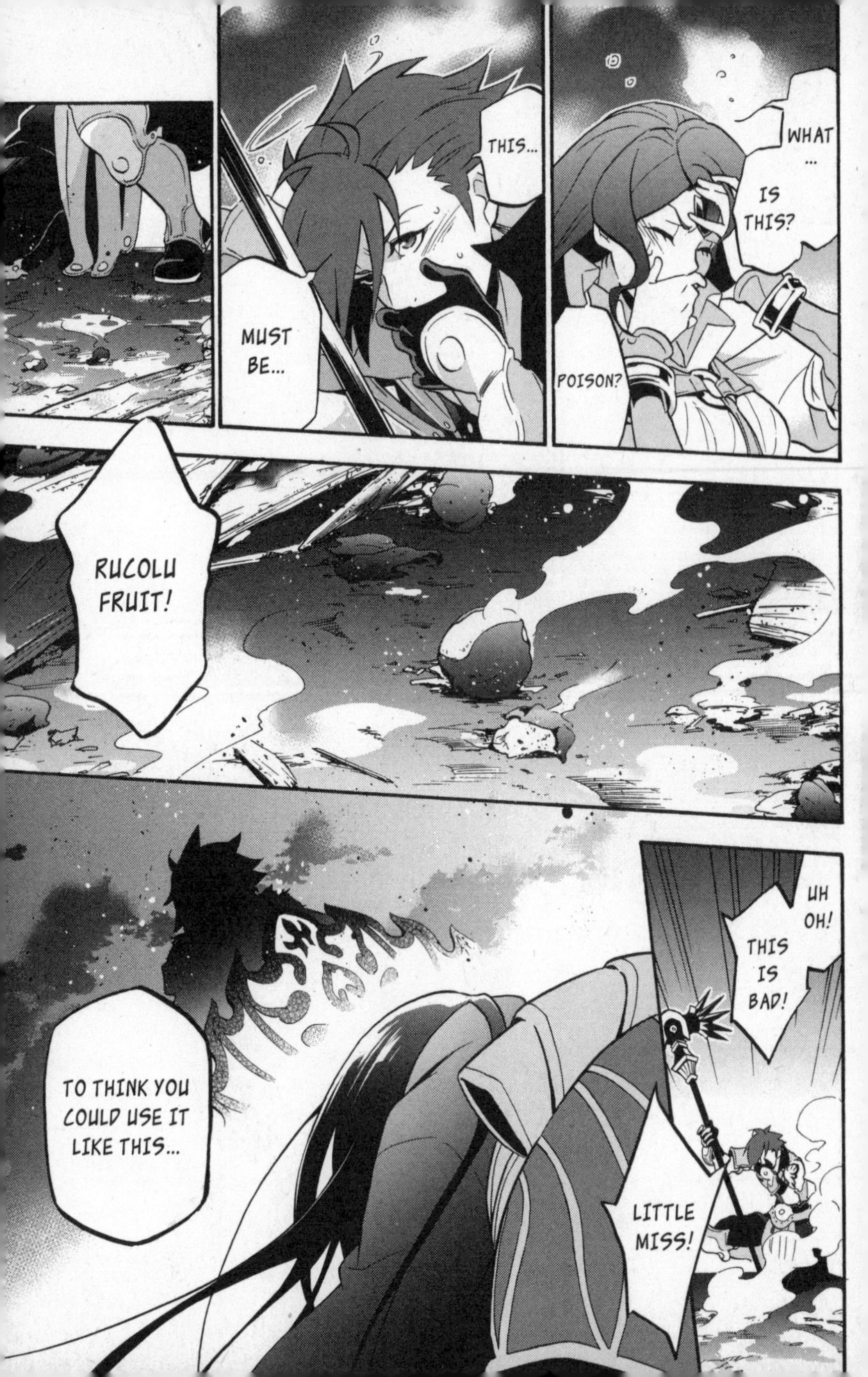
WHAT... IS THIS?
POISON?
THIS...
MUST BE...
RUCOLU FRUIT!
UH OH! THIS IS BAD!
TO THINK YOU COULD USE IT LIKE THIS...
LITTLE MISS!

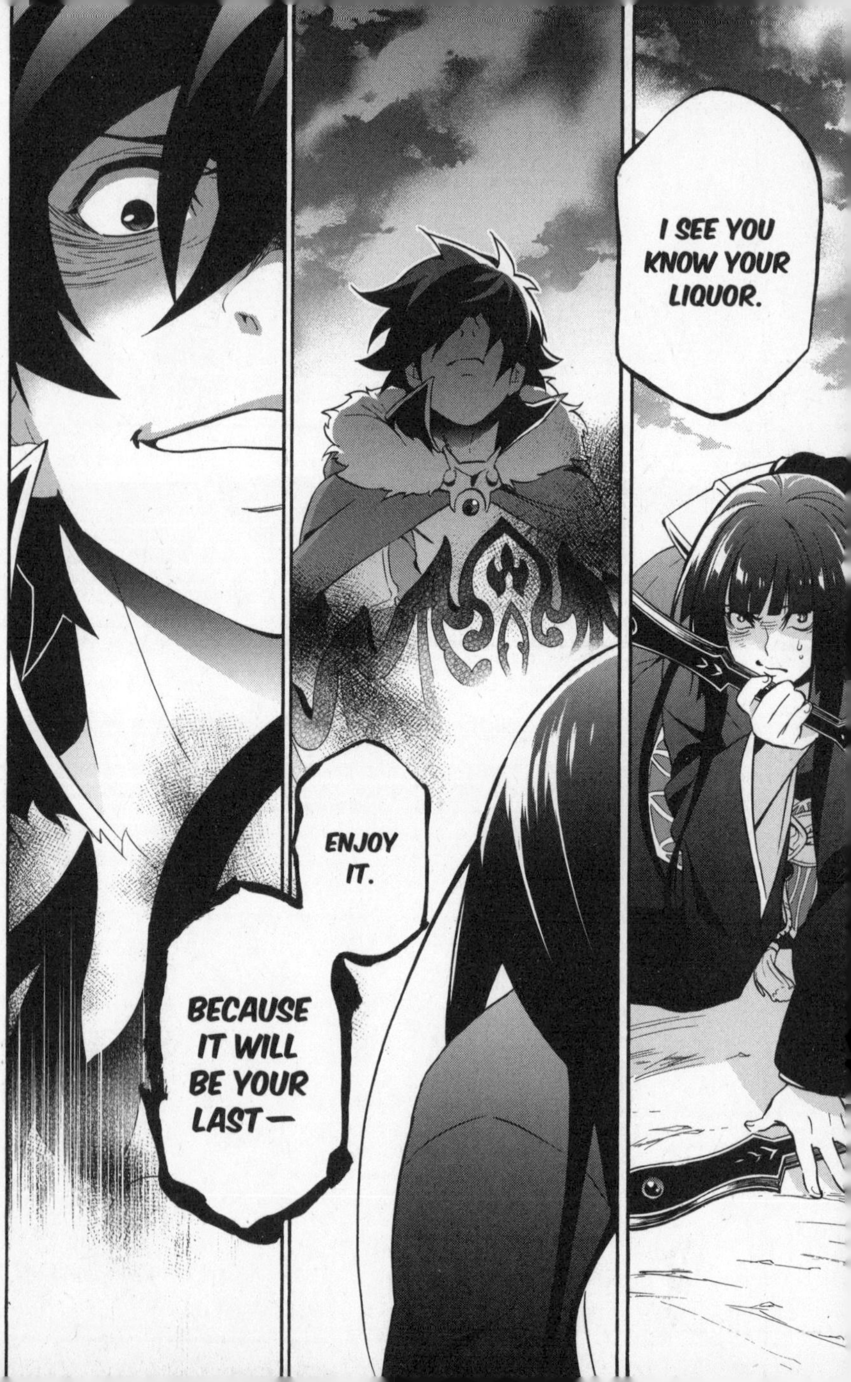
I SEE YOU KNOW YOUR LIQUOR.
ENJOY IT.
BECAUSE IT WILL BE YOUR LAST—

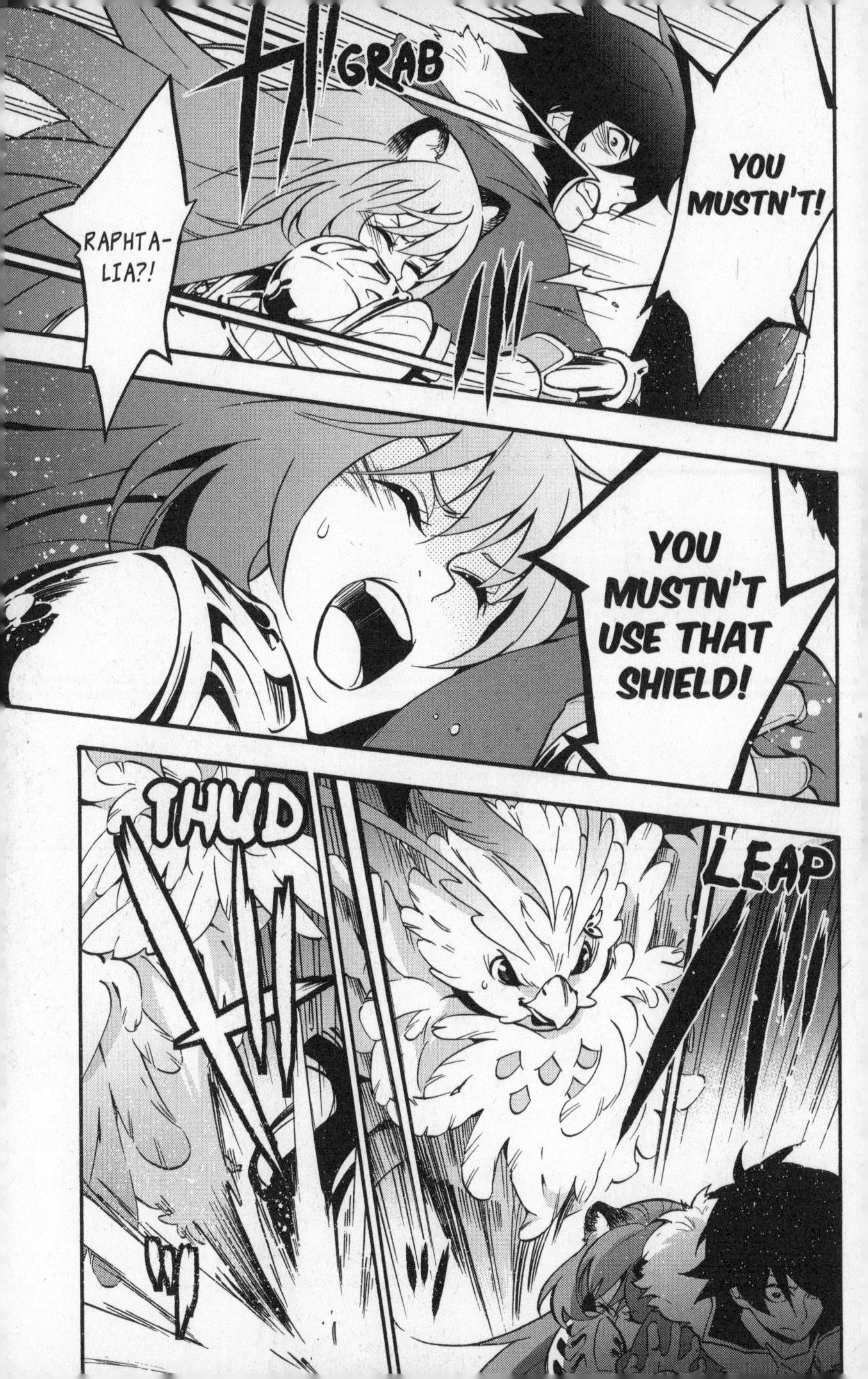
GRAB
YOU MUSTN'T!
RAPHTA-LIA?!
YOU MUSTN'T USE THAT SHIELD!
LEAP
THUD

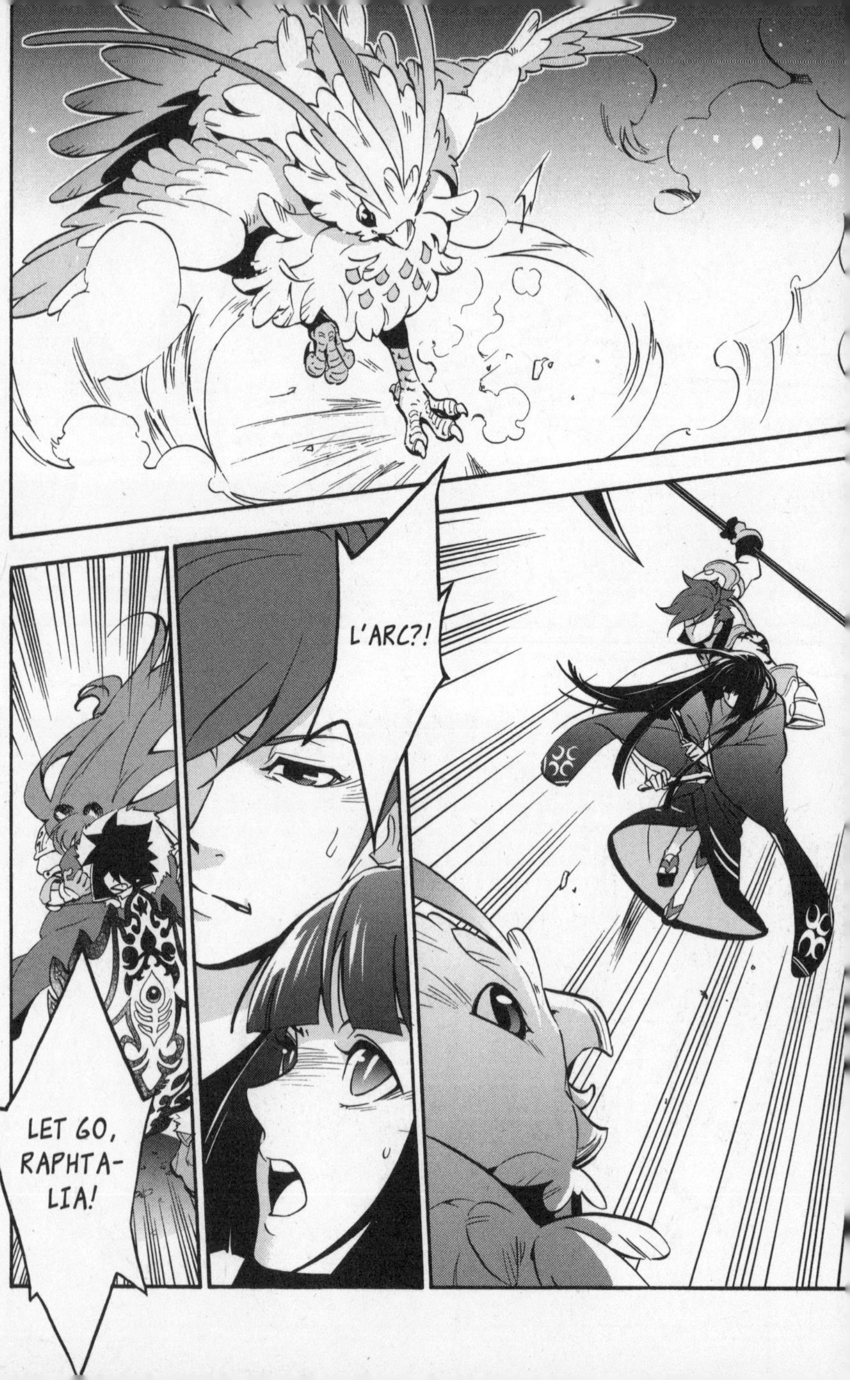
L'ARC?!
LET GO, RAPHTA-LIA!

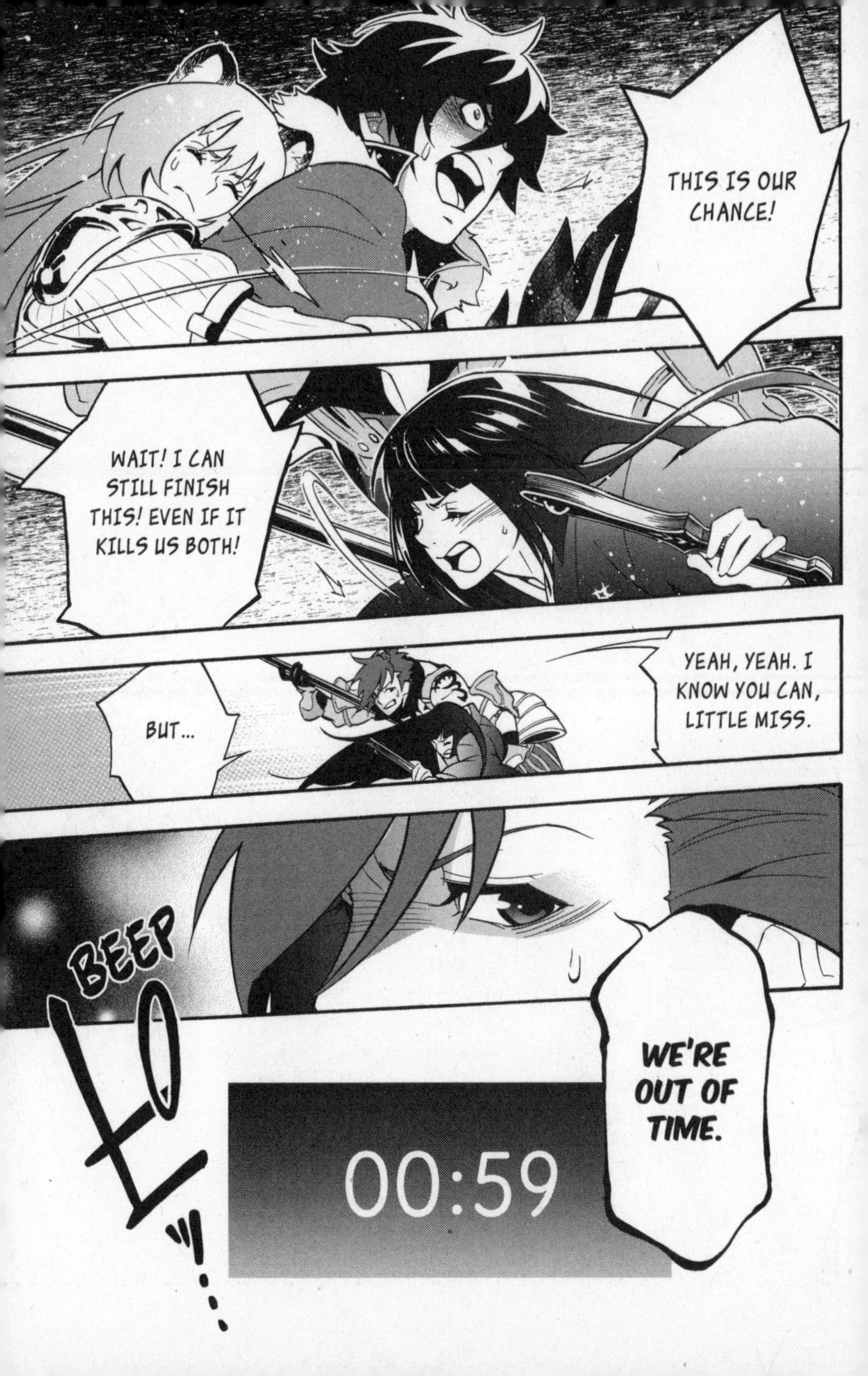
THIS IS OUR CHANCE!
WAIT! I CAN STILL FINISH THIS! EVEN IF IT KILLS US BOTH!
YEAH, YEAH. I KNOW YOU CAN, LITTLE MISS.
BUT...
WE'RE OUT OF TIME.
BEEP
00:59

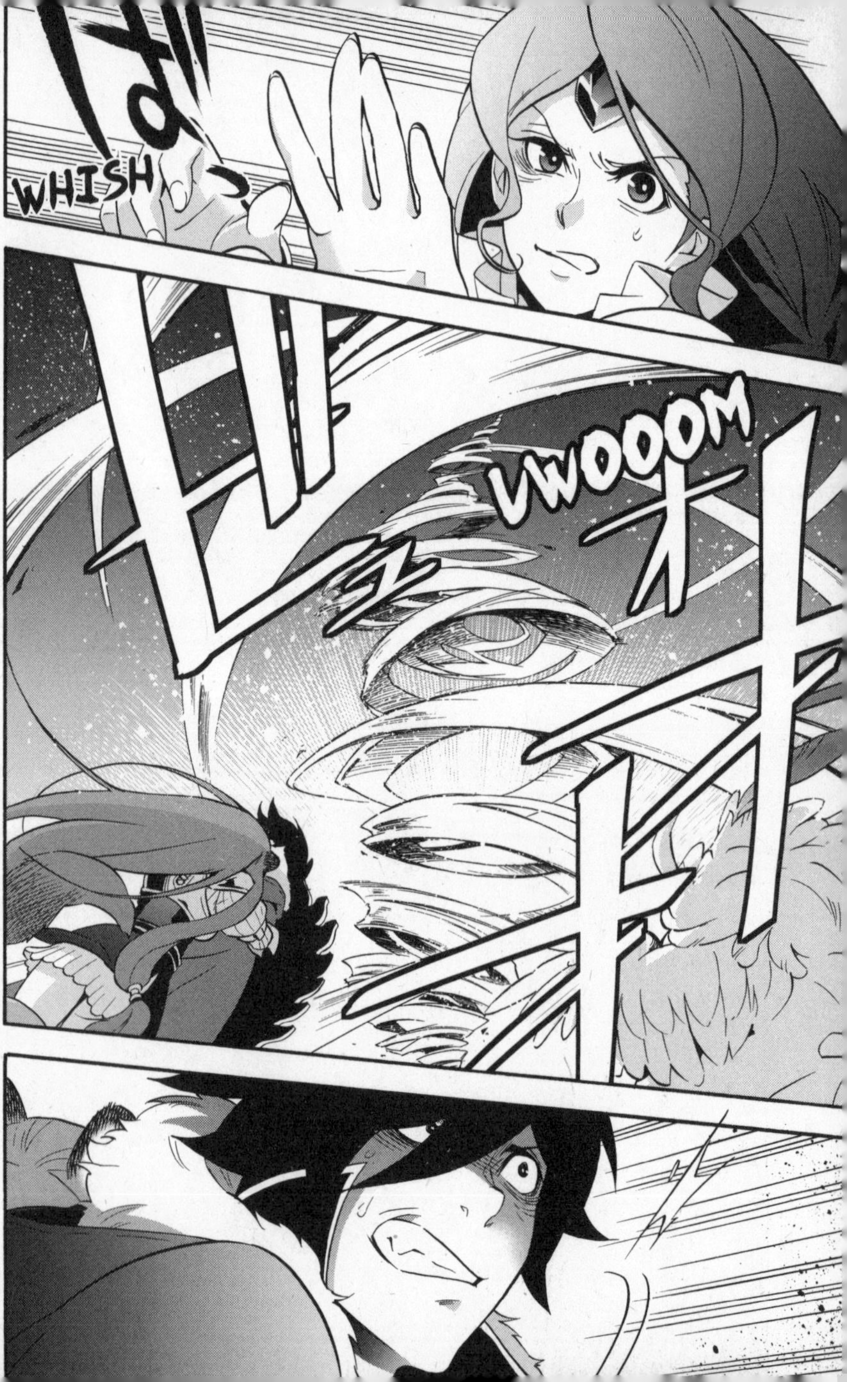
WHISH
VWOOOM

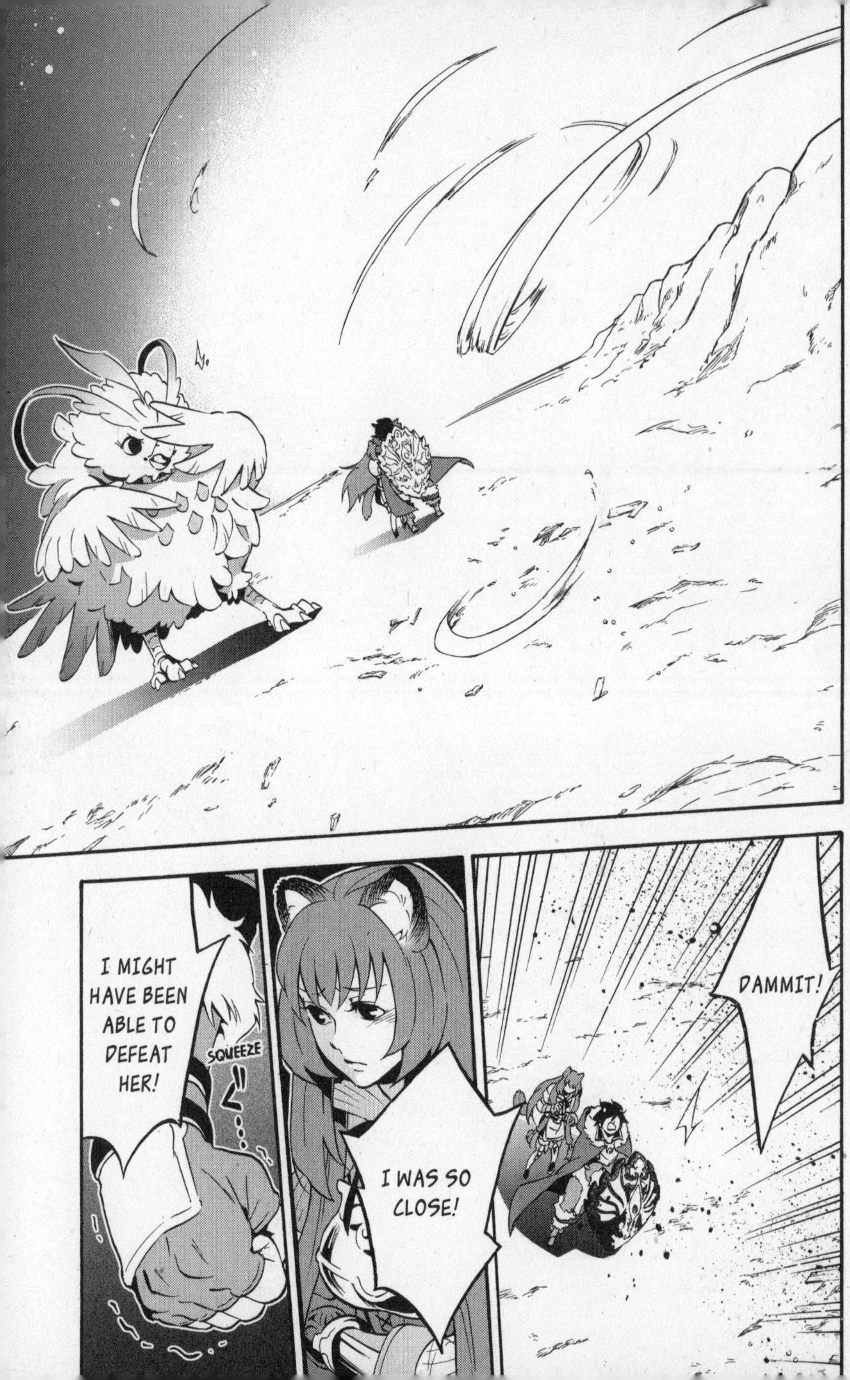
DAMMIT!
I WAS SO CLOSE!
I MIGHT HAVE BEEN ABLE TO DEFEAT HER!
SQUEEZE

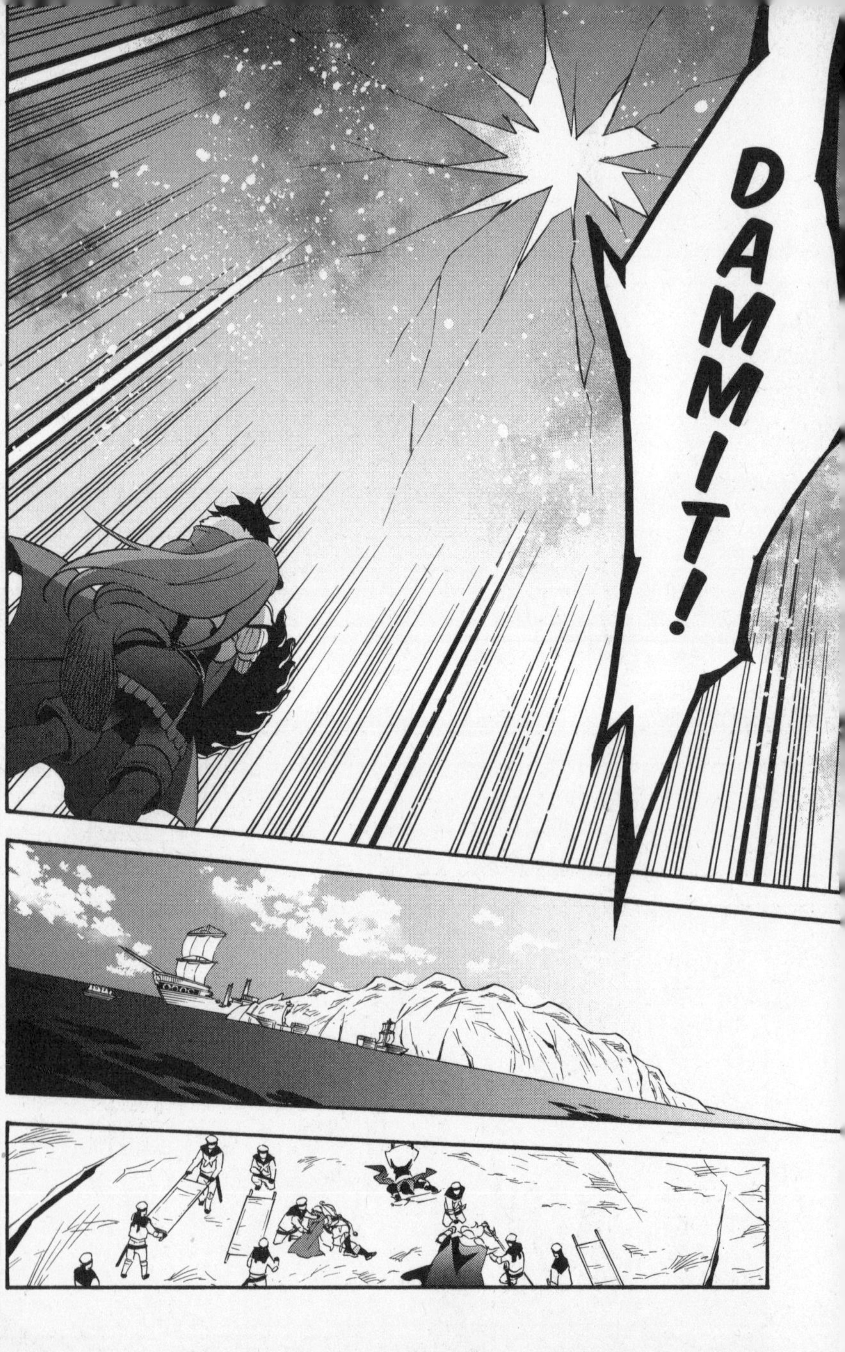
DAMMIT!

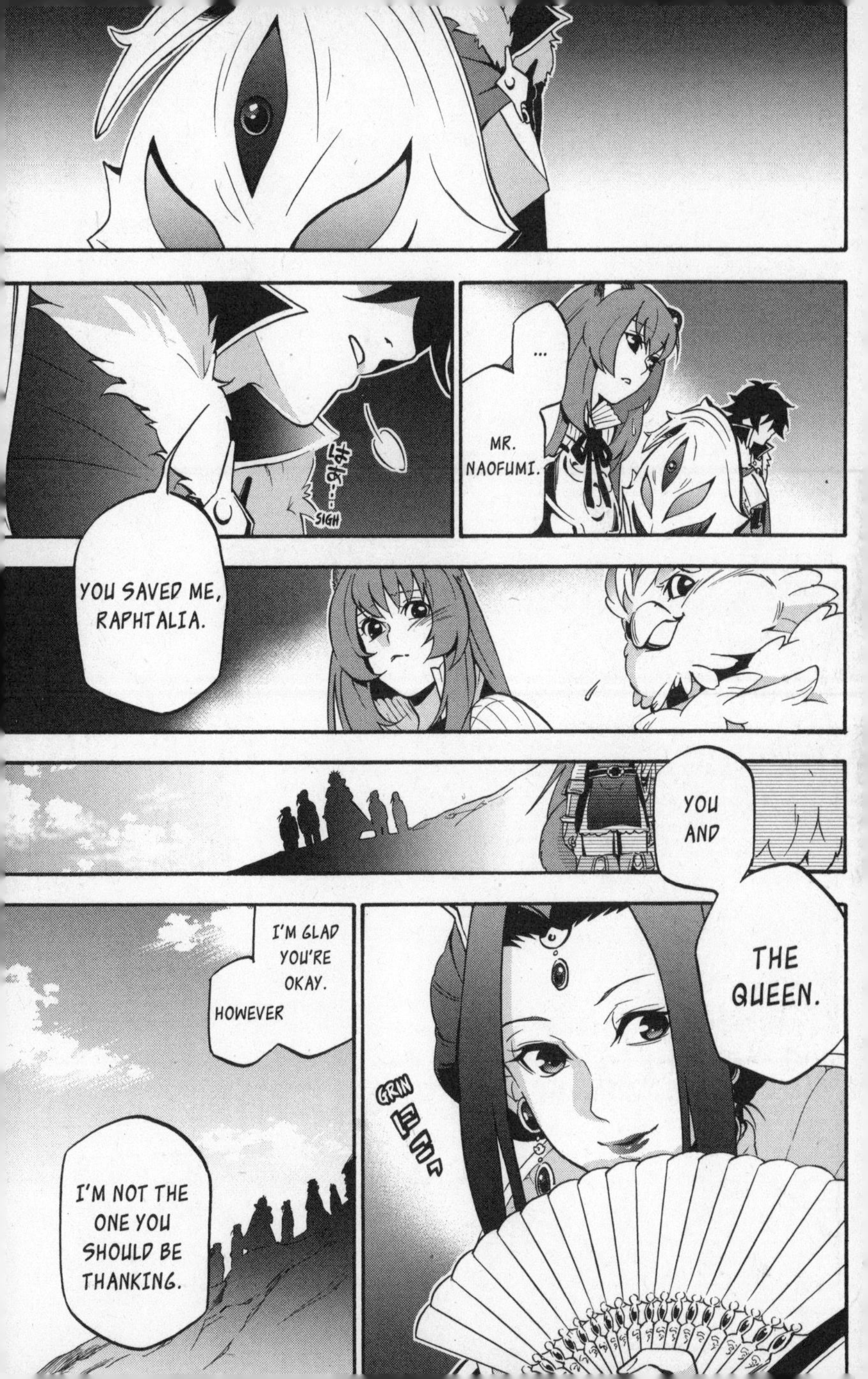
...
MR. NAOFUMI.
SIGH
YOU SAVED ME, RAPHTALIA.
YOU AND
THE QUEEN.
GRIN
I'M GLAD YOU'RE OKAY.
HOWEVER
I'M NOT THE ONE YOU SHOULD BE THANKING.

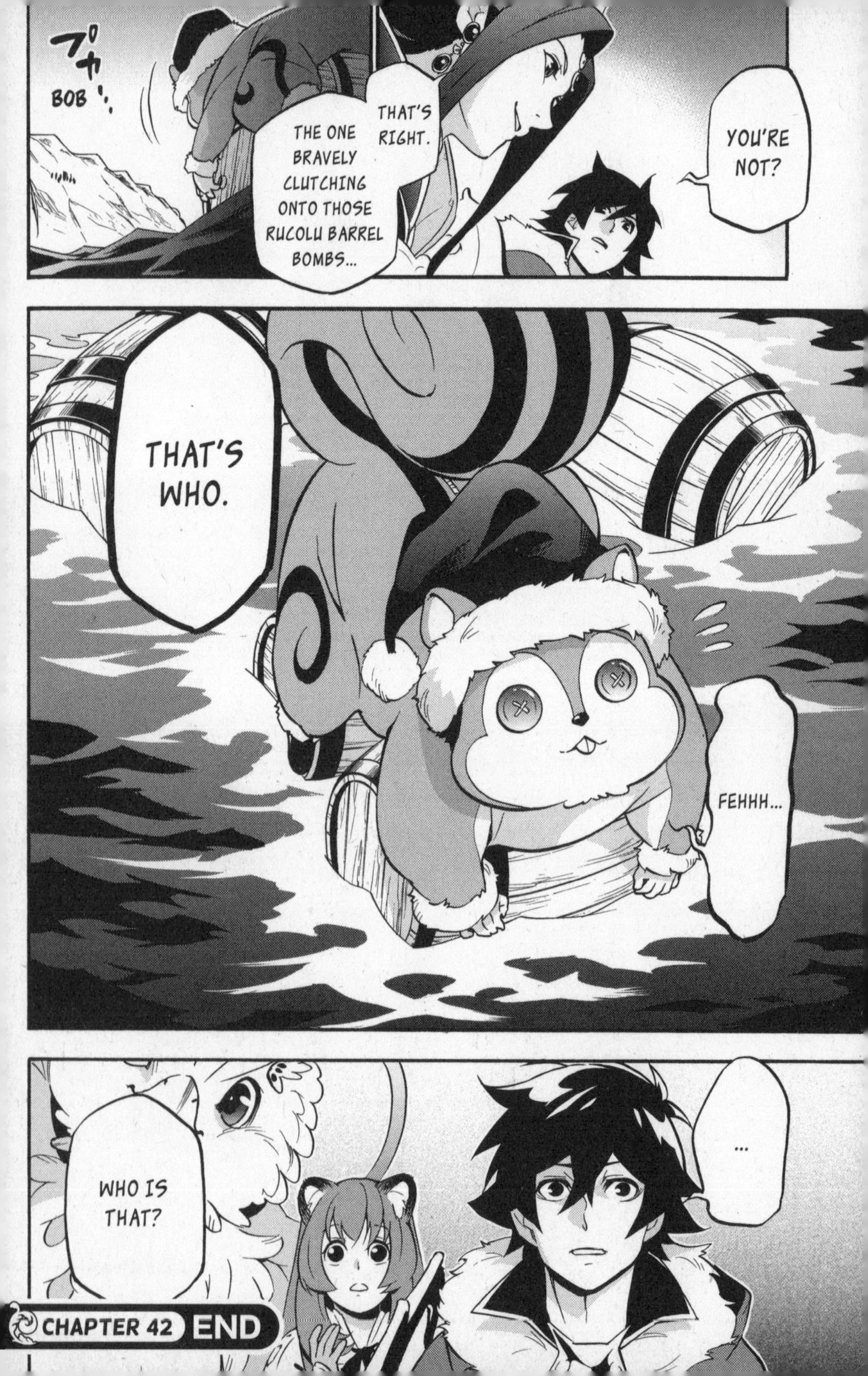

YOU'RE NOT?
THAT'S RIGHT.
THE ONE BRAVELY CLUTCHING ONTO THOSE RUCOLU BARREL BOMBS...
プヤ
BOB
THAT'S WHO.
FEHHH...
...
WHO IS THAT?
CHAPTER 42 END

THE RISING OF THE SHIELD HERO

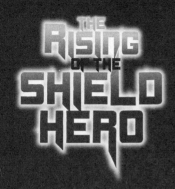

THE RISING OF THE SHIELD HERO

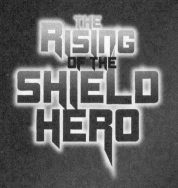

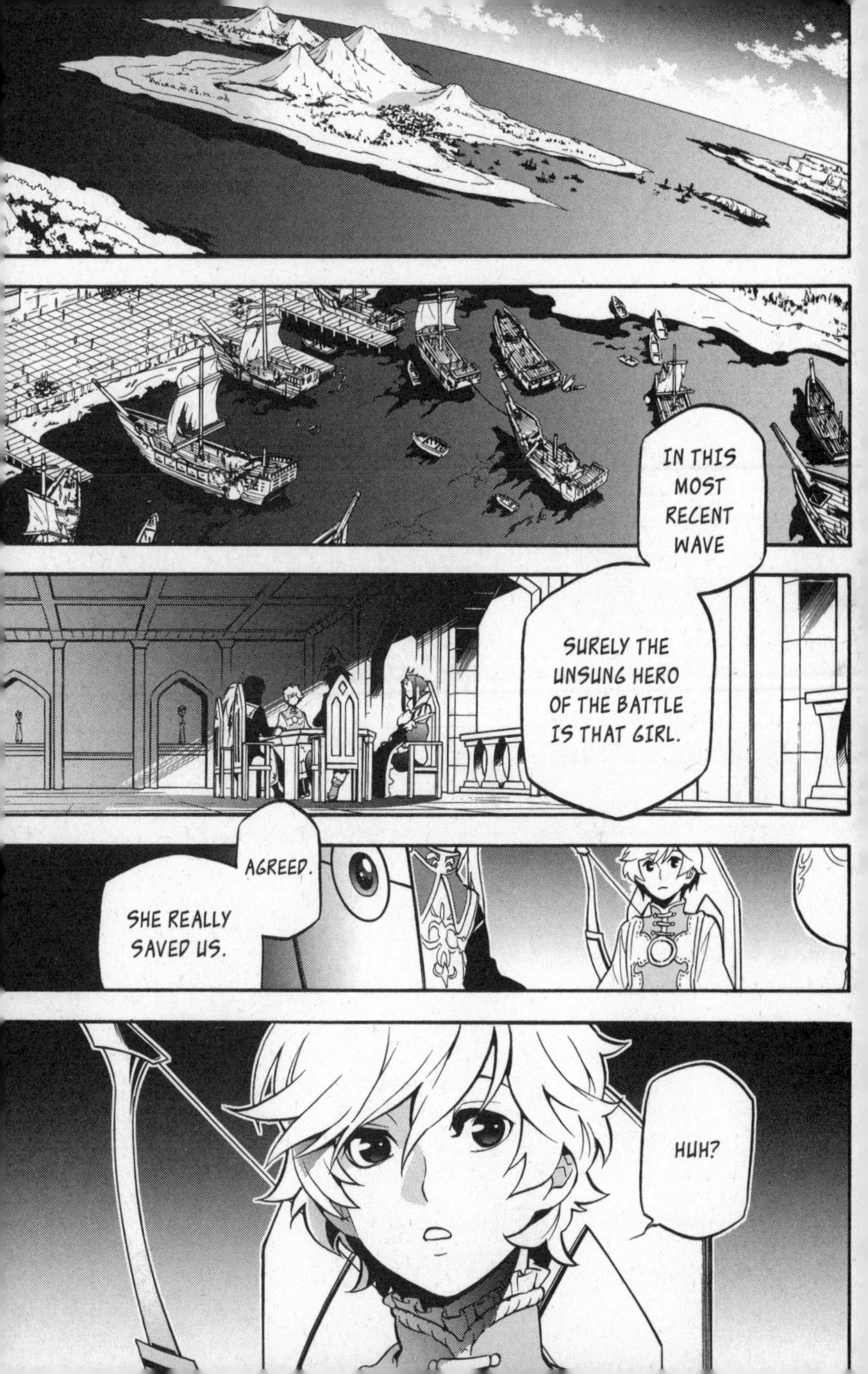
IN THIS MOST RECENT WAVE
SURELY THE UNSUNG HERO OF THE BATTLE IS THAT GIRL.
AGREED.
SHE REALLY SAVED US.
HUH?

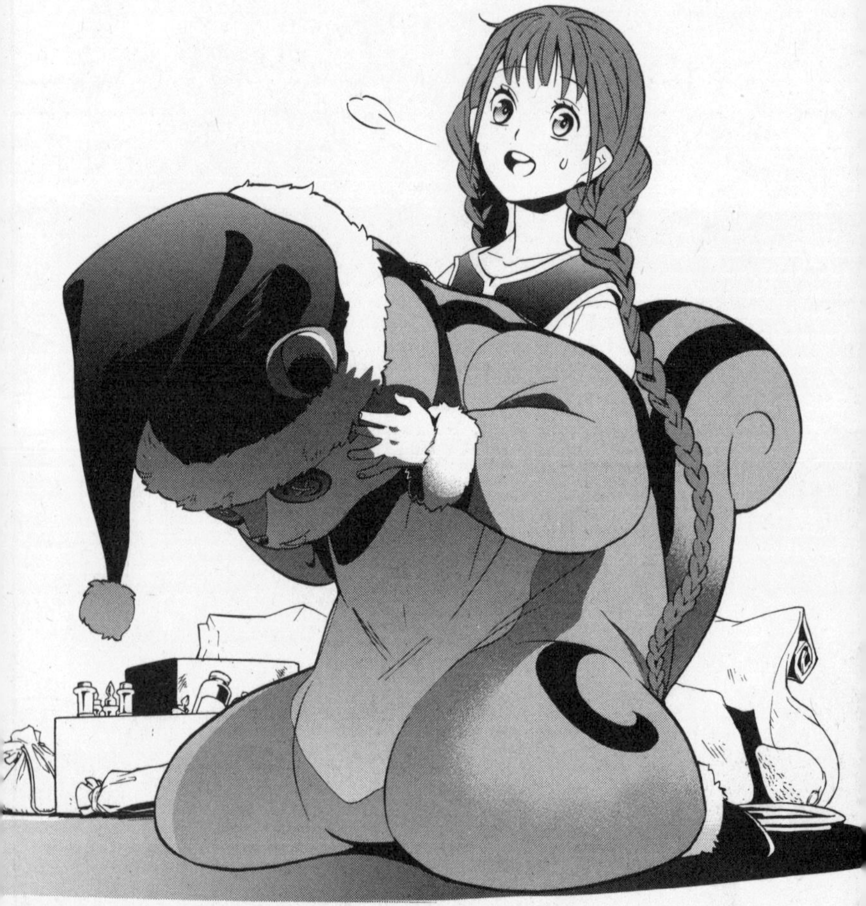

# CHAPTER 43 AN UNFORTUNATE GIRL

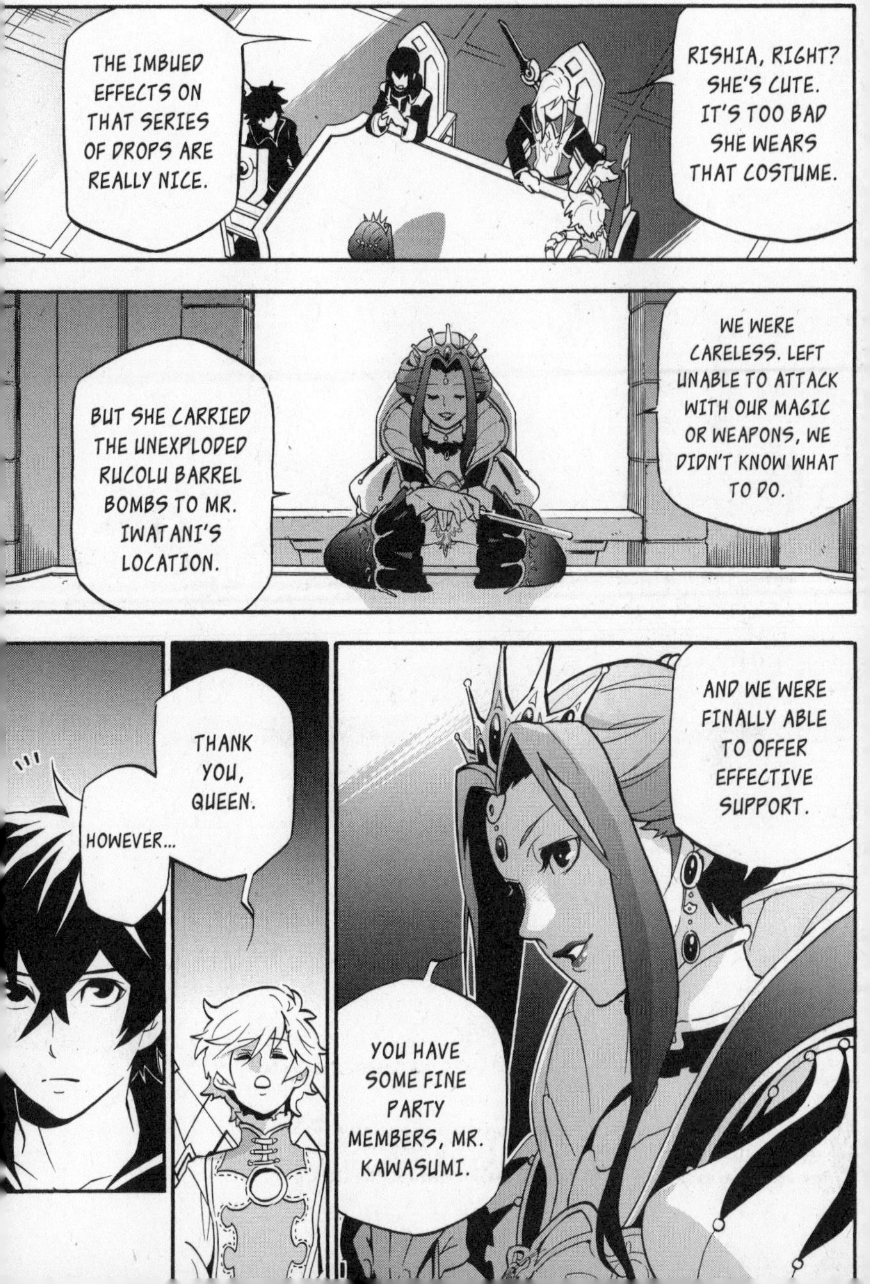
RISHIA, RIGHT? SHE'S CUTE. IT'S TOO BAD SHE WEARS THAT COSTUME.
THE IMBUED EFFECTS ON THAT SERIES OF DROPS ARE REALLY NICE.
WE WERE CARELESS. LEFT UNABLE TO ATTACK WITH OUR MAGIC OR WEAPONS, WE DIDN'T KNOW WHAT TO DO.
BUT SHE CARRIED THE UNEXPLODED RUCOLU BARREL BOMBS TO MR. IWATANI'S LOCATION.
AND WE WERE FINALLY ABLE TO OFFER EFFECTIVE SUPPORT.
YOU HAVE SOME FINE PARTY MEMBERS, MR. KAWASUMI.
THANK YOU, QUEEN.
HOWEVER...

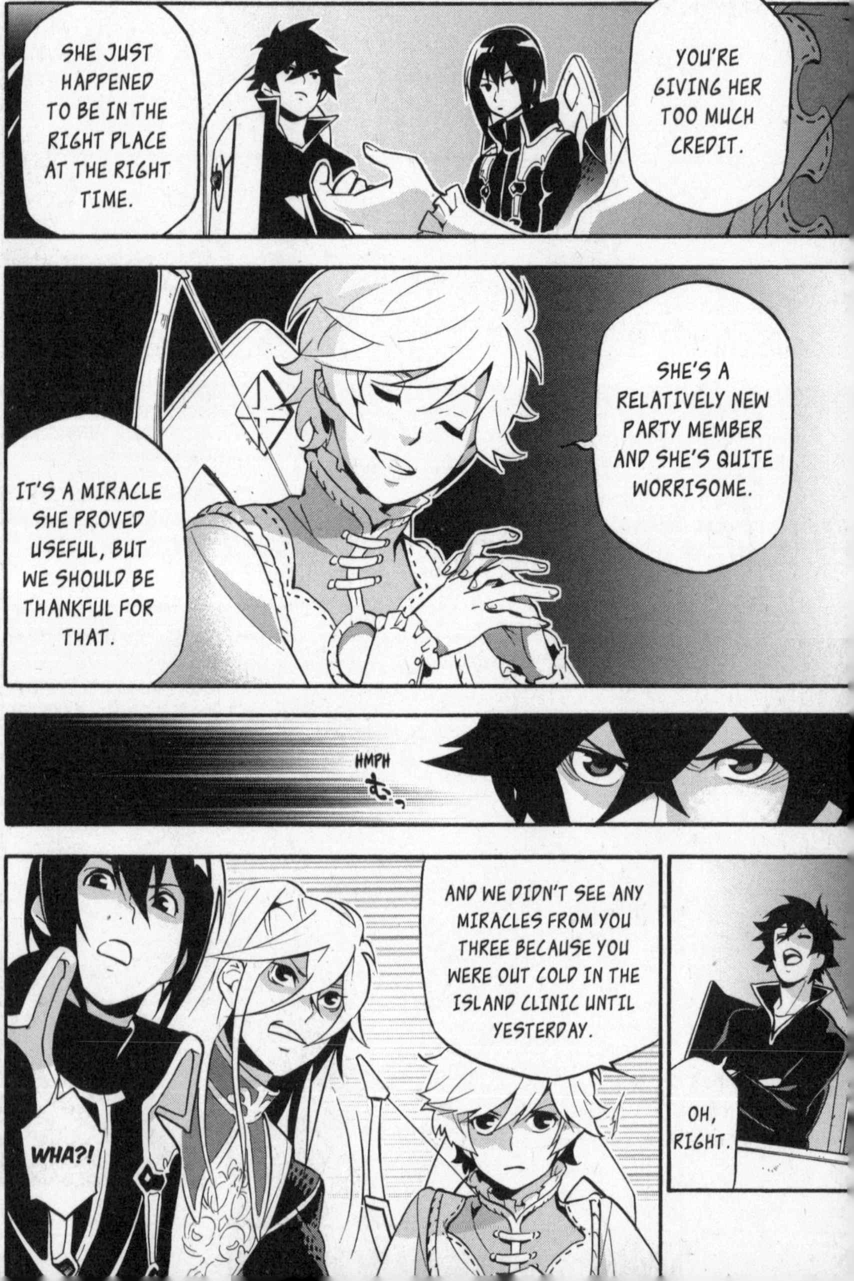
YOU'RE GIVING HER TOO MUCH CREDIT.
SHE JUST HAPPENED TO BE IN THE RIGHT PLACE AT THE RIGHT TIME.
SHE'S A RELATIVELY NEW PARTY MEMBER AND SHE'S QUITE WORRISOME.
IT'S A MIRACLE SHE PROVED USEFUL, BUT WE SHOULD BE THANKFUL FOR THAT.
HMPH
OH, RIGHT.
AND WE DIDN'T SEE ANY MIRACLES FROM YOU THREE BECAUSE YOU WERE OUT COLD IN THE ISLAND CLINIC UNTIL YESTERDAY.
WHA?!

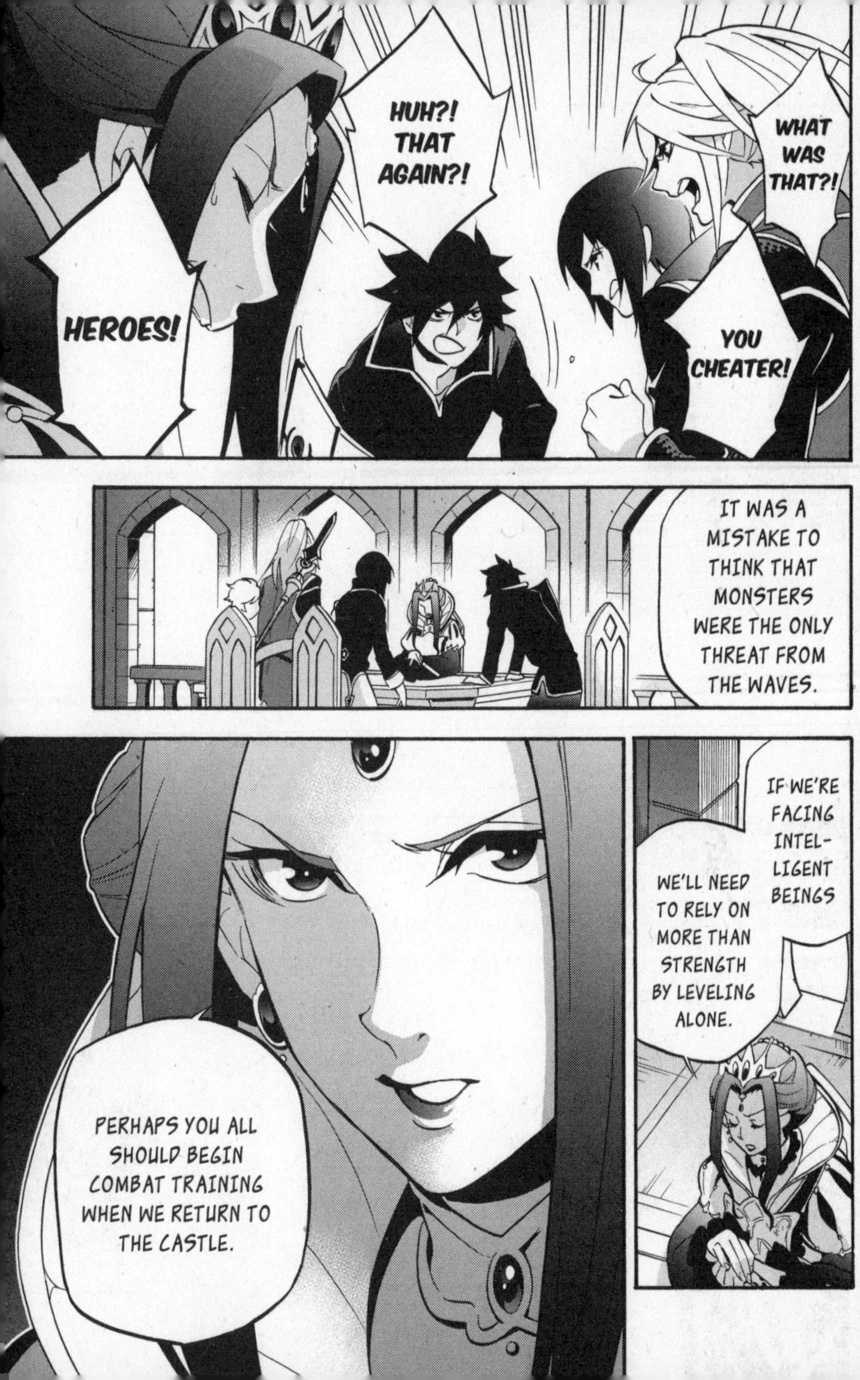
WHAT WAS THAT?!
HUH?! THAT AGAIN?!
YOU CHEATER!
HEROES!
IT WAS A MISTAKE TO THINK THAT MONSTERS WERE THE ONLY THREAT FROM THE WAVES.
IF WE'RE FACING INTEL-LIGENT BEINGS
WE'LL NEED TO RELY ON MORE THAN STRENGTH BY LEVELING ALONE.
PERHAPS YOU ALL SHOULD BEGIN COMBAT TRAINING WHEN WE RETURN TO THE CASTLE.

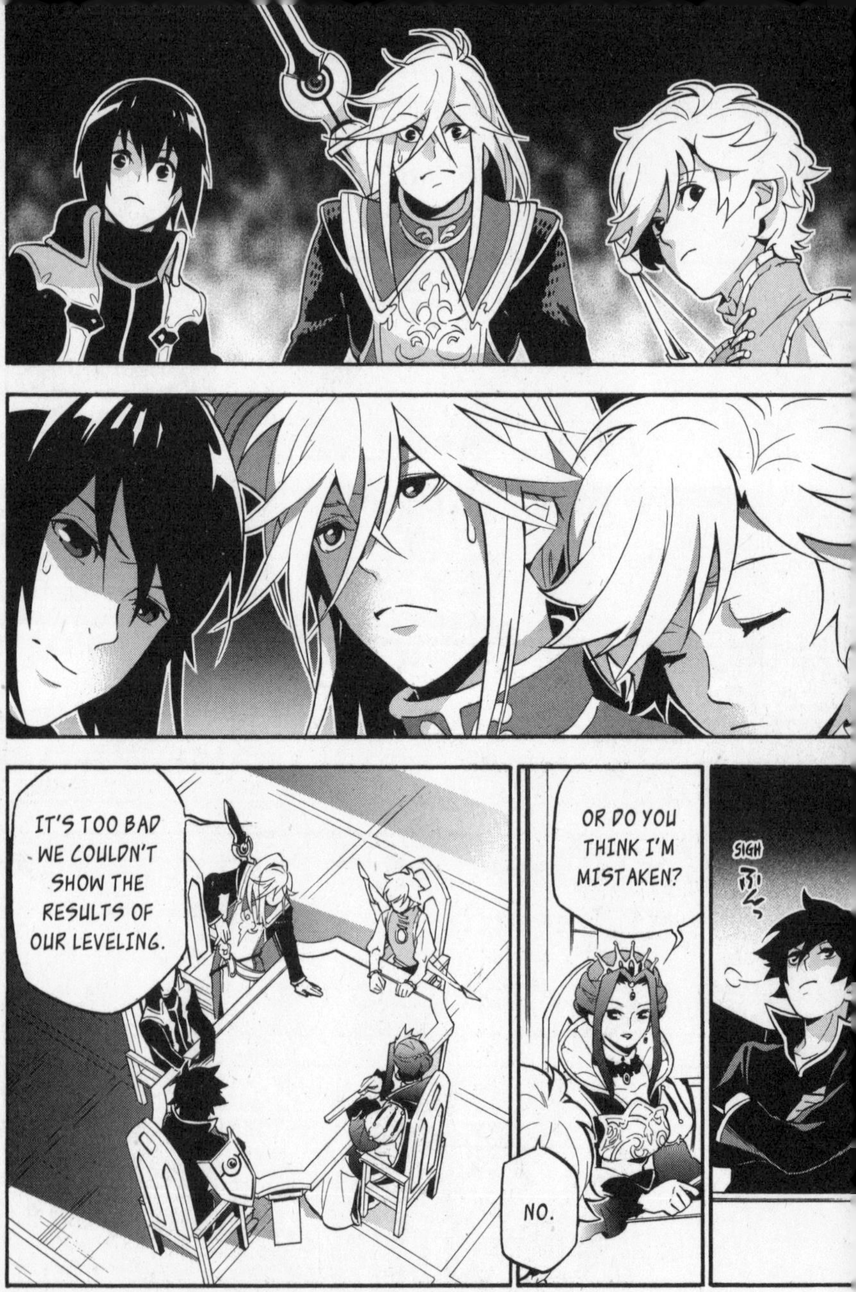
SIGH
OR DO YOU THINK I'M MISTAKEN?
NO.
IT'S TOO BAD WE COULDN'T SHOW THE RESULTS OF OUR LEVELING.

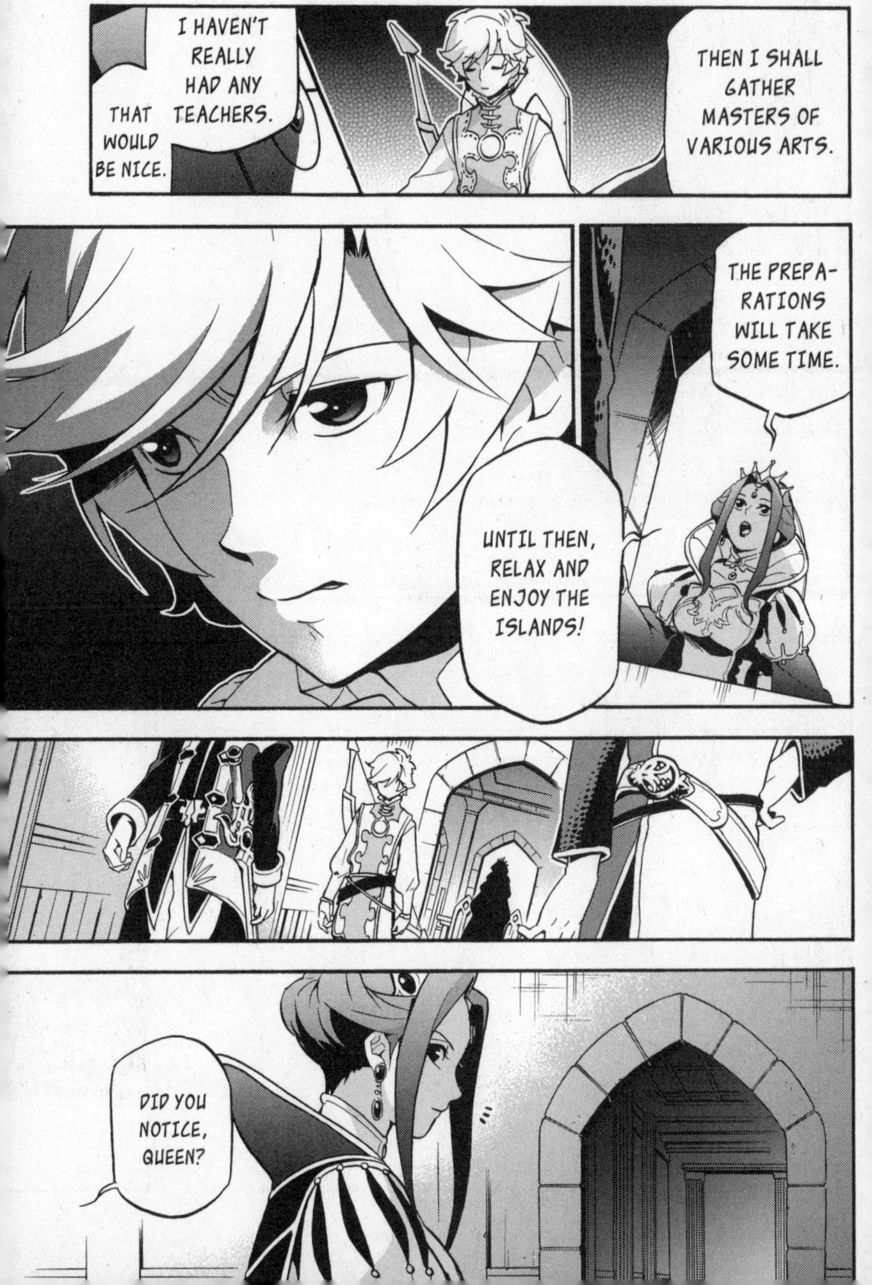
THEN I SHALL GATHER MASTERS OF VARIOUS ARTS.
I HAVEN'T REALLY HAD ANY TEACHERS.
THAT WOULD BE NICE.
THE PREPA-RATIONS WILL TAKE SOME TIME.
UNTIL THEN, RELAX AND ENJOY THE ISLANDS!
DID YOU NOTICE, QUEEN?

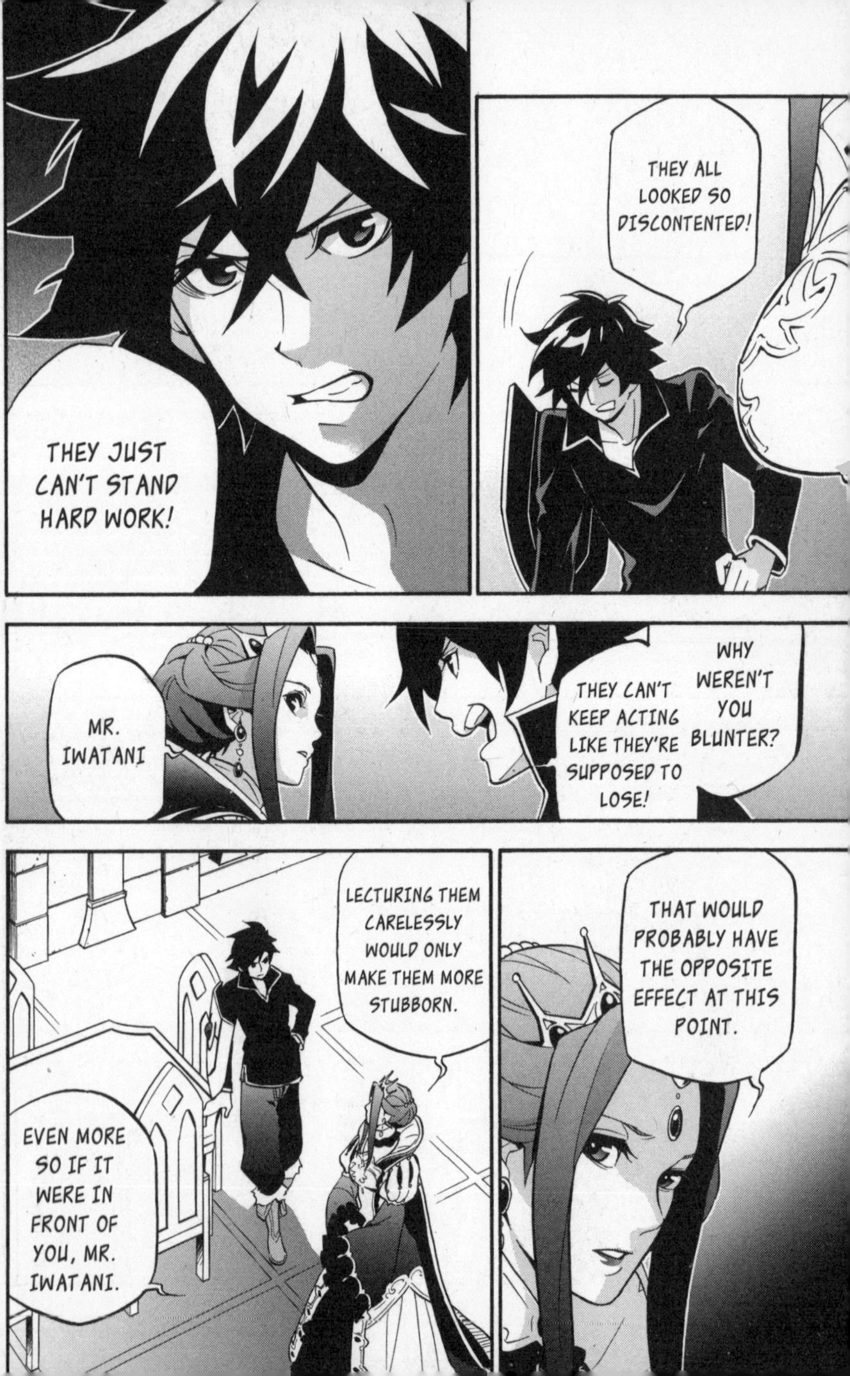
THEY ALL LOOKED SO DISCONTENTED!
THEY JUST CAN'T STAND HARD WORK!
WHY WEREN'T YOU BLUNTER?
THEY CAN'T KEEP ACTING LIKE THEY'RE SUPPOSED TO LOSE!
MR. IWATANI
THAT WOULD PROBABLY HAVE THE OPPOSITE EFFECT AT THIS POINT.
LECTURING THEM CARELESSLY WOULD ONLY MAKE THEM MORE STUBBORN.
EVEN MORE SO IF IT WERE IN FRONT OF YOU, MR. IWATANI.

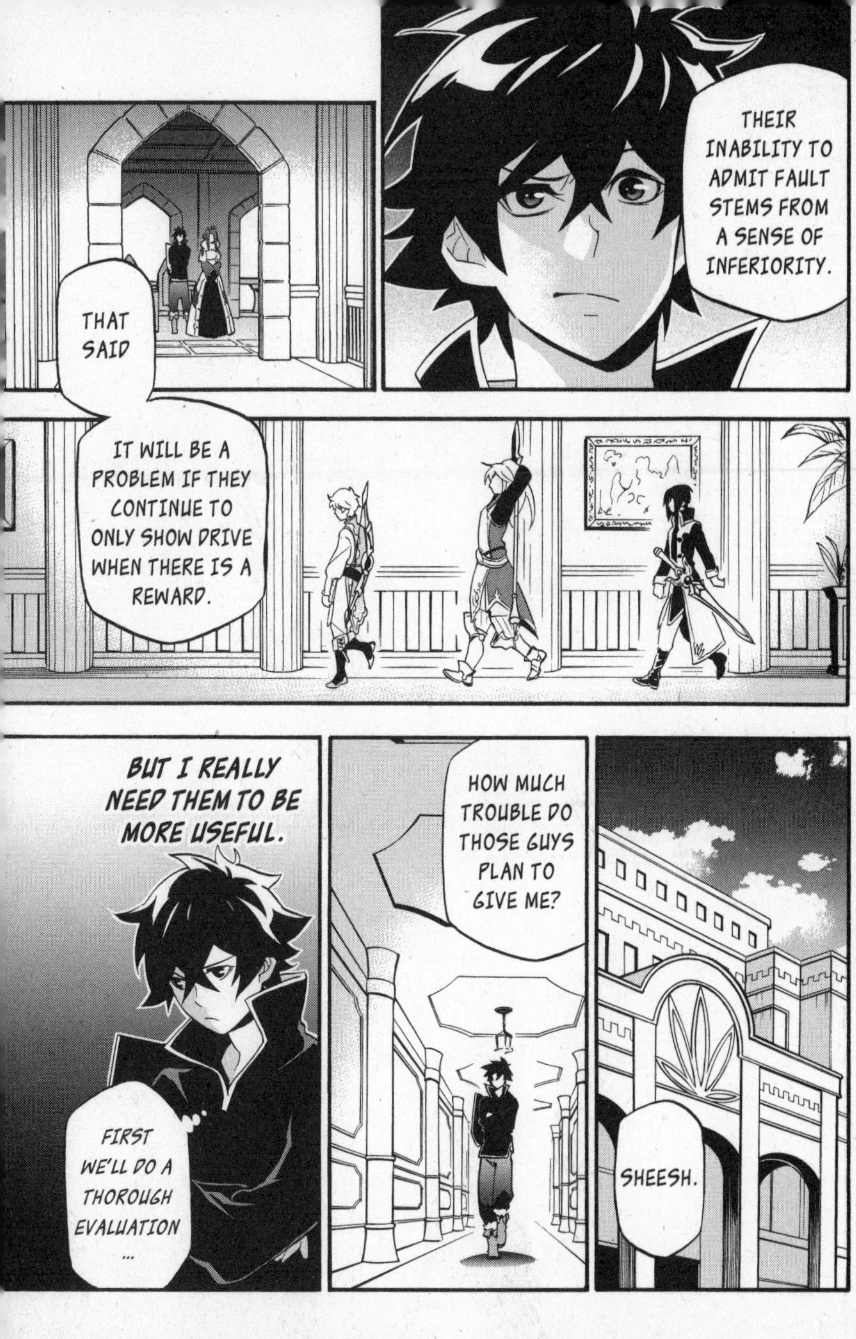
THEIR INABILITY TO ADMIT FAULT STEMS FROM A SENSE OF INFERIORITY.
THAT SAID
IT WILL BE A PROBLEM IF THEY CONTINUE TO ONLY SHOW DRIVE WHEN THERE IS A REWARD.
SHEESH.
HOW MUCH TROUBLE DO THOSE GUYS PLAN TO GIVE ME?
BUT I REALLY NEED THEM TO BE MORE USEFUL.
FIRST WE'LL DO A THOROUGH EVALUATION ...

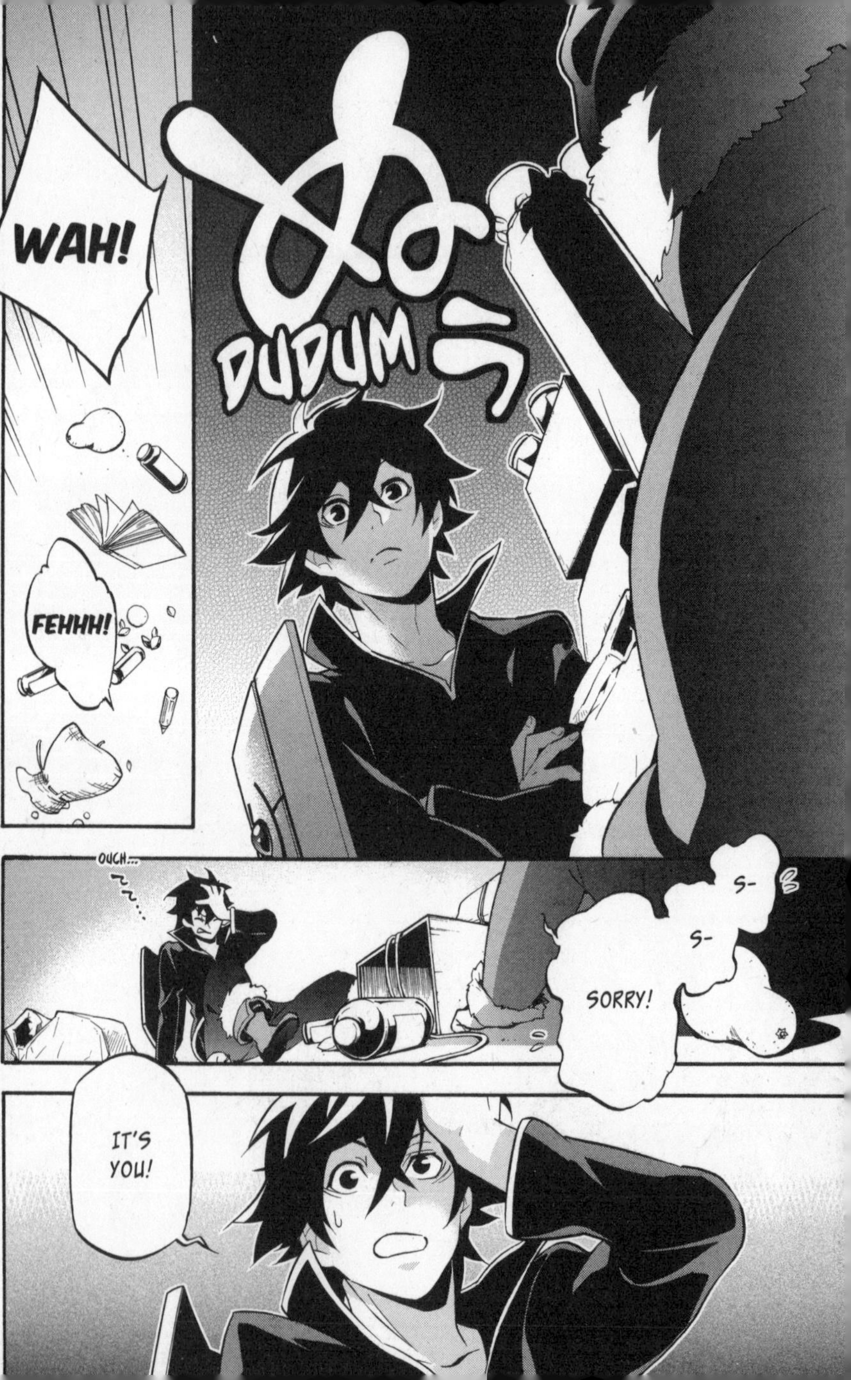
WAH!
DUDUM
FEHHH!
OUCH...
S- S- SORRY!
IT'S YOU!

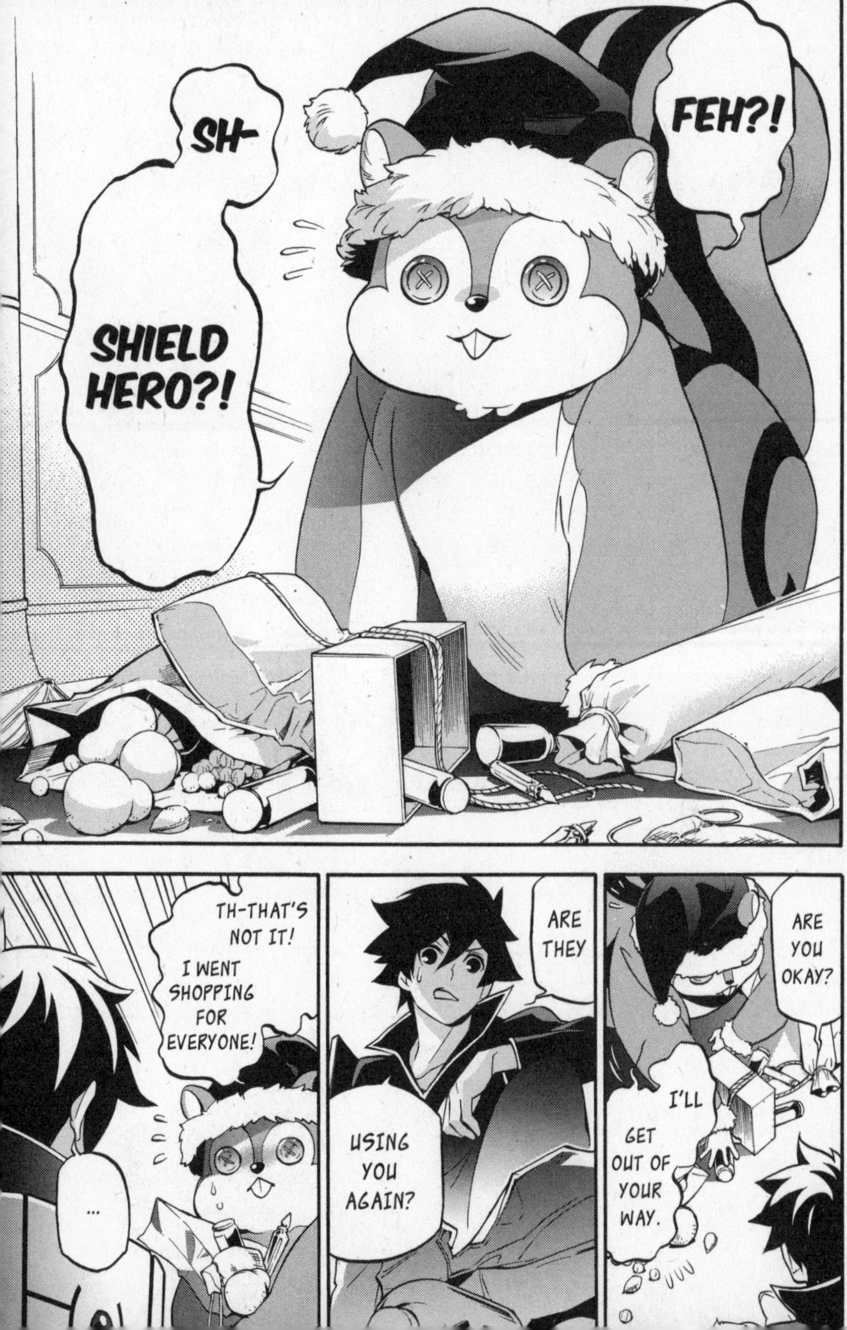

FEH?!
SH- SHIELD HERO?!
ARE YOU OKAY?
I'LL GET OUT OF YOUR WAY.
ARE THEY USING YOU AGAIN?
TH-THAT'S NOT IT! I WENT SHOPPING FOR EVERYONE!
...

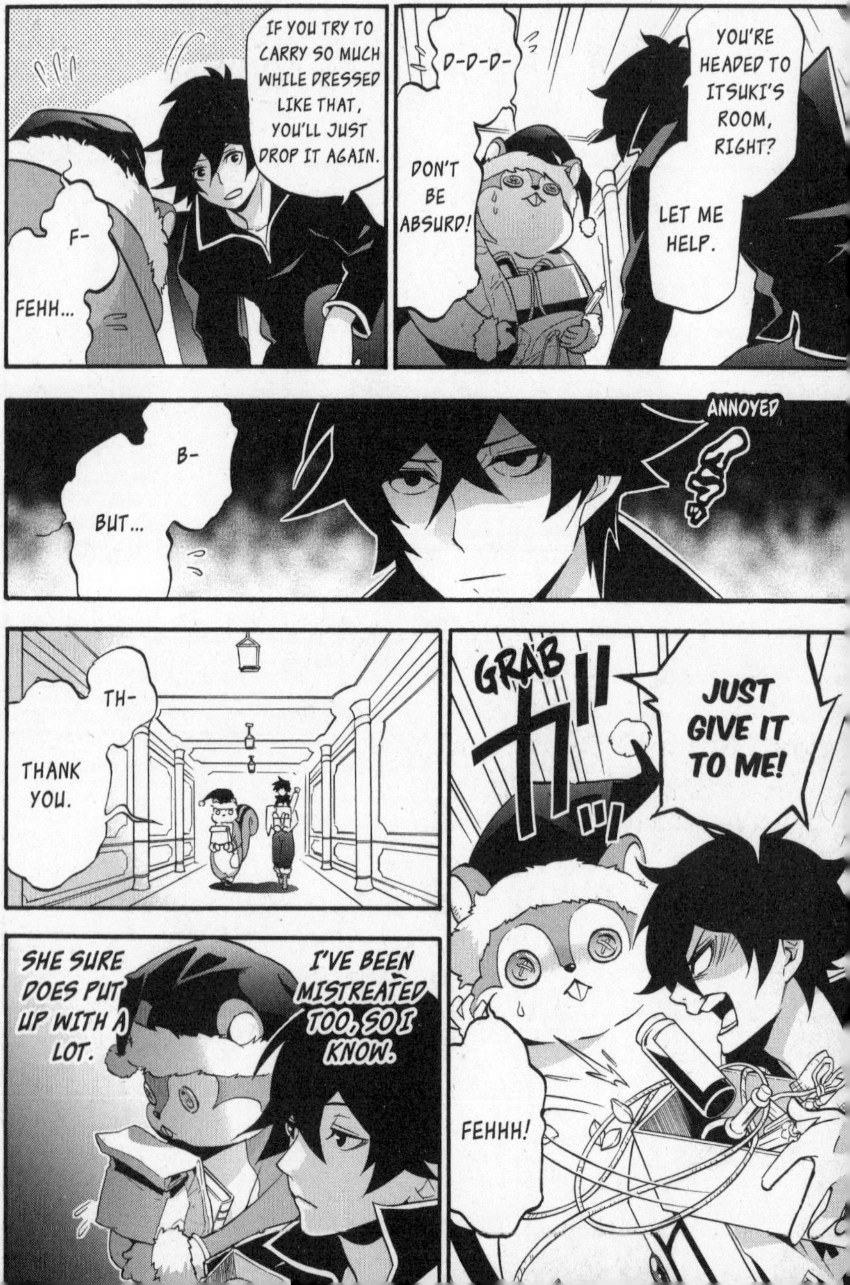
YOU'RE HEADED TO ITSUKI'S ROOM, RIGHT?
D-D-D-
LET ME HELP.
DON'T BE ABSURD!
IF YOU TRY TO CARRY SO MUCH WHILE DRESSED LIKE THAT, YOU'LL JUST DROP IT AGAIN.
F-
FEHH...
ANNOYED
B-
BUT...
GRAB
JUST GIVE IT TO ME!
FEHHH!
TH-
THANK YOU.
I'VE BEEN MISTREATED TOO, SO I KNOW.
SHE SURE DOES PUT UP WITH A LOT.

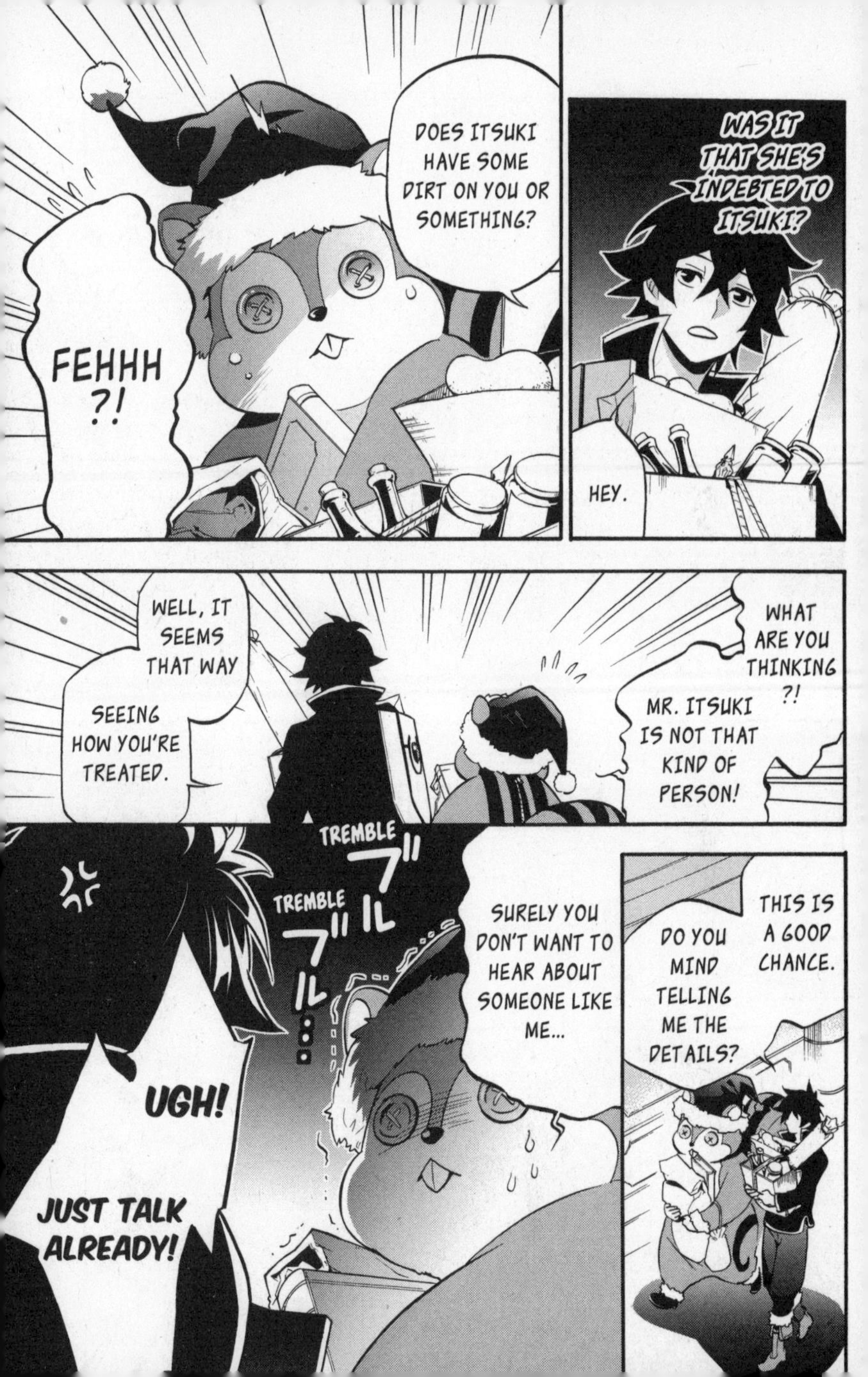
WAS IT THAT SHE'S INDEBTED TO ITSUKI?
HEY.
DOES ITSUKI HAVE SOME DIRT ON YOU OR SOMETHING?
FEHHH ?!
WHAT ARE YOU THINKING ?!
MR. ITSUKI IS NOT THAT KIND OF PERSON!
WELL, IT SEEMS THAT WAY
SEEING HOW YOU'RE TREATED.
THIS IS A GOOD CHANCE.
DO YOU MIND TELLING ME THE DETAILS?
SURELY YOU DON'T WANT TO HEAR ABOUT SOMEONE LIKE ME...
TREMBLE ブル
TREMBLE ブル
UGH!
JUST TALK ALREADY!

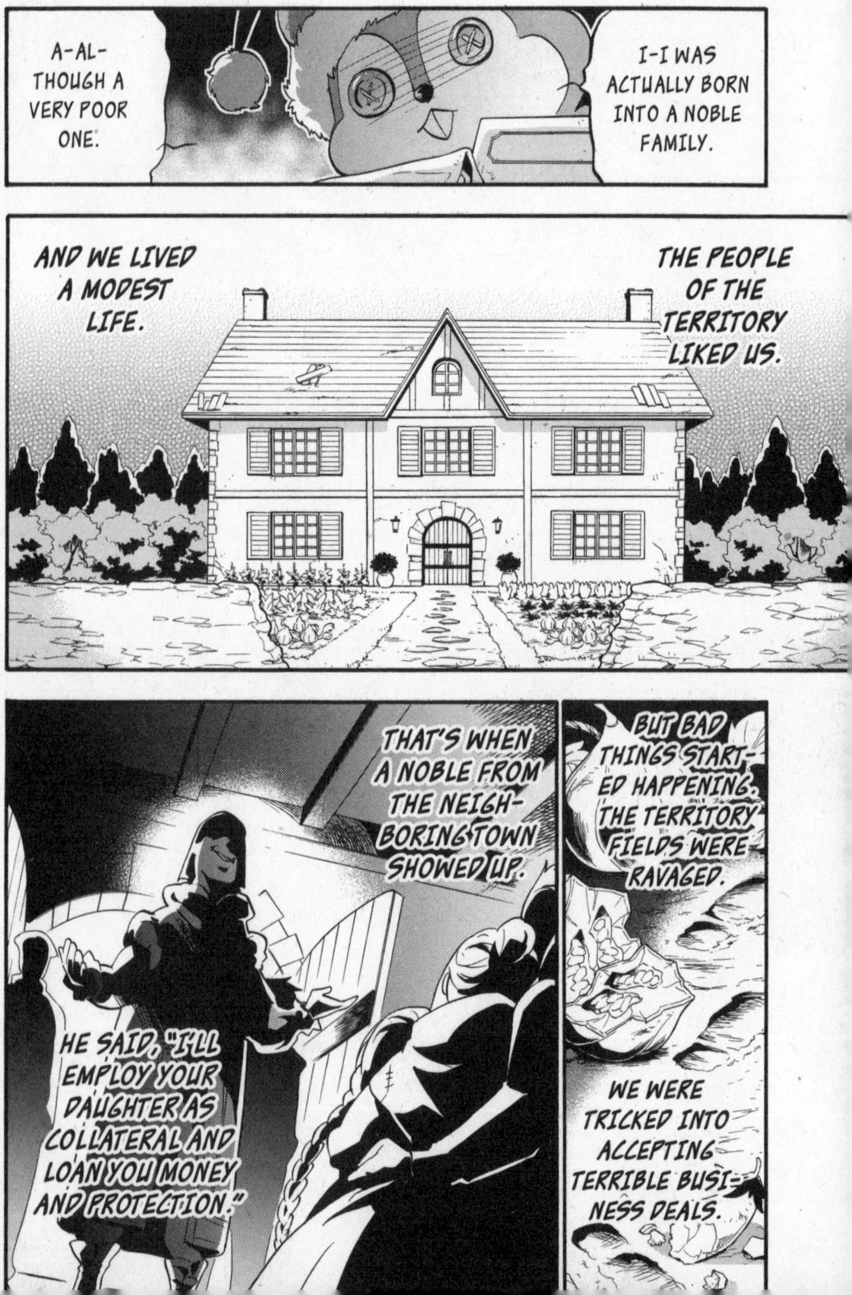
I-I WAS ACTUALLY BORN INTO A NOBLE FAMILY.
A-ALTHOUGH A VERY POOR ONE.
THE PEOPLE OF THE TERRITORY LIKED US.
AND WE LIVED A MODEST LIFE.
BUT BAD THINGS STARTED HAPPENING. THE TERRITORY FIELDS WERE RAVAGED.
WE WERE TRICKED INTO ACCEPTING TERRIBLE BUSINESS DEALS.
THAT'S WHEN A NOBLE FROM THE NEIGHBORING TOWN SHOWED UP.
HE SAID, "I'LL EMPLOY YOUR DAUGHTER AS COLLATERAL AND LOAN YOU MONEY AND PROTECTION."

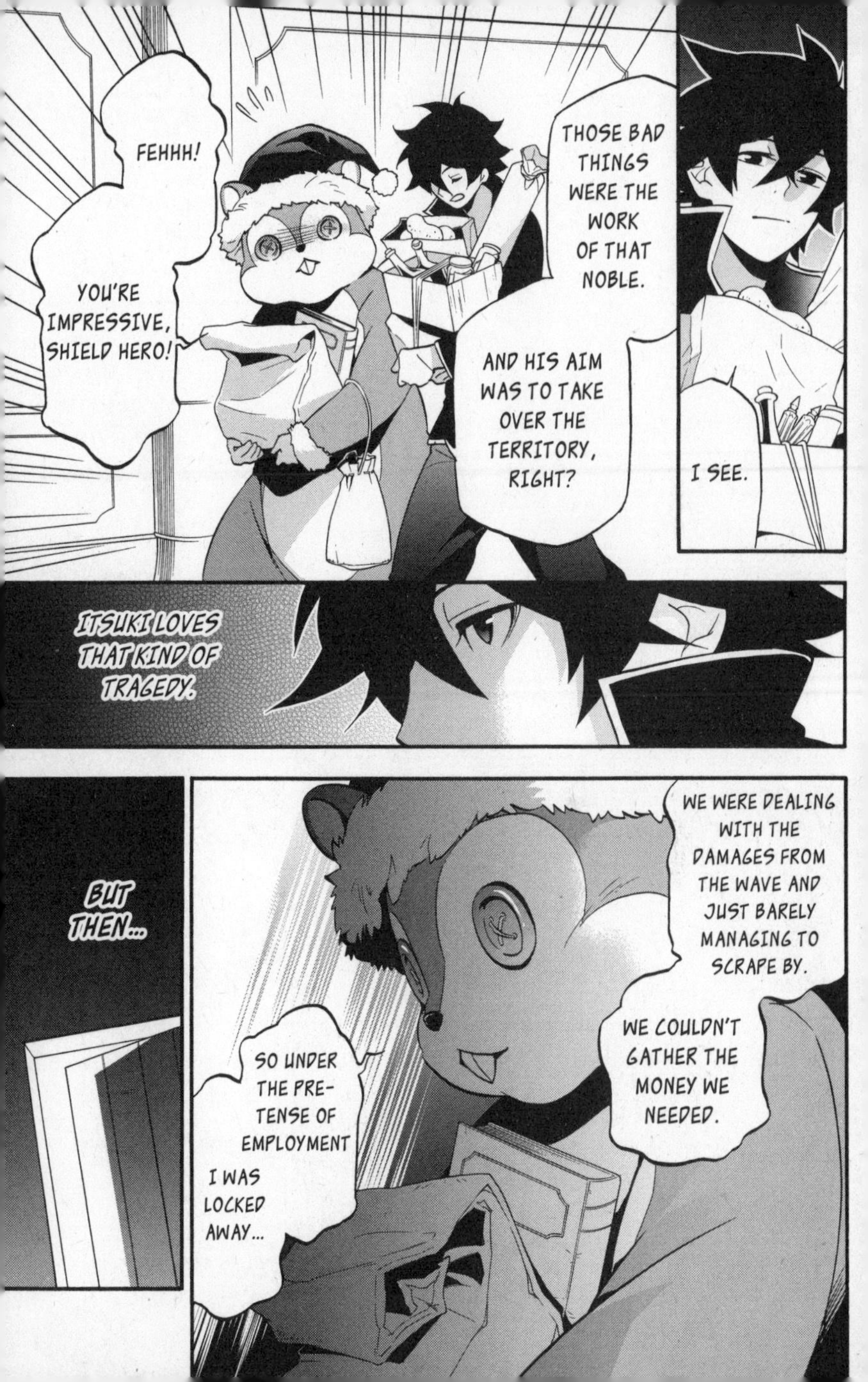
I SEE.
THOSE BAD THINGS WERE THE WORK OF THAT NOBLE.
AND HIS AIM WAS TO TAKE OVER THE TERRITORY, RIGHT?
FEHHH!
YOU'RE IMPRESSIVE, SHIELD HERO!
ITSUKI LOVES THAT KIND OF TRAGEDY.
WE WERE DEALING WITH THE DAMAGES FROM THE WAVE AND JUST BARELY MANAGING TO SCRAPE BY.
WE COULDN'T GATHER THE MONEY WE NEEDED.
SO UNDER THE PRE-TENSE OF EMPLOYMENT
I WAS LOCKED AWAY...
BUT THEN...

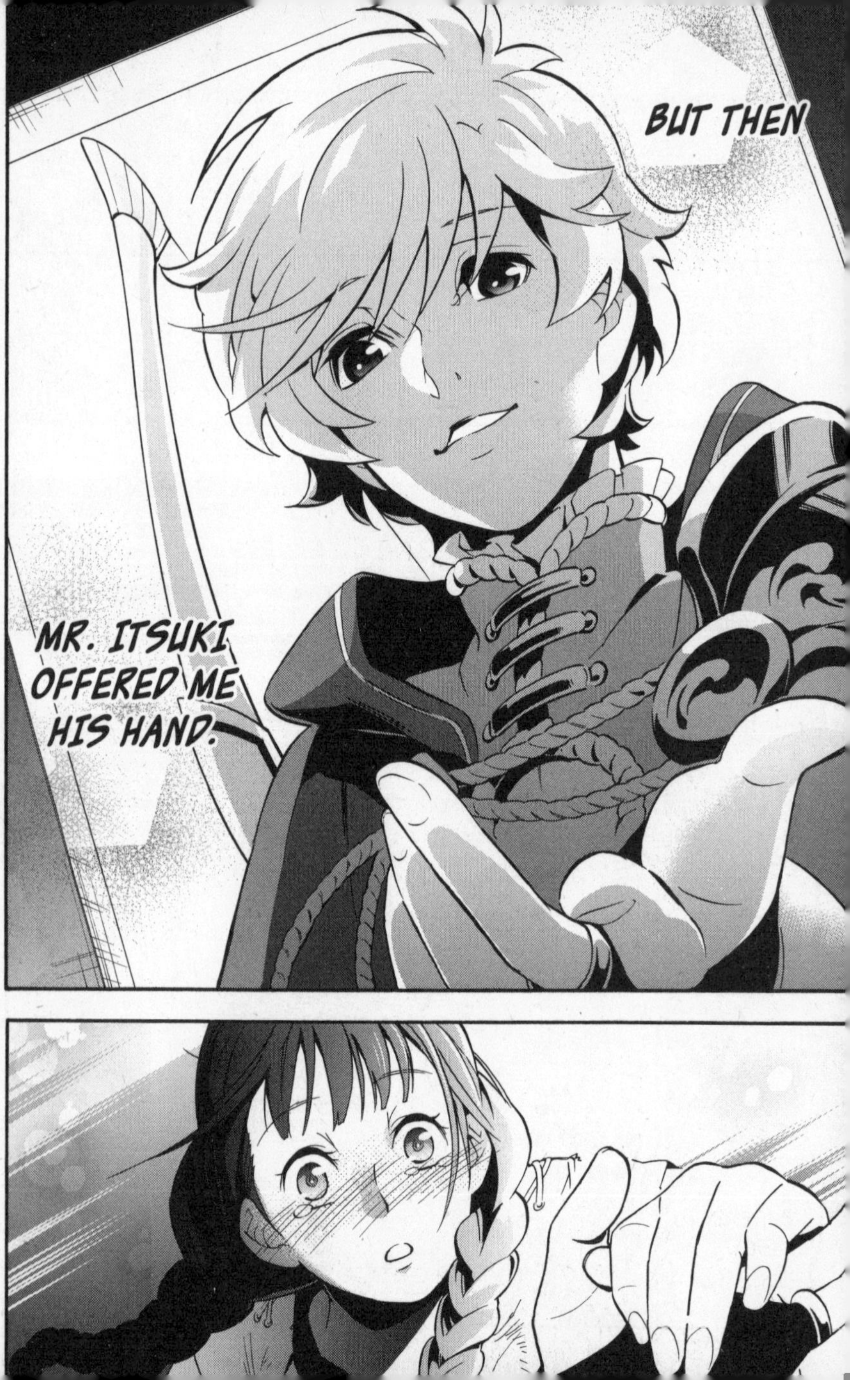
BUT THEN
MR. ITSUKI OFFERED ME HIS HAND.

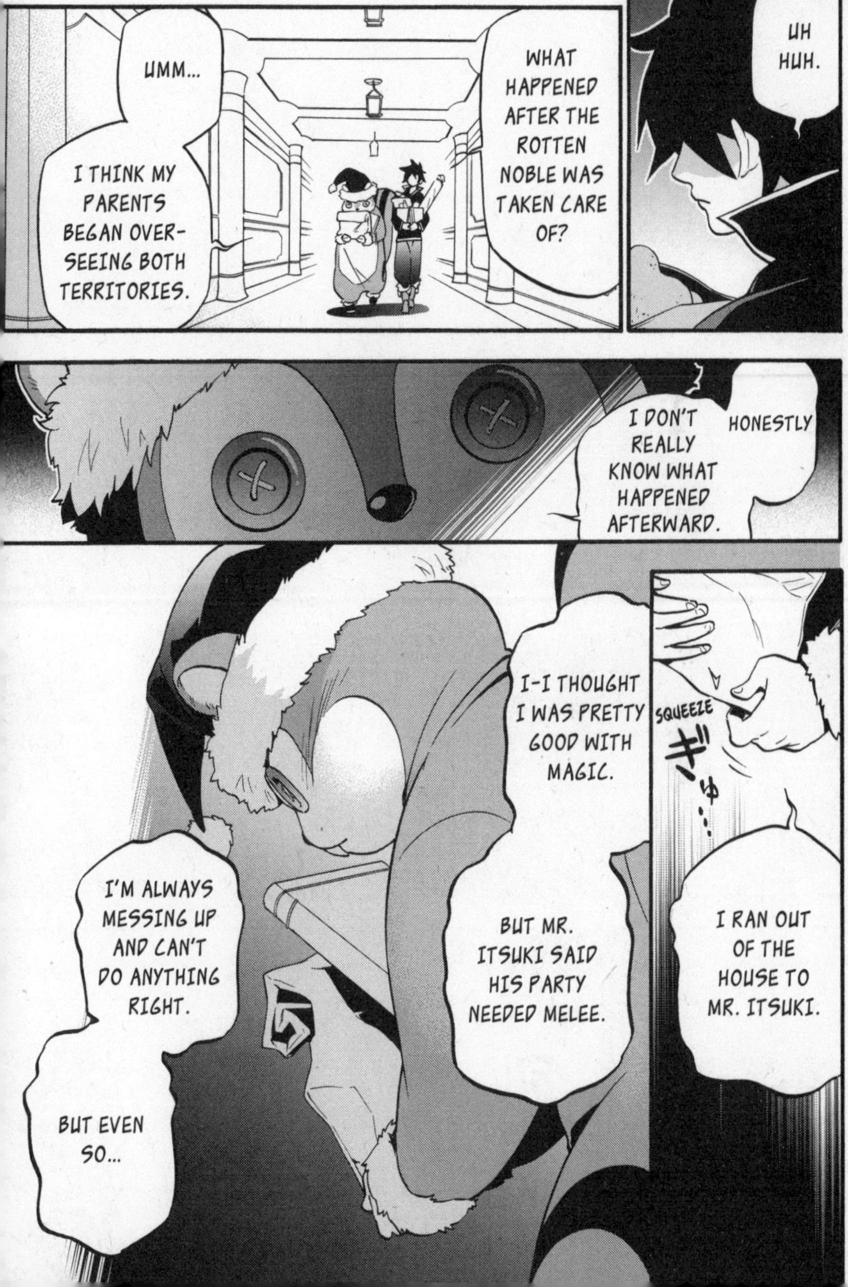
UH HUH.
WHAT HAPPENED AFTER THE ROTTEN NOBLE WAS TAKEN CARE OF?
UMM...
I THINK MY PARENTS BEGAN OVER-SEEING BOTH TERRITORIES.
HONESTLY
I DON'T REALLY KNOW WHAT HAPPENED AFTERWARD.
SQUEEZE
ぎゅ…
I RAN OUT OF THE HOUSE TO MR. ITSUKI.
I-I THOUGHT I WAS PRETTY GOOD WITH MAGIC.
BUT MR. ITSUKI SAID HIS PARTY NEEDED MELEE.
I'M ALWAYS MESSING UP AND CAN'T DO ANYTHING RIGHT.
BUT EVEN SO...

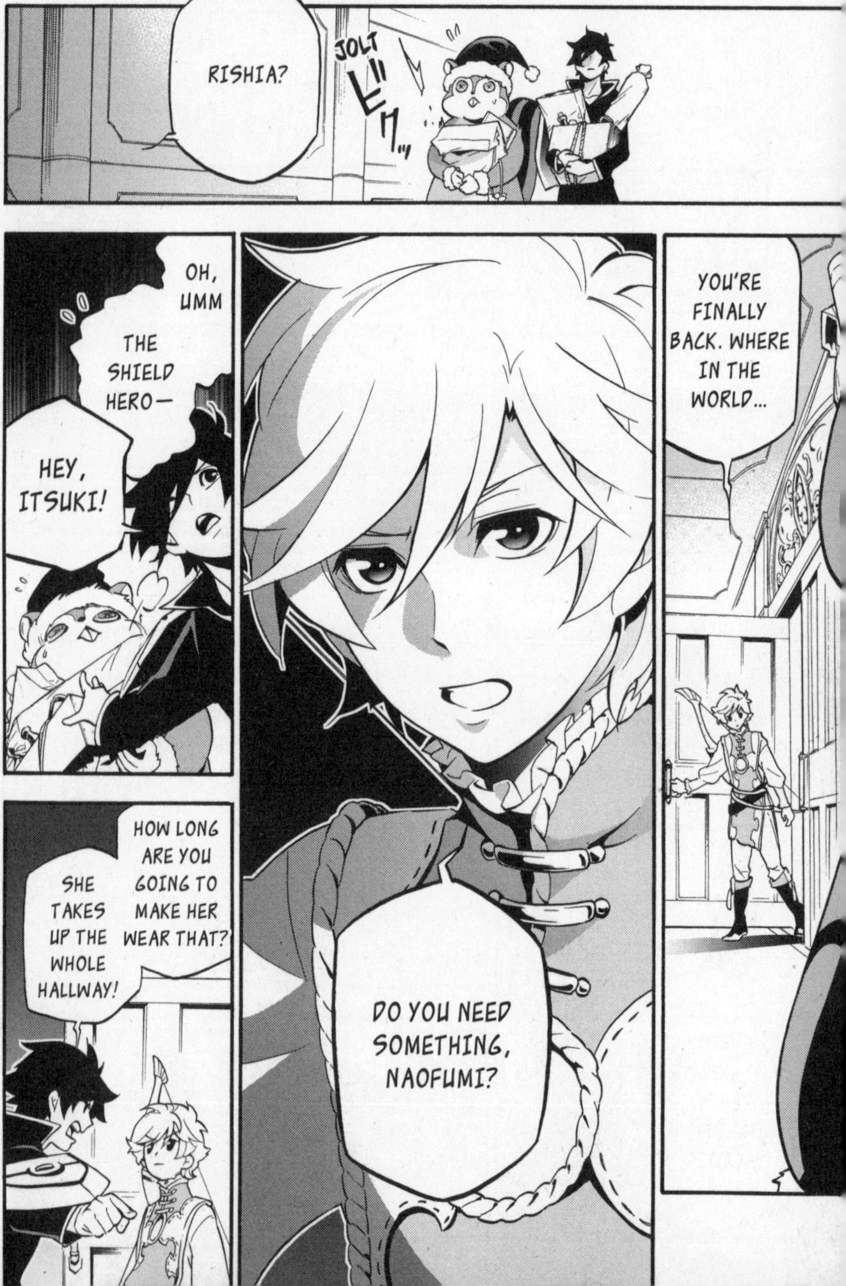
RISHIA?
JOLT
YOU'RE FINALLY BACK. WHERE IN THE WORLD...
DO YOU NEED SOMETHING, NAOFUMI?
OH, UMM
THE SHIELD HERO—
HEY, ITSUKI!
HOW LONG ARE YOU GOING TO MAKE HER WEAR THAT?
SHE TAKES UP THE WHOLE HALLWAY!

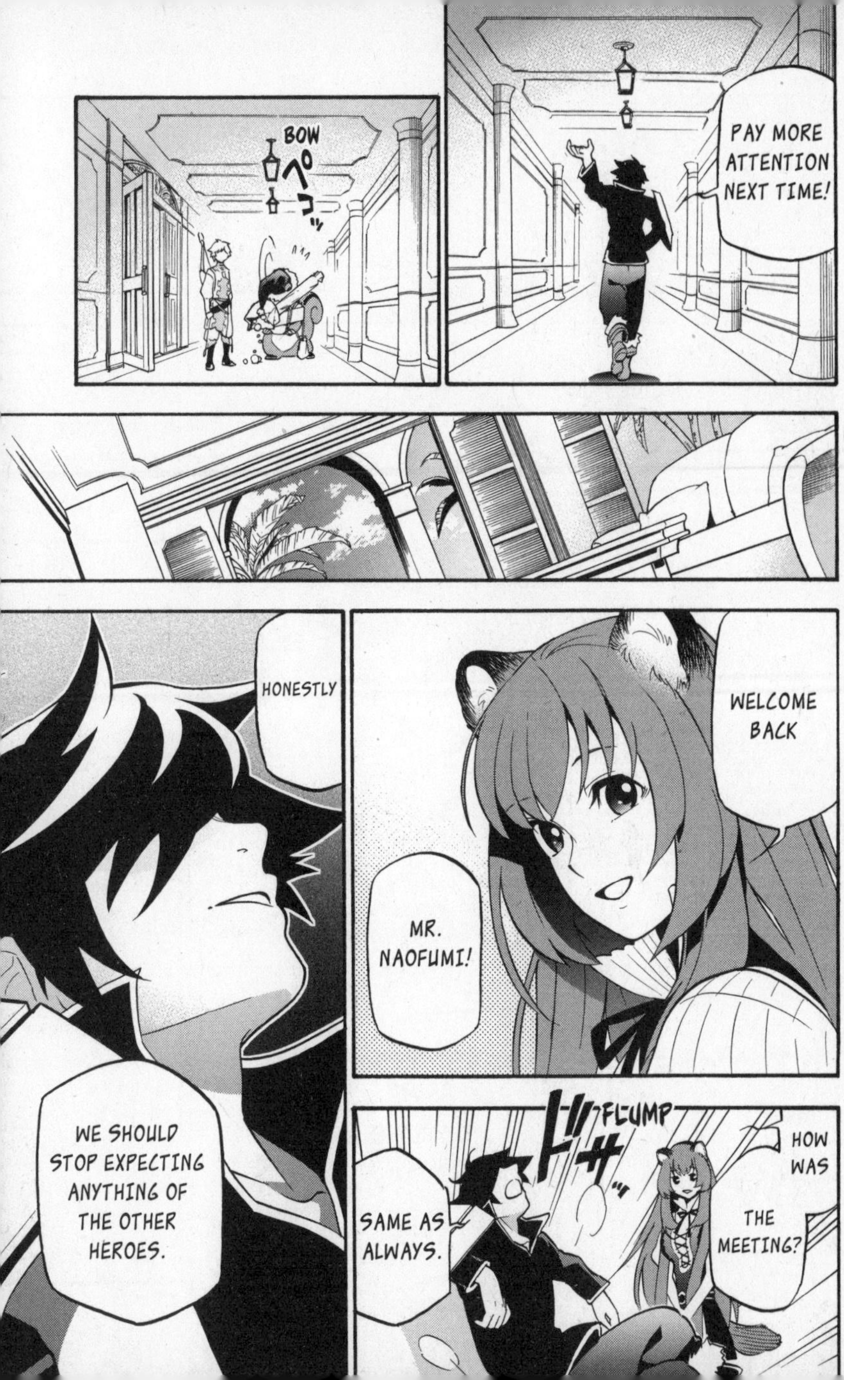
PAY MORE ATTENTION NEXT TIME!
BOW
ペコッ
WELCOME BACK
MR. NAOFUMI!
HOW WAS THE MEETING?
FLUMP
ドサッ
SAME AS ALWAYS.
HONESTLY
WE SHOULD STOP EXPECTING ANYTHING OF THE OTHER HEROES.

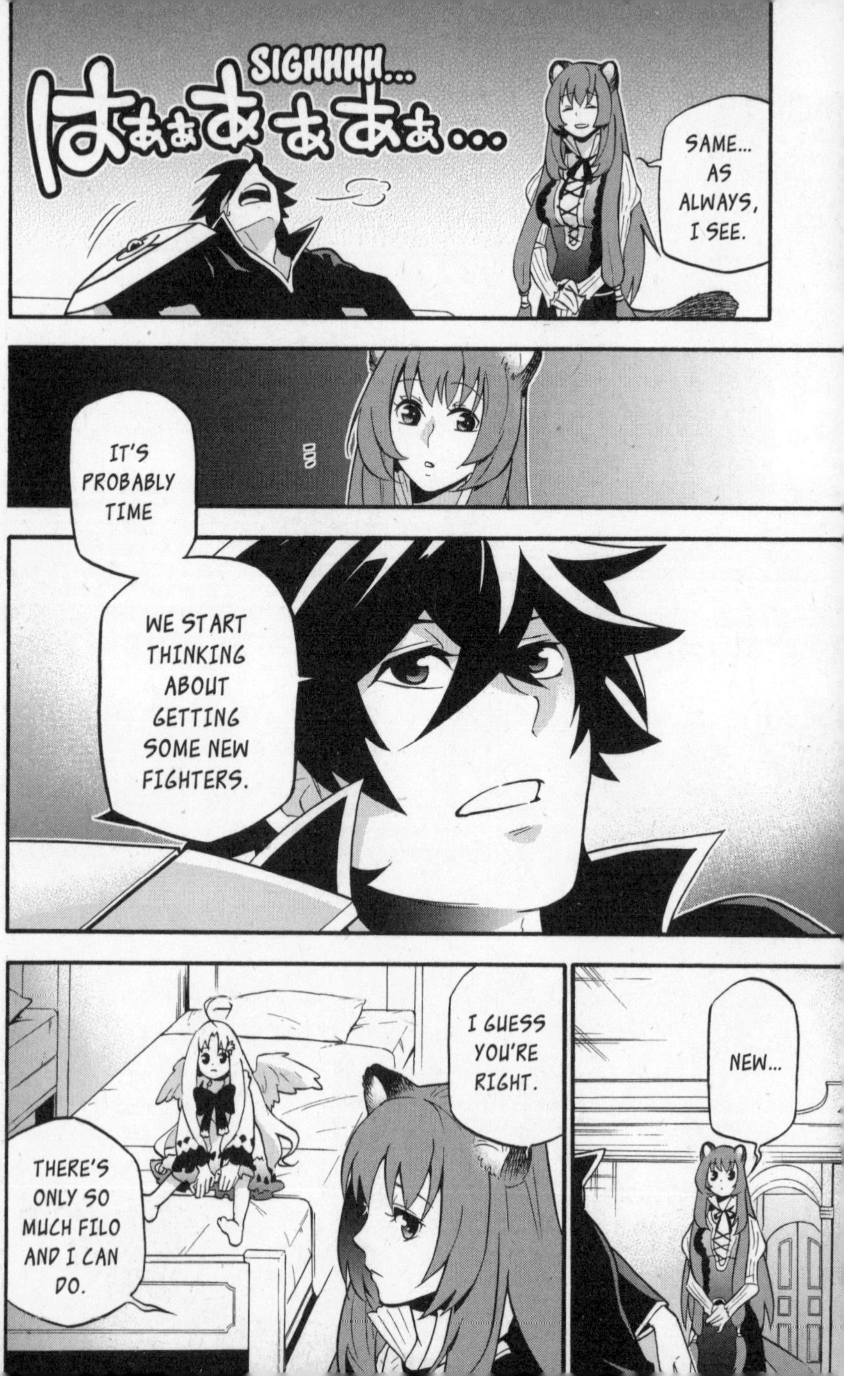
SIGHHHH...
はぁぁあぁあぁ...
SAME... AS ALWAYS, I SEE.
...
IT'S PROBABLY TIME
WE START THINKING ABOUT GETTING SOME NEW FIGHTERS.
NEW...
I GUESS YOU'RE RIGHT.
THERE'S ONLY SO MUCH FILO AND I CAN DO.

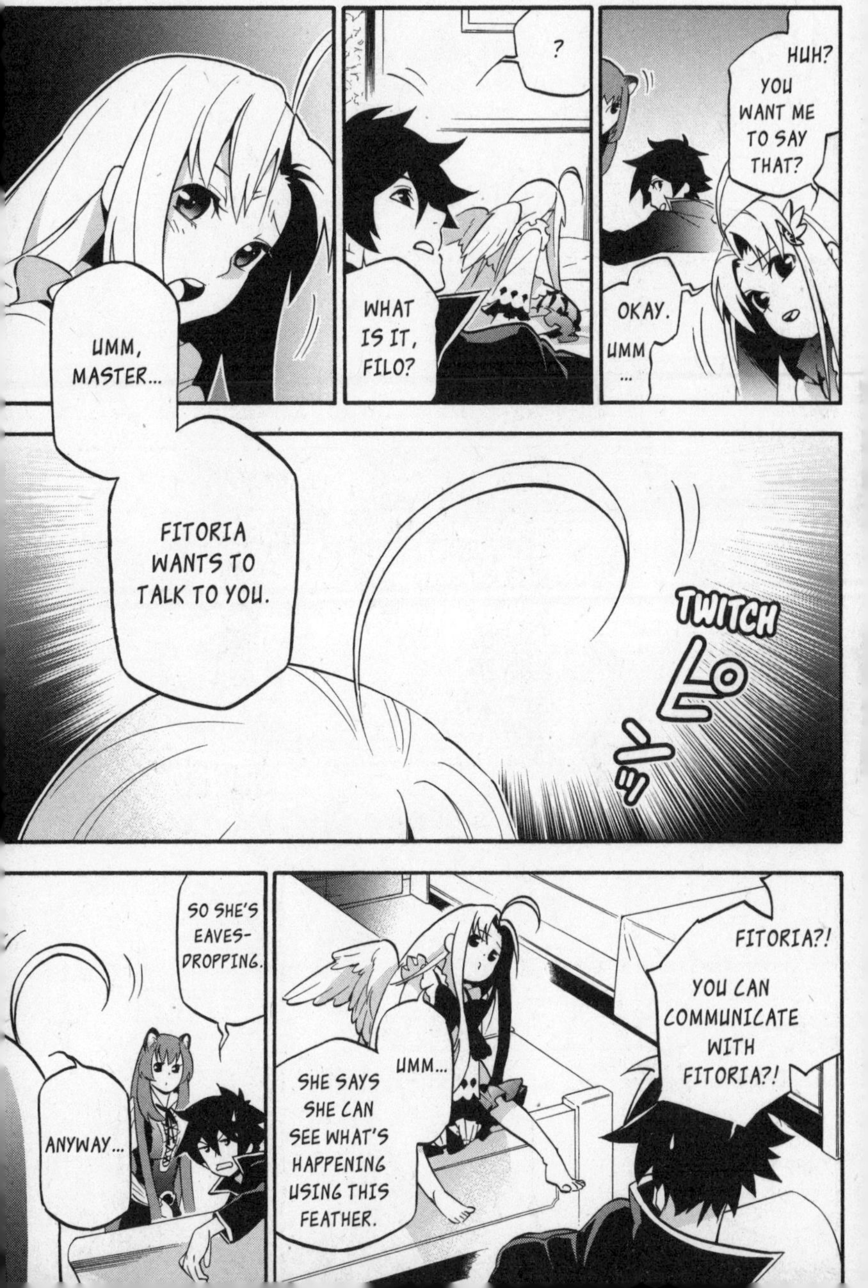
HUH? YOU WANT ME TO SAY THAT?
OKAY.
UMM ...
?
WHAT IS IT, FILO?
UMM, MASTER...
FITORIA WANTS TO TALK TO YOU.
TWITCH
FITORIA?!
YOU CAN COMMUNICATE WITH FITORIA?!
UMM...
SHE SAYS SHE CAN SEE WHAT'S HAPPENING USING THIS FEATHER.
SO SHE'S EAVES-DROPPING.
ANYWAY...

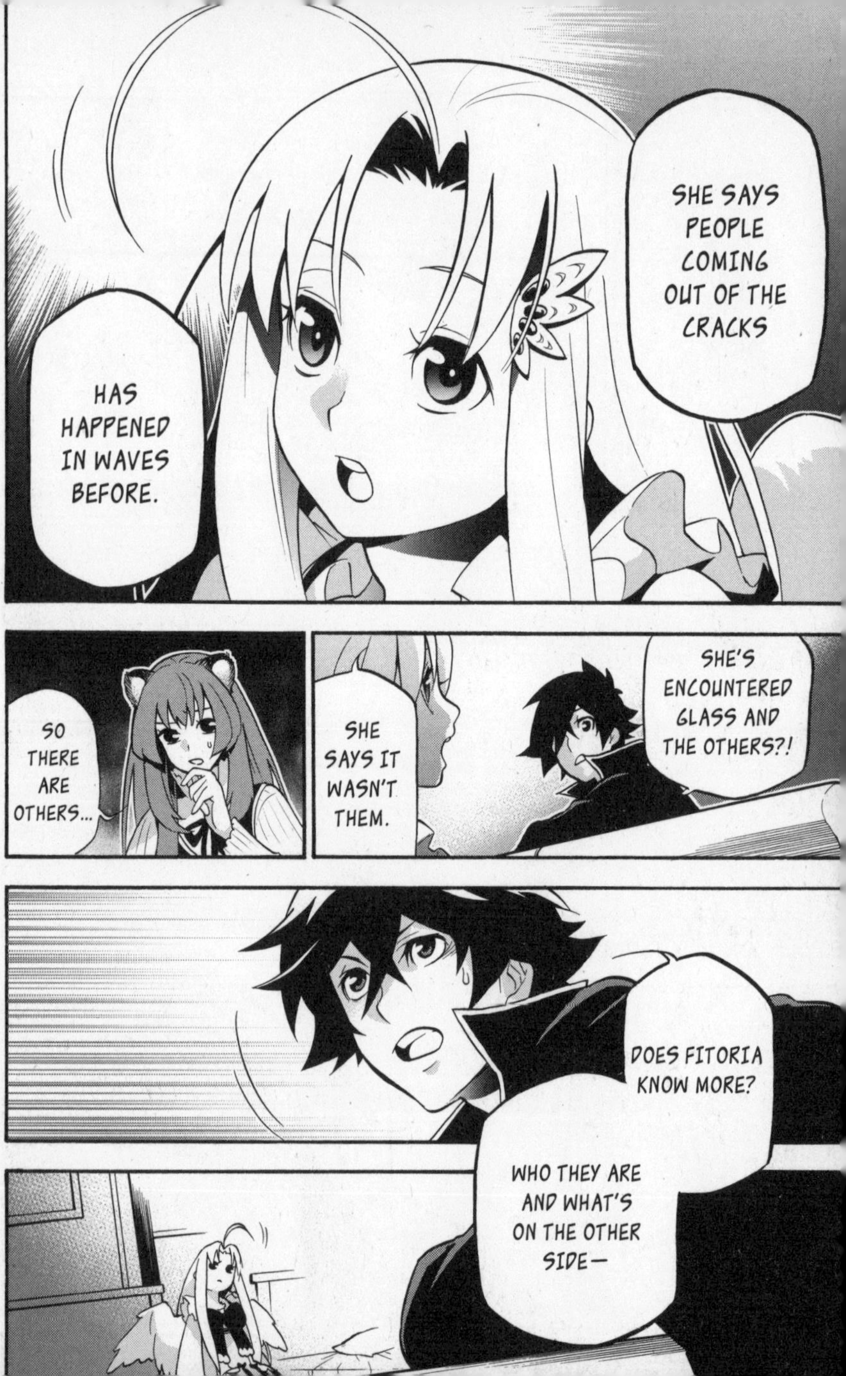
SHE SAYS PEOPLE COMING OUT OF THE CRACKS
HAS HAPPENED IN WAVES BEFORE.
SHE'S ENCOUNTERED GLASS AND THE OTHERS?!
SHE SAYS IT WASN'T THEM.
SO THERE ARE OTHERS...
DOES FITORIA KNOW MORE?
WHO THEY ARE AND WHAT'S ON THE OTHER SIDE—

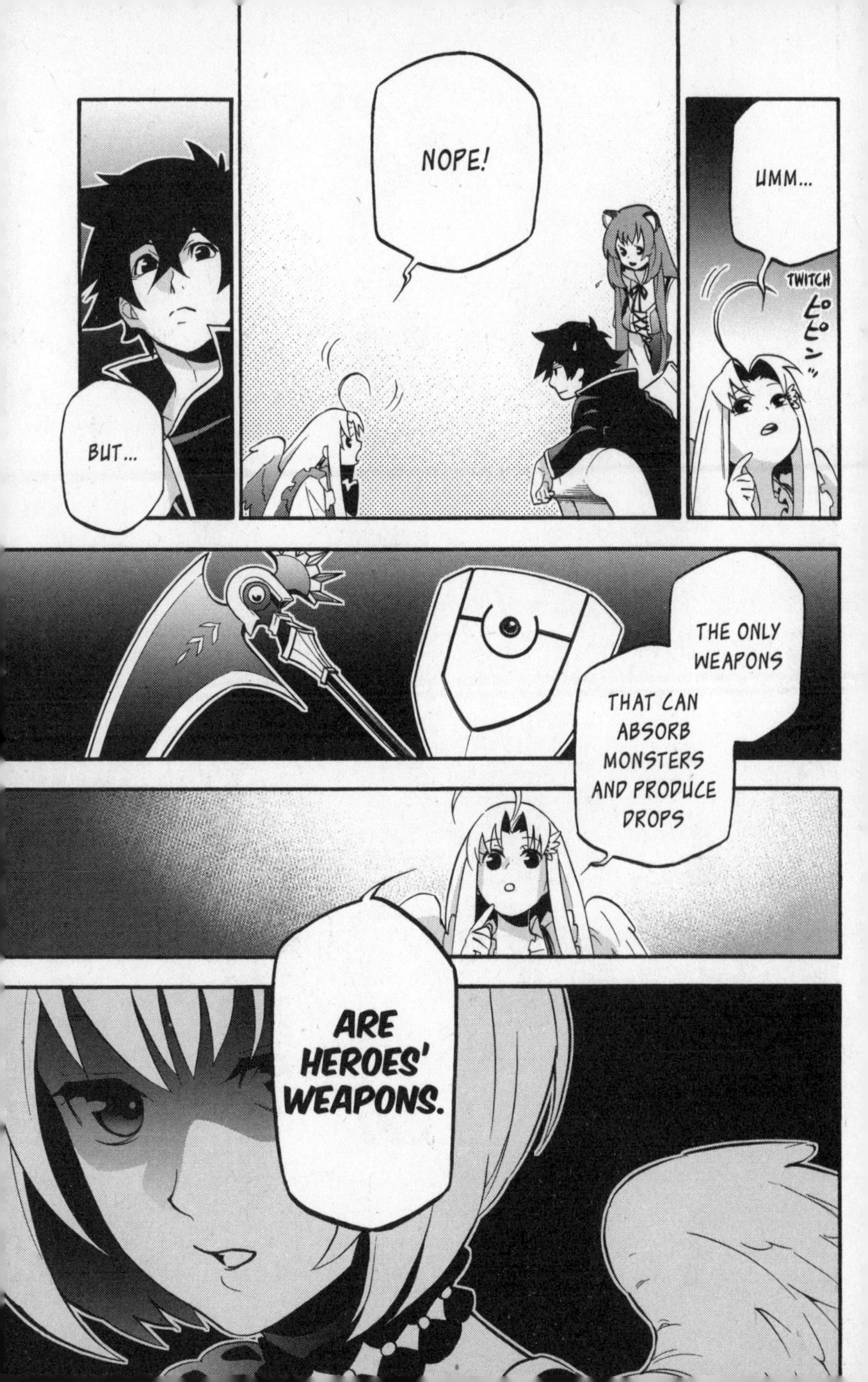
UMM...
TWITCH
ピピン‥
NOPE!
BUT...
THE ONLY WEAPONS
THAT CAN ABSORB MONSTERS AND PRODUCE DROPS
ARE HEROES' WEAPONS.

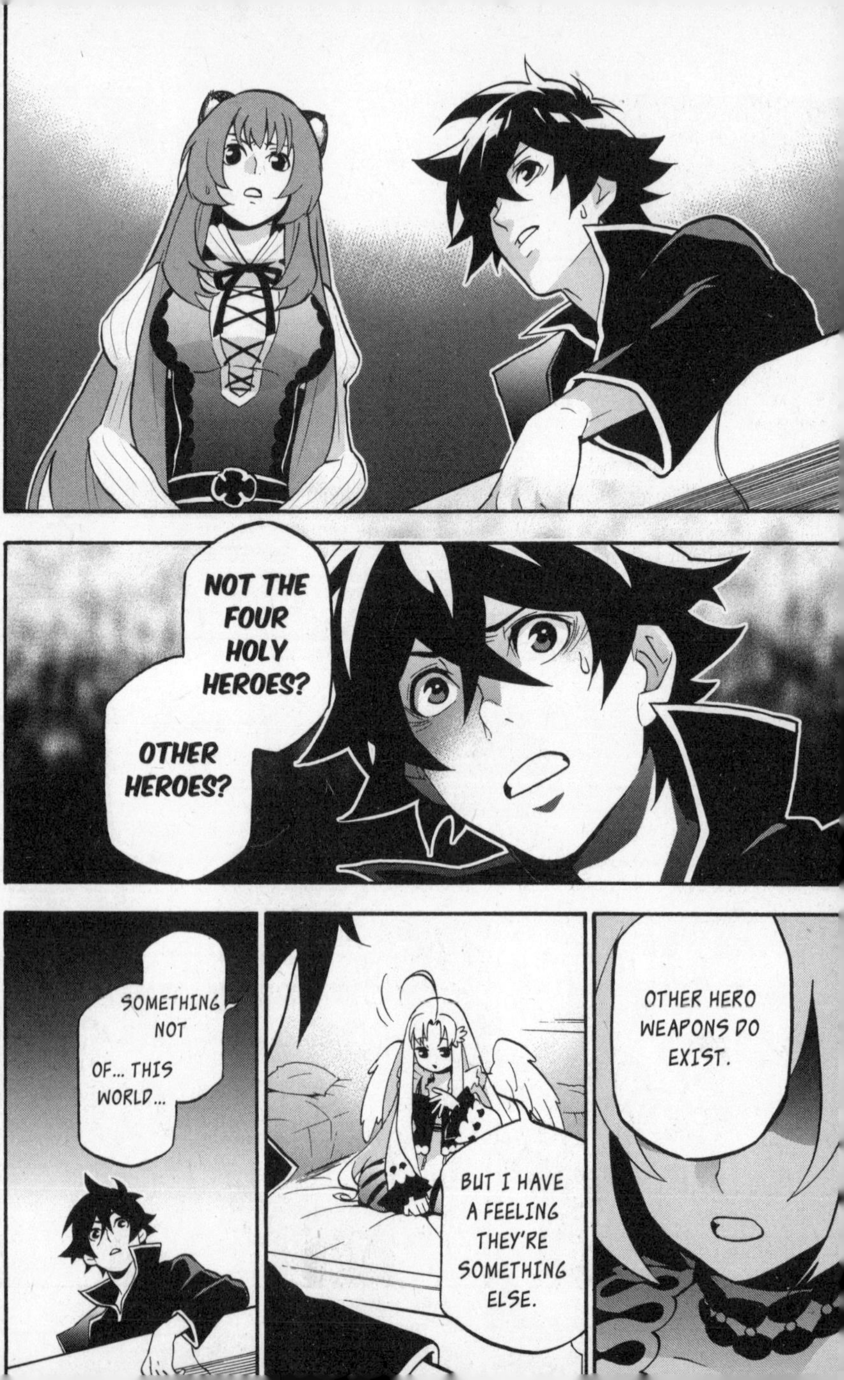
NOT THE FOUR HOLY HEROES?
OTHER HEROES?
OTHER HERO WEAPONS DO EXIST.
BUT I HAVE A FEELING THEY'RE SOMETHING ELSE.
SOMETHING NOT OF... THIS WORLD...

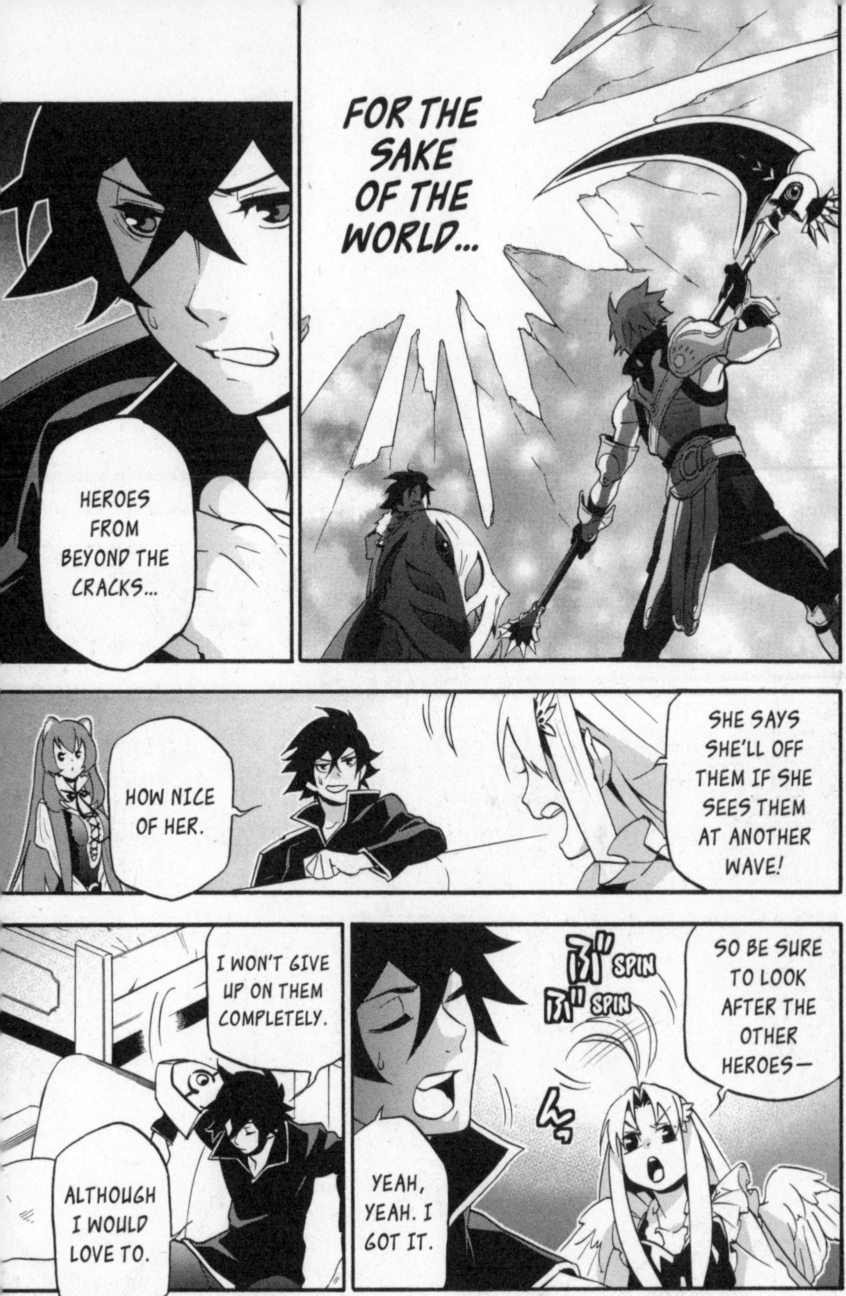
FOR THE SAKE OF THE WORLD...
HEROES FROM BEYOND THE CRACKS...
SHE SAYS SHE'LL OFF THEM IF SHE SEES THEM AT ANOTHER WAVE!
HOW NICE OF HER.
SO BE SURE TO LOOK AFTER THE OTHER HEROES—
ぶ SPIN
ぶ SPIN
ん
YEAH, YEAH. I GOT IT.
I WON'T GIVE UP ON THEM COMPLETELY.
ALTHOUGH I WOULD LOVE TO.

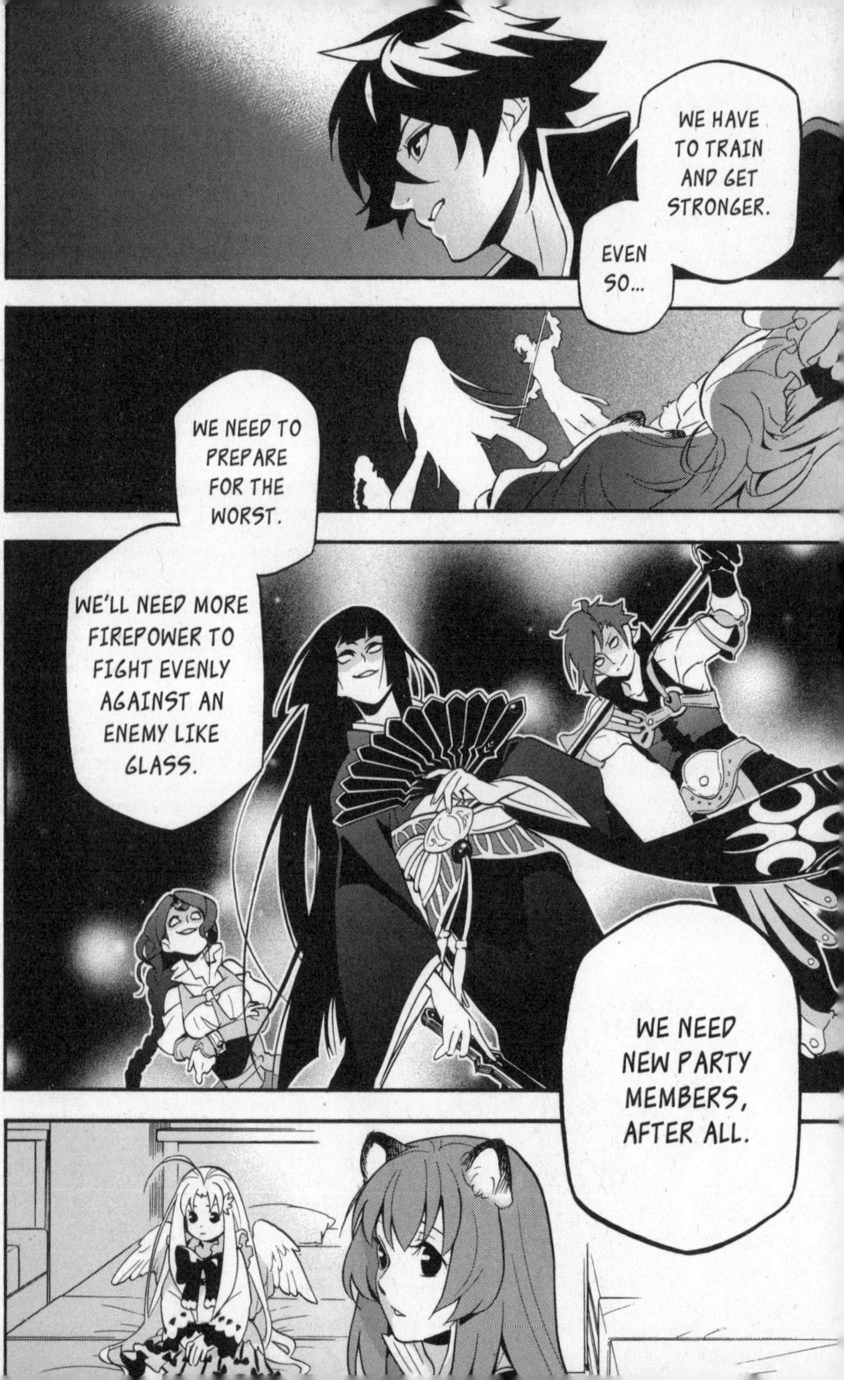
WE HAVE TO TRAIN AND GET STRONGER.
EVEN SO...
WE NEED TO PREPARE FOR THE WORST.
WE'LL NEED MORE FIREPOWER TO FIGHT EVENLY AGAINST AN ENEMY LIKE GLASS.
WE NEED NEW PARTY MEMBERS, AFTER ALL.

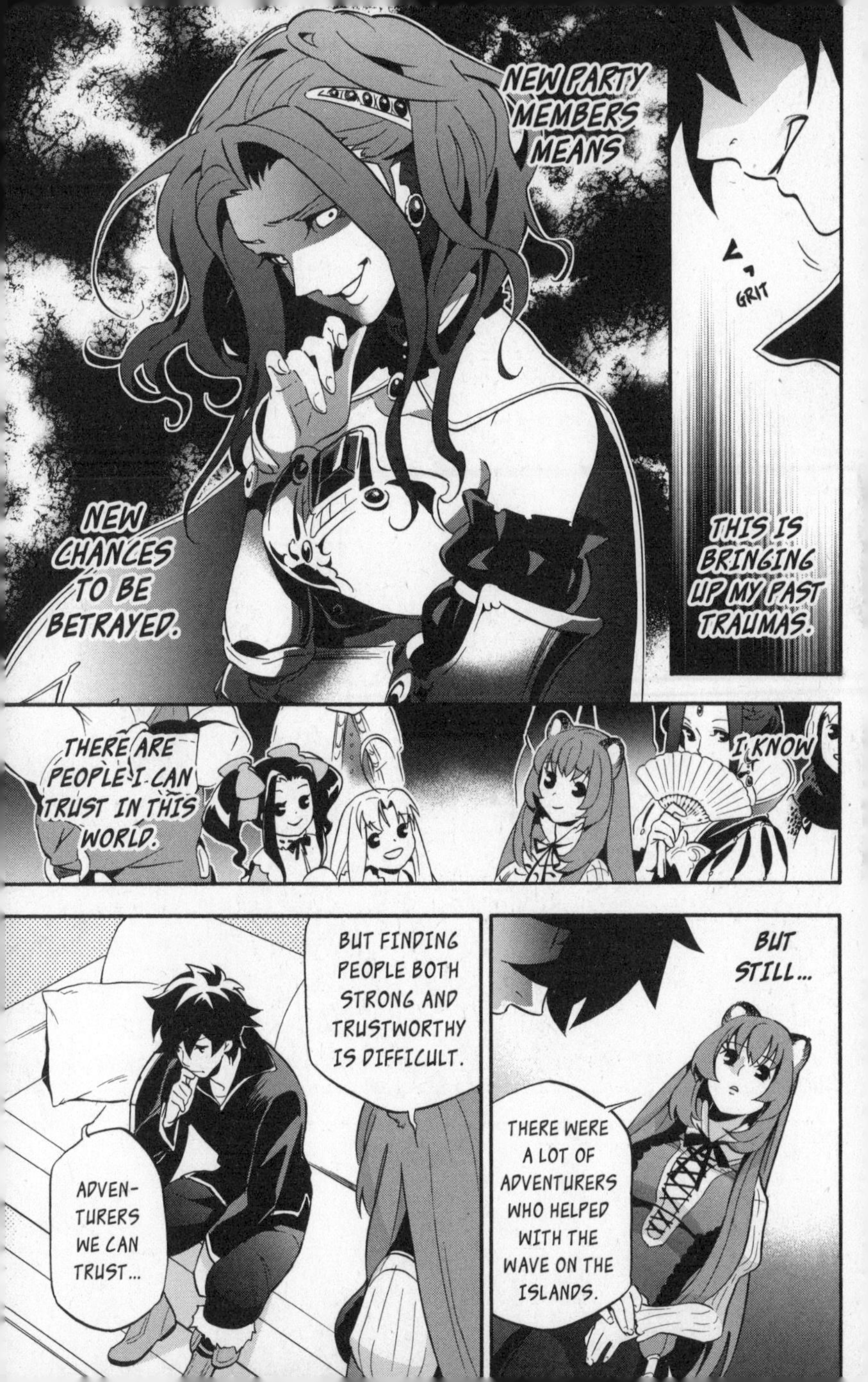
GRIT
THIS IS BRINGING UP MY PAST TRAUMAS.
NEW PARTY MEMBERS MEANS
NEW CHANCES TO BE BETRAYED.
I KNOW
THERE ARE PEOPLE I CAN TRUST IN THIS WORLD.
BUT STILL...
THERE WERE A LOT OF ADVENTURERS WHO HELPED WITH THE WAVE ON THE ISLANDS.
BUT FINDING PEOPLE BOTH STRONG AND TRUSTWORTHY IS DIFFICULT.
ADVEN-TURERS WE CAN TRUST...

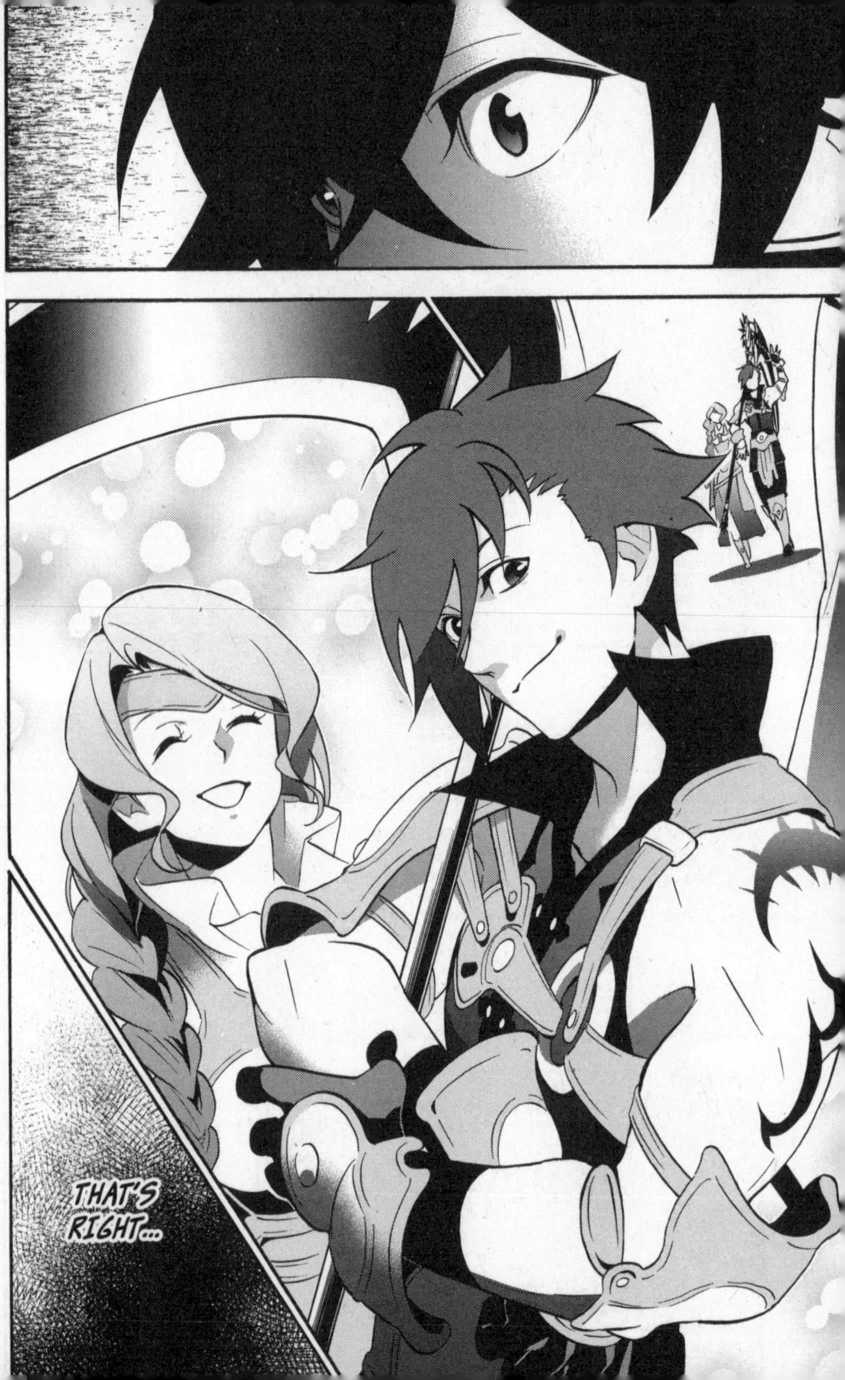
THAT'S RIGHT...

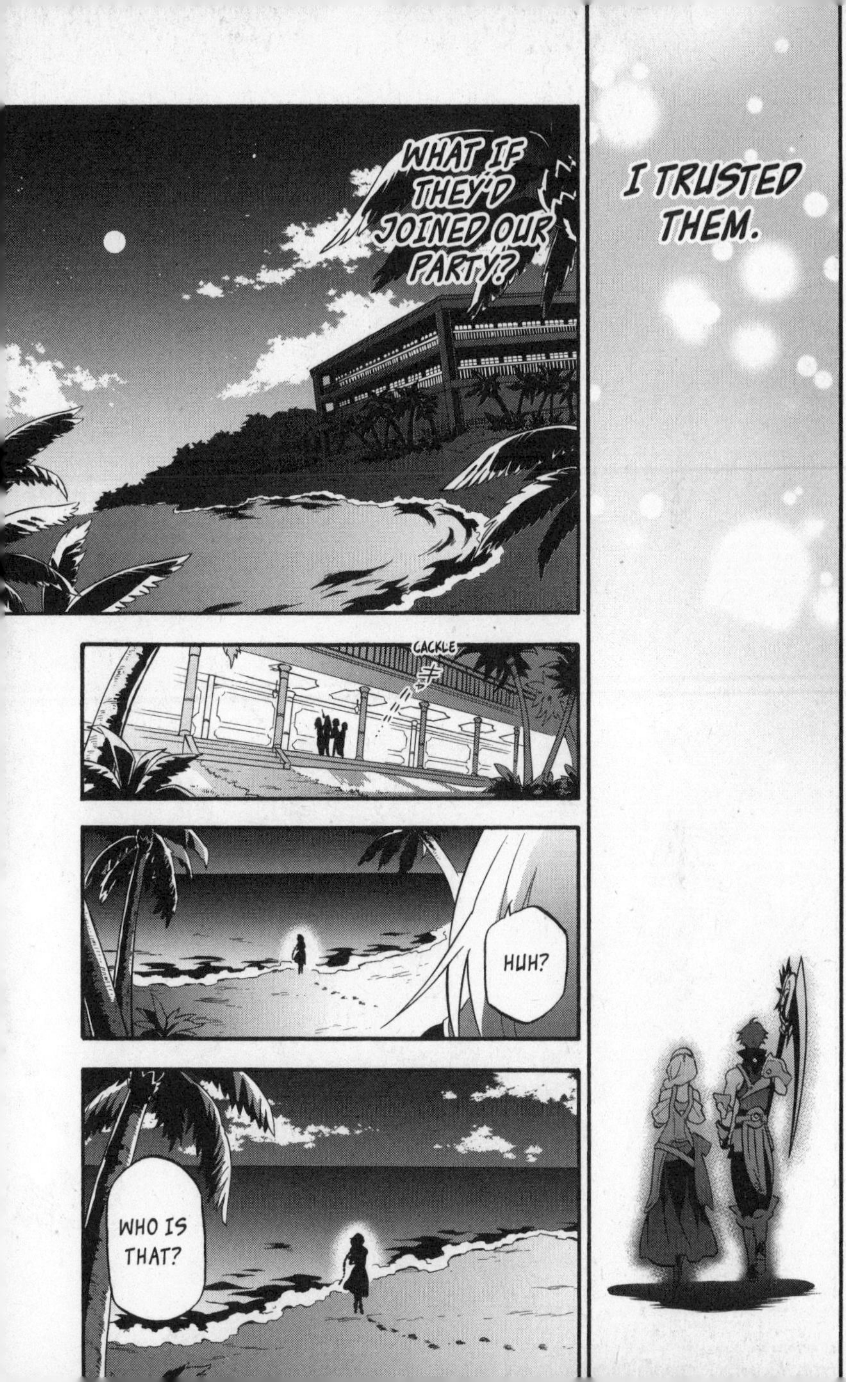
I TRUSTED THEM.
WHAT IF THEY'D JOINED OUR PARTY?
CACKLE
HUH?
WHO IS THAT?

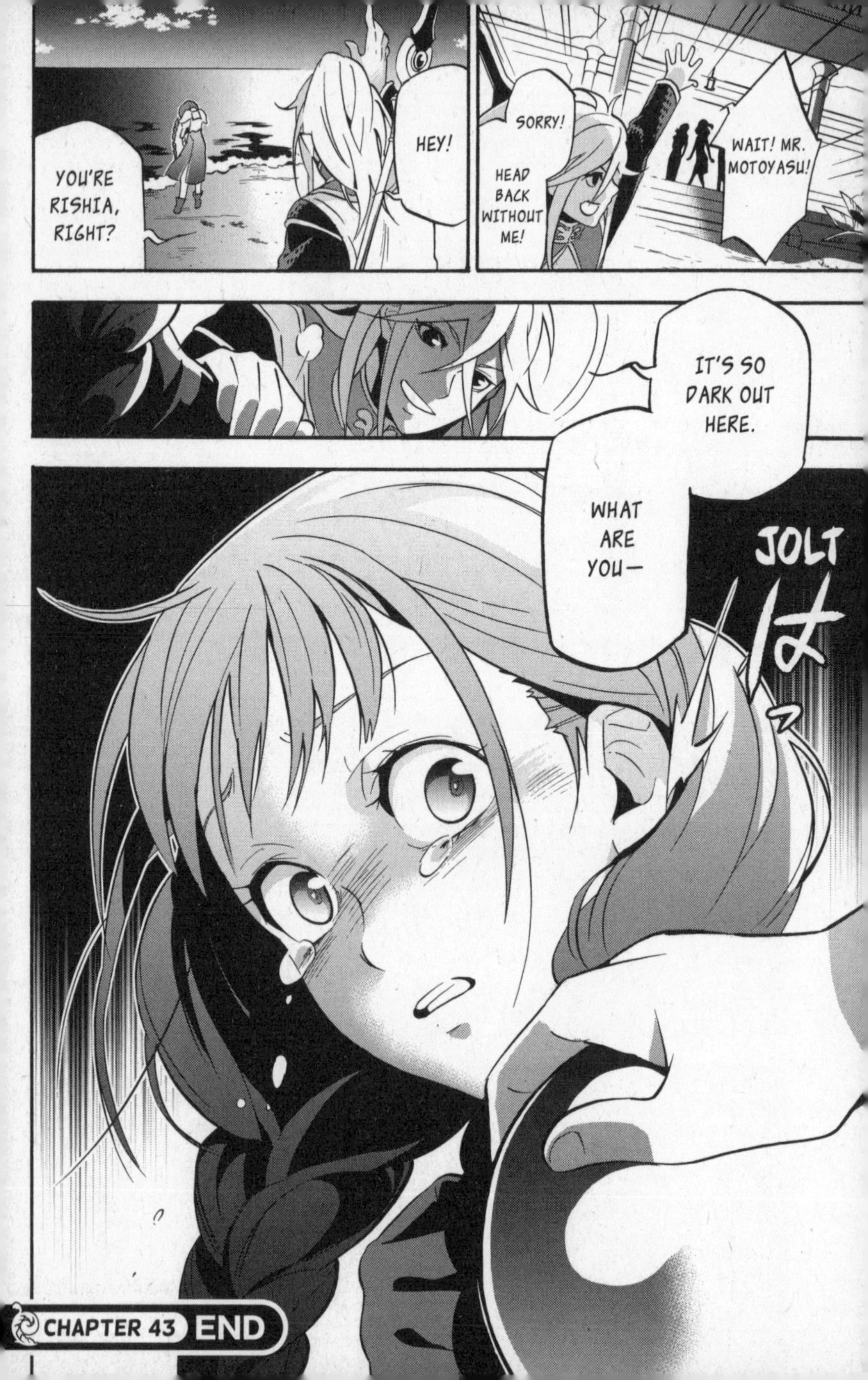
WAIT! MR. MOTOYASU!
SORRY!
HEAD BACK WITHOUT ME!
HEY!
YOU'RE RISHIA, RIGHT?
IT'S SO DARK OUT HERE.
WHAT ARE YOU—
JOLT
は
CHAPTER 43 END

# THE RISING OF THE SHIELD HERO

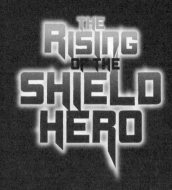

THE RISING OF THE SHIELD HERO

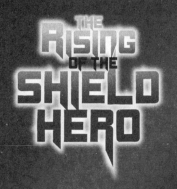

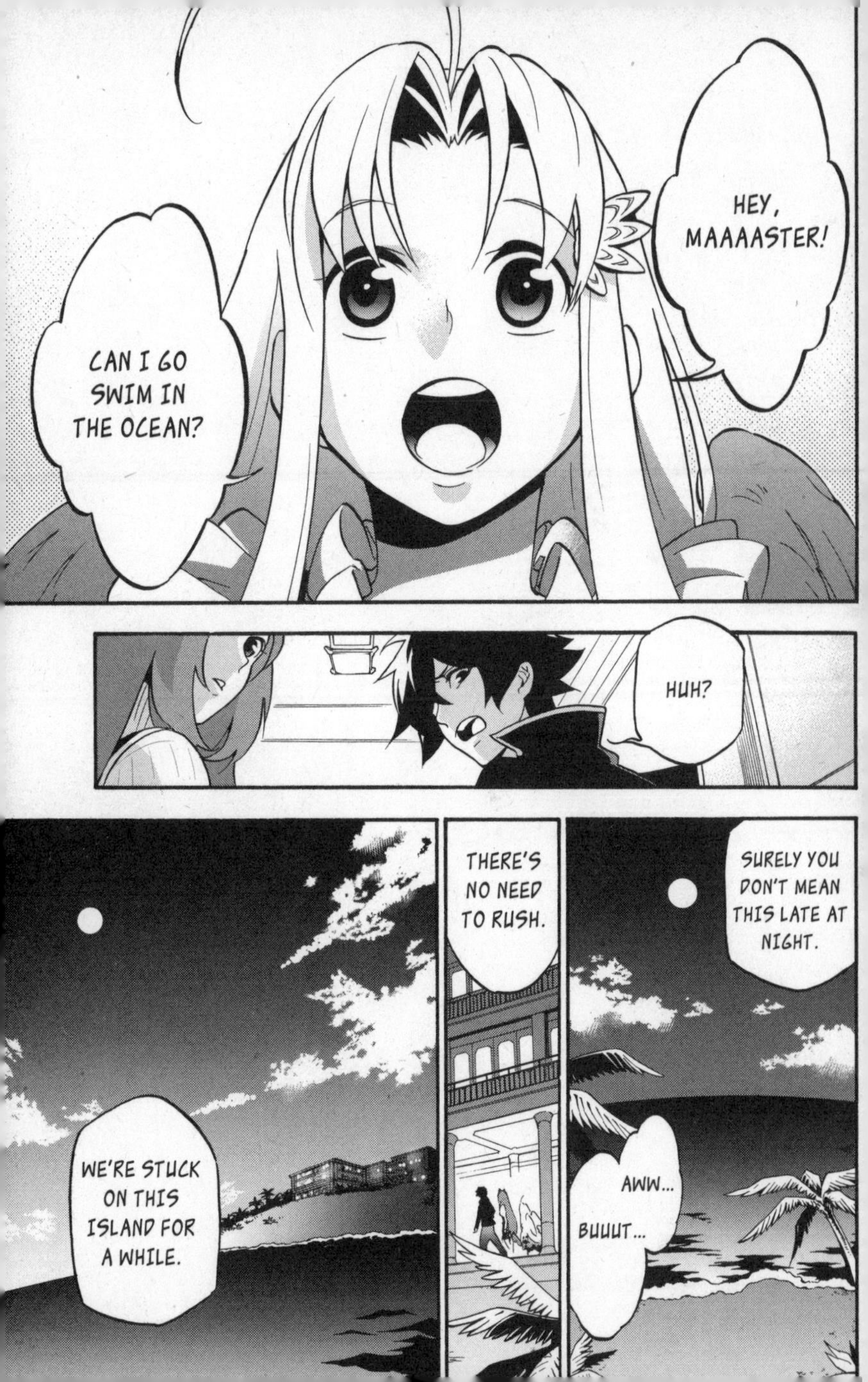
HEY, MAAAASTER!
CAN I GO SWIM IN THE OCEAN?
HUH?
SURELY YOU DON'T MEAN THIS LATE AT NIGHT.
AWW... BUUUT...
THERE'S NO NEED TO RUSH.
WE'RE STUCK ON THIS ISLAND FOR A WHILE.

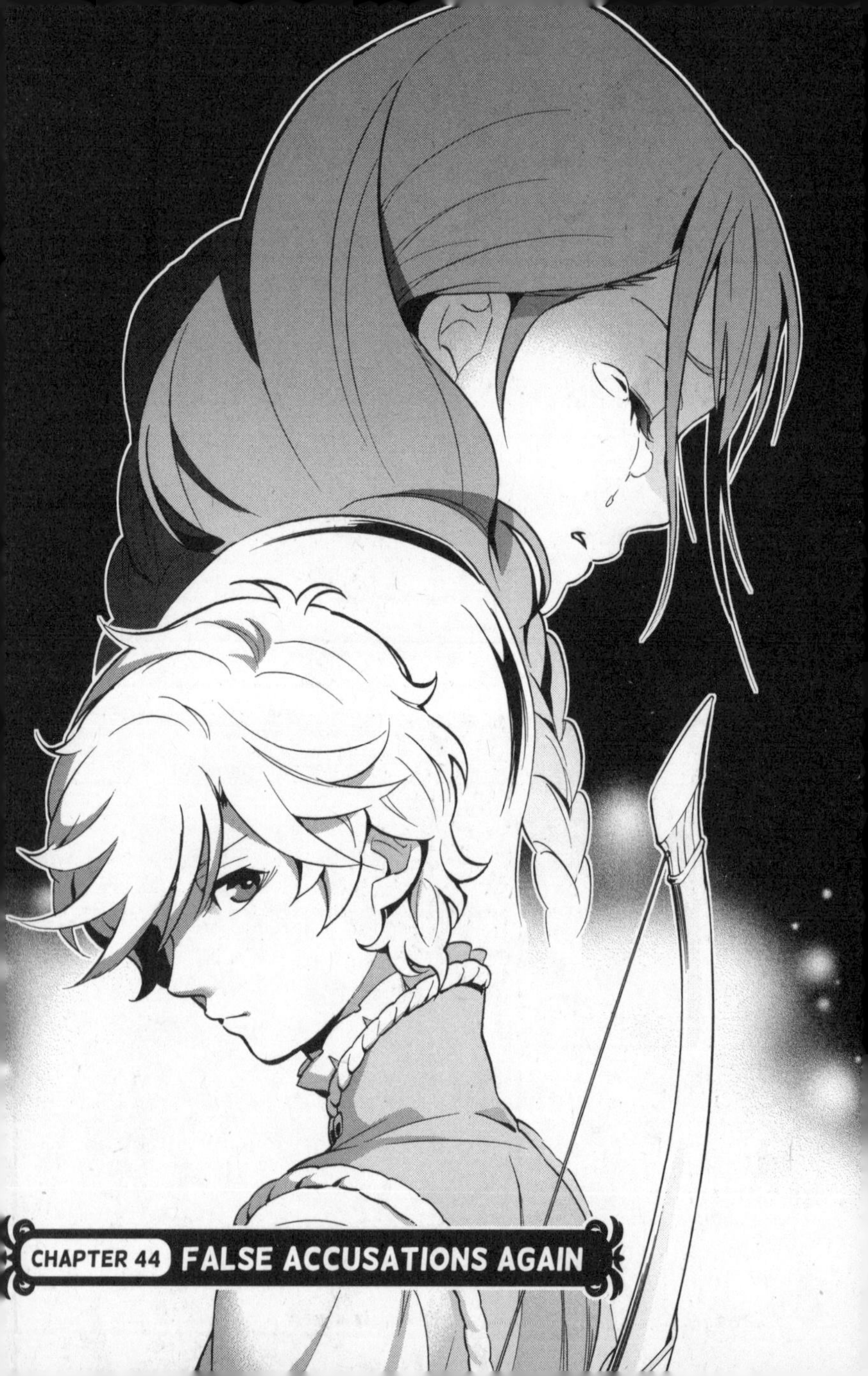
CHAPTER 44 FALSE ACCUSATIONS AGAIN

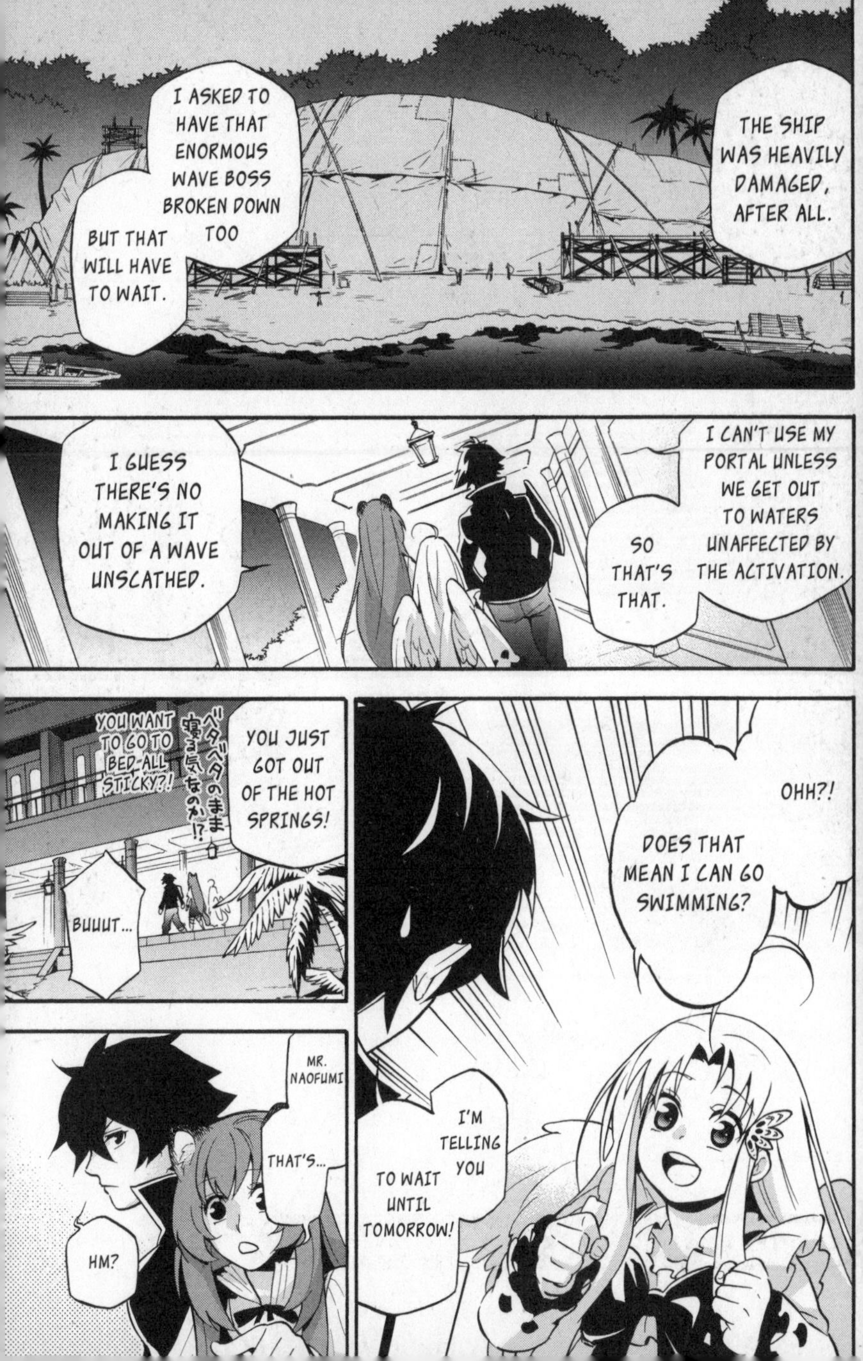
THE SHIP WAS HEAVILY DAMAGED, AFTER ALL.
I ASKED TO HAVE THAT ENORMOUS WAVE BOSS BROKEN DOWN TOO
BUT THAT WILL HAVE TO WAIT.
I CAN'T USE MY PORTAL UNLESS WE GET OUT TO WATERS UNAFFECTED BY THE ACTIVATION.
SO THAT'S THAT.
I GUESS THERE'S NO MAKING IT OUT OF A WAVE UNSCATHED.
OHH?!
DOES THAT MEAN I CAN GO SWIMMING?
I'M TELLING YOU
TO WAIT UNTIL TOMORROW!
YOU JUST GOT OUT OF THE HOT SPRINGS!
YOU WANT TO GO TO BED ALL STICKY?!
ベタベタのまま寝る気なのか!?
BUUUT...
MR. NAOFUMI
THAT'S...
HM?

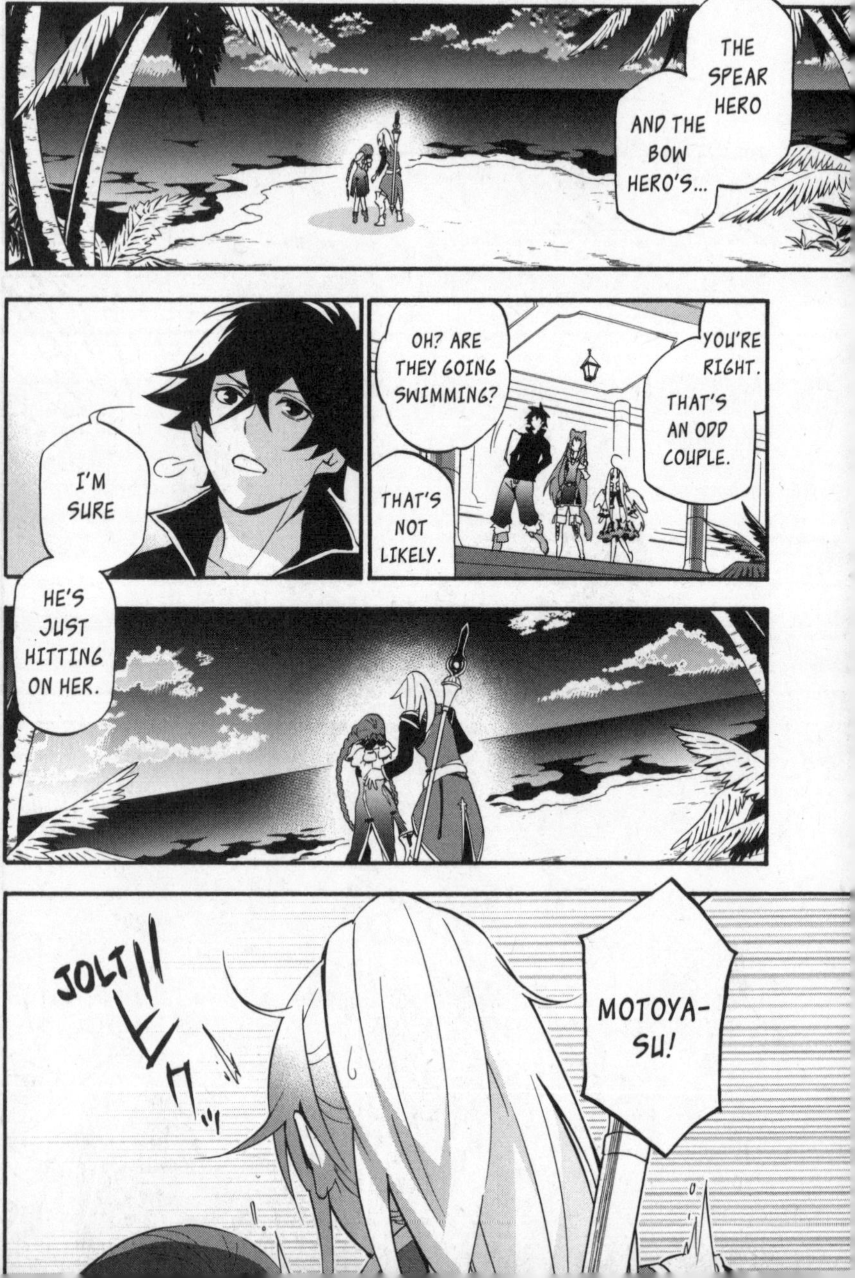
THE SPEAR HERO
AND THE BOW HERO'S...
YOU'RE RIGHT. THAT'S AN ODD COUPLE.
OH? ARE THEY GOING SWIMMING?
THAT'S NOT LIKELY.
I'M SURE
HE'S JUST HITTING ON HER.
MOTOYA-SU!
JOLT

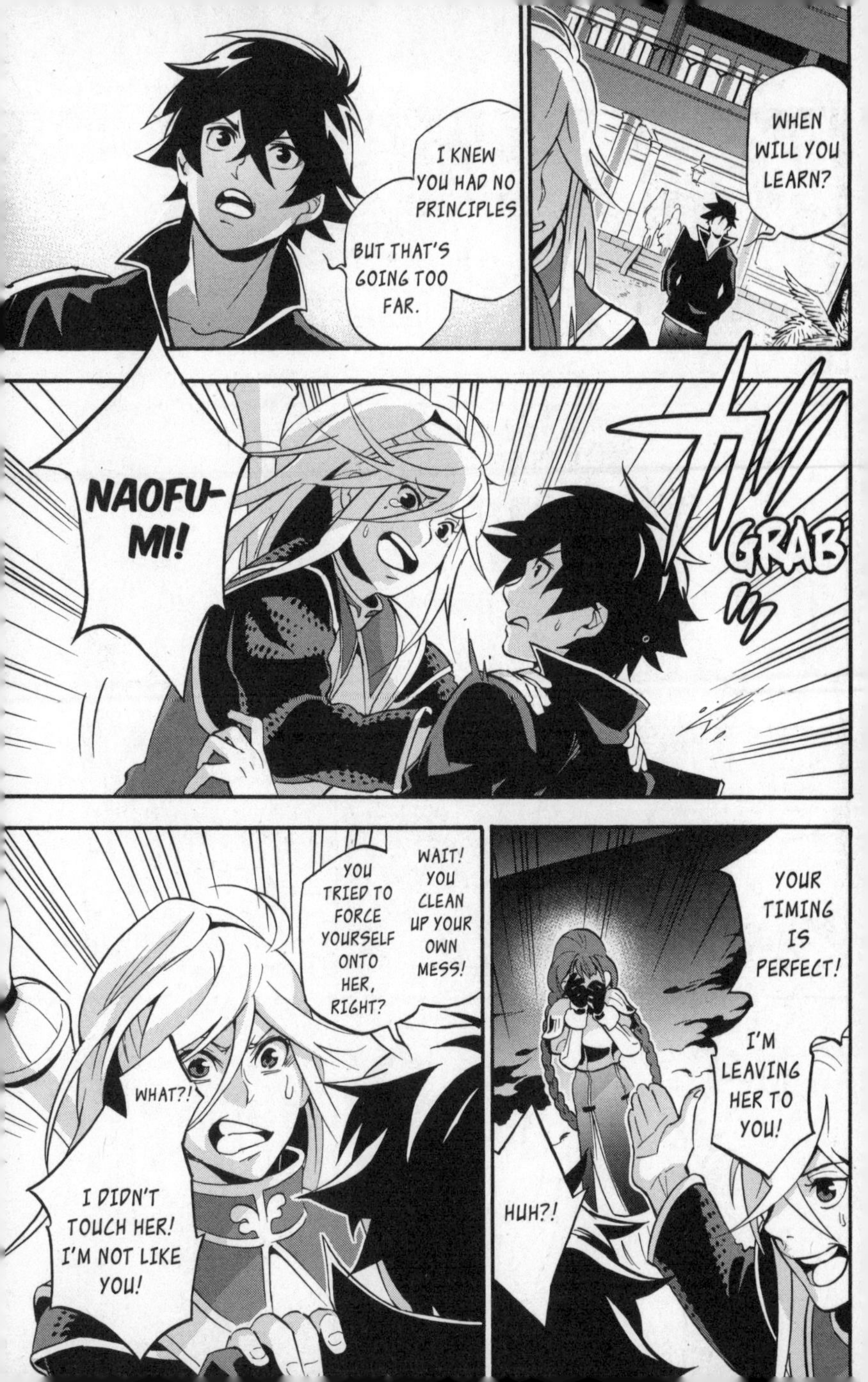
WHEN WILL YOU LEARN?
I KNEW YOU HAD NO PRINCIPLES
BUT THAT'S GOING TOO FAR.
GRAB
NAOFU-MI!
YOUR TIMING IS PERFECT!
I'M LEAVING HER TO YOU!
HUH?!
WAIT! YOU CLEAN UP YOUR OWN MESS!
YOU TRIED TO FORCE YOURSELF ONTO HER, RIGHT?
WHAT?!
I DIDN'T TOUCH HER! I'M NOT LIKE YOU!

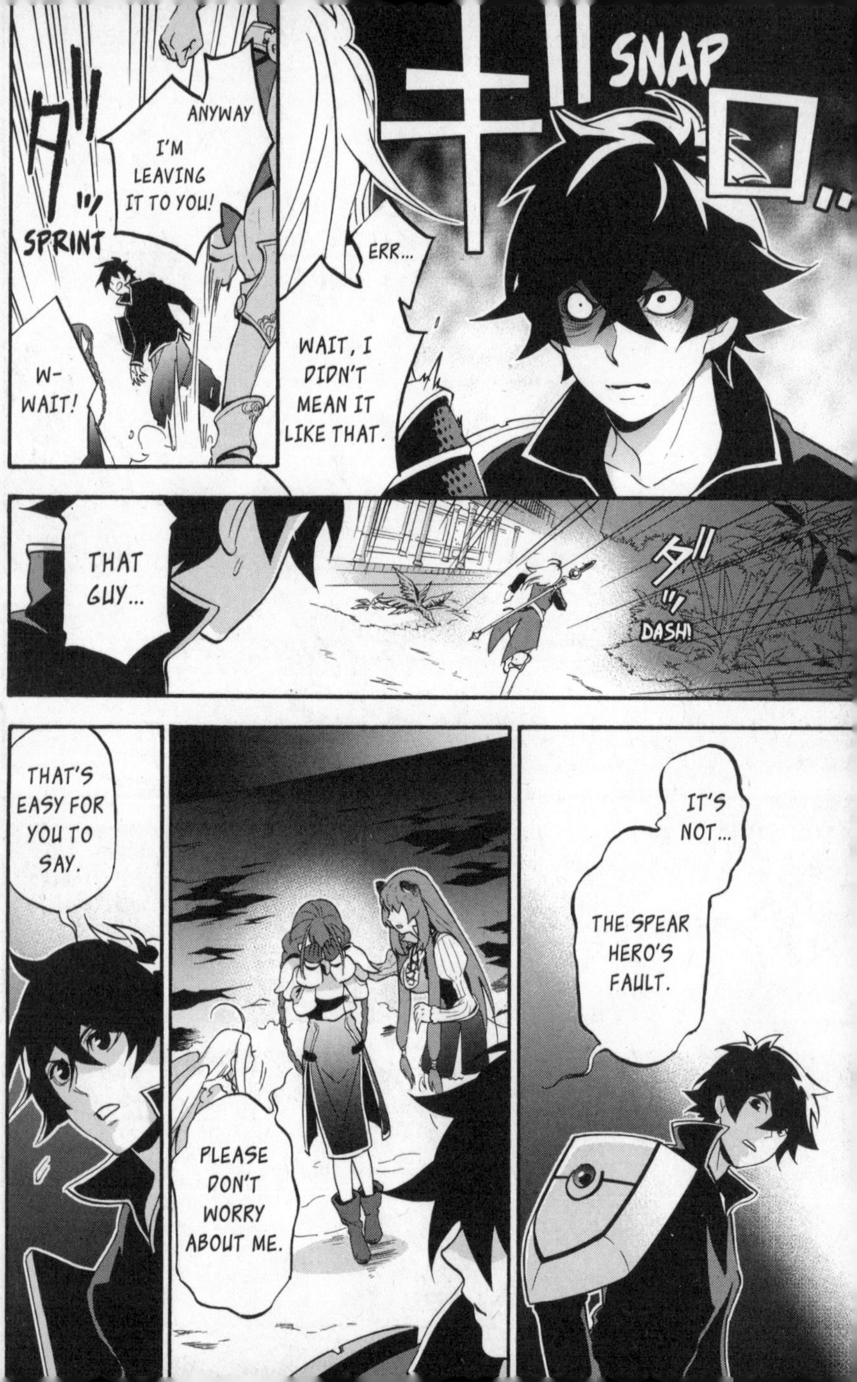
SNAP
ERR...
WAIT, I DIDN'T MEAN IT LIKE THAT.
ANYWAY I'M LEAVING IT TO YOU!
SPRINT
W-WAIT!
DASH!
THAT GUY...
IT'S NOT... THE SPEAR HERO'S FAULT.
PLEASE DON'T WORRY ABOUT ME.
THAT'S EASY FOR YOU TO SAY.

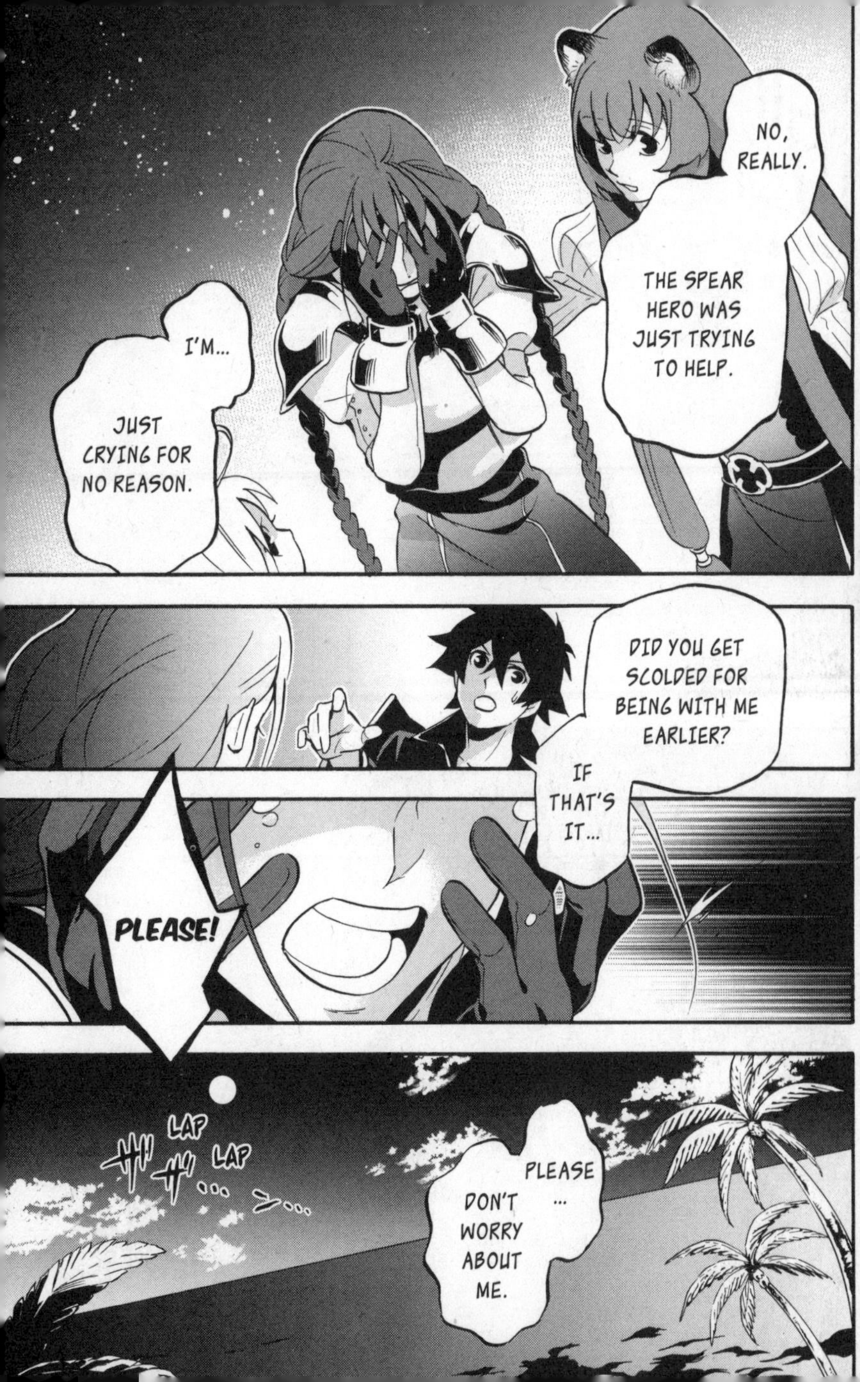
NO, REALLY.
THE SPEAR HERO WAS JUST TRYING TO HELP.
I'M...
JUST CRYING FOR NO REASON.
DID YOU GET SCOLDED FOR BEING WITH ME EARLIER?
IF THAT'S IT...
PLEASE!
PLEASE...
DON'T WORRY ABOUT ME.
LAP
LAP

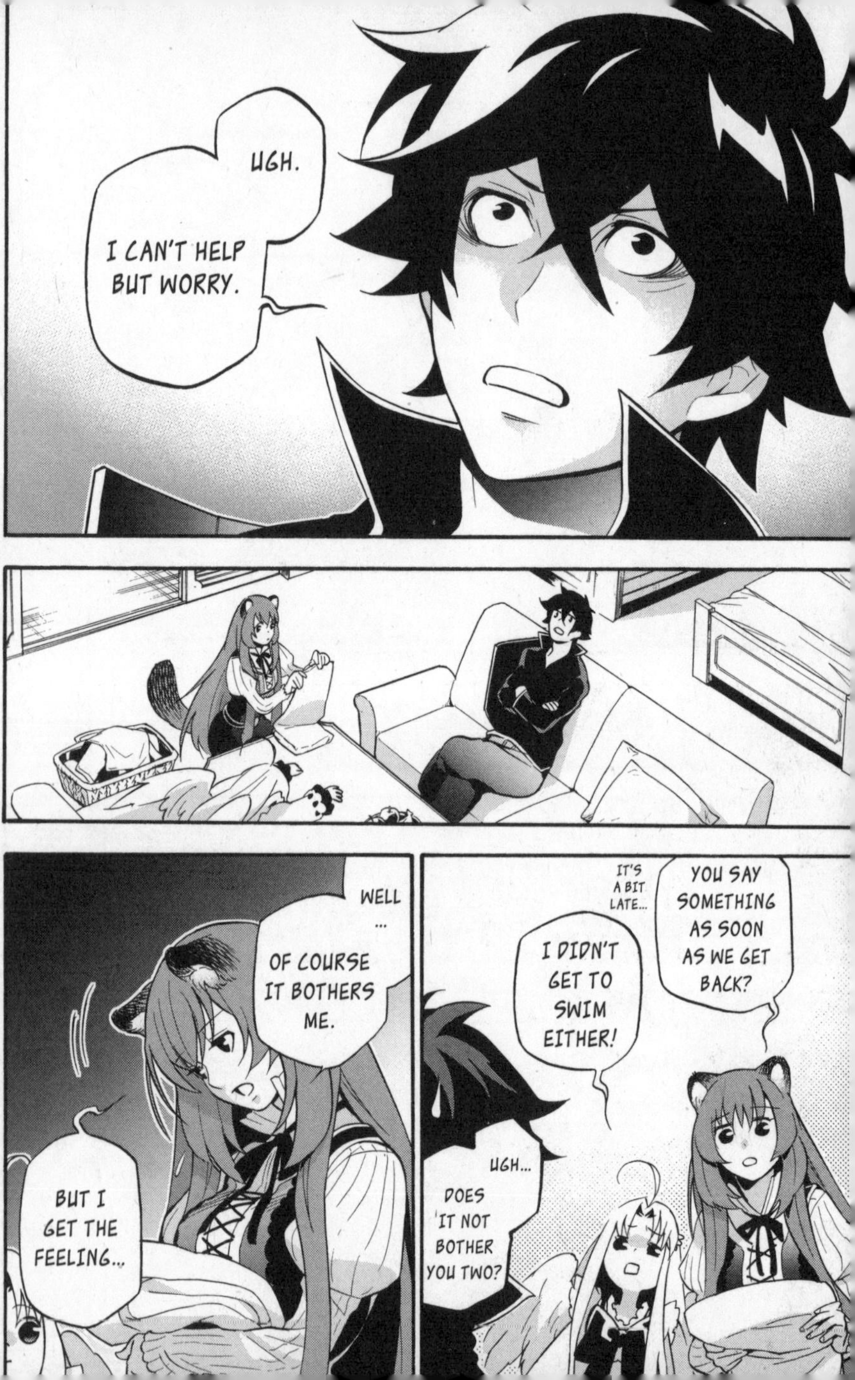
UGH.
I CAN'T HELP BUT WORRY.
YOU SAY SOMETHING AS SOON AS WE GET BACK?
IT'S A BIT LATE...
I DIDN'T GET TO SWIM EITHER!
UGH...
DOES IT NOT BOTHER YOU TWO?
WELL ...
OF COURSE IT BOTHERS ME.
BUT I GET THE FEELING...

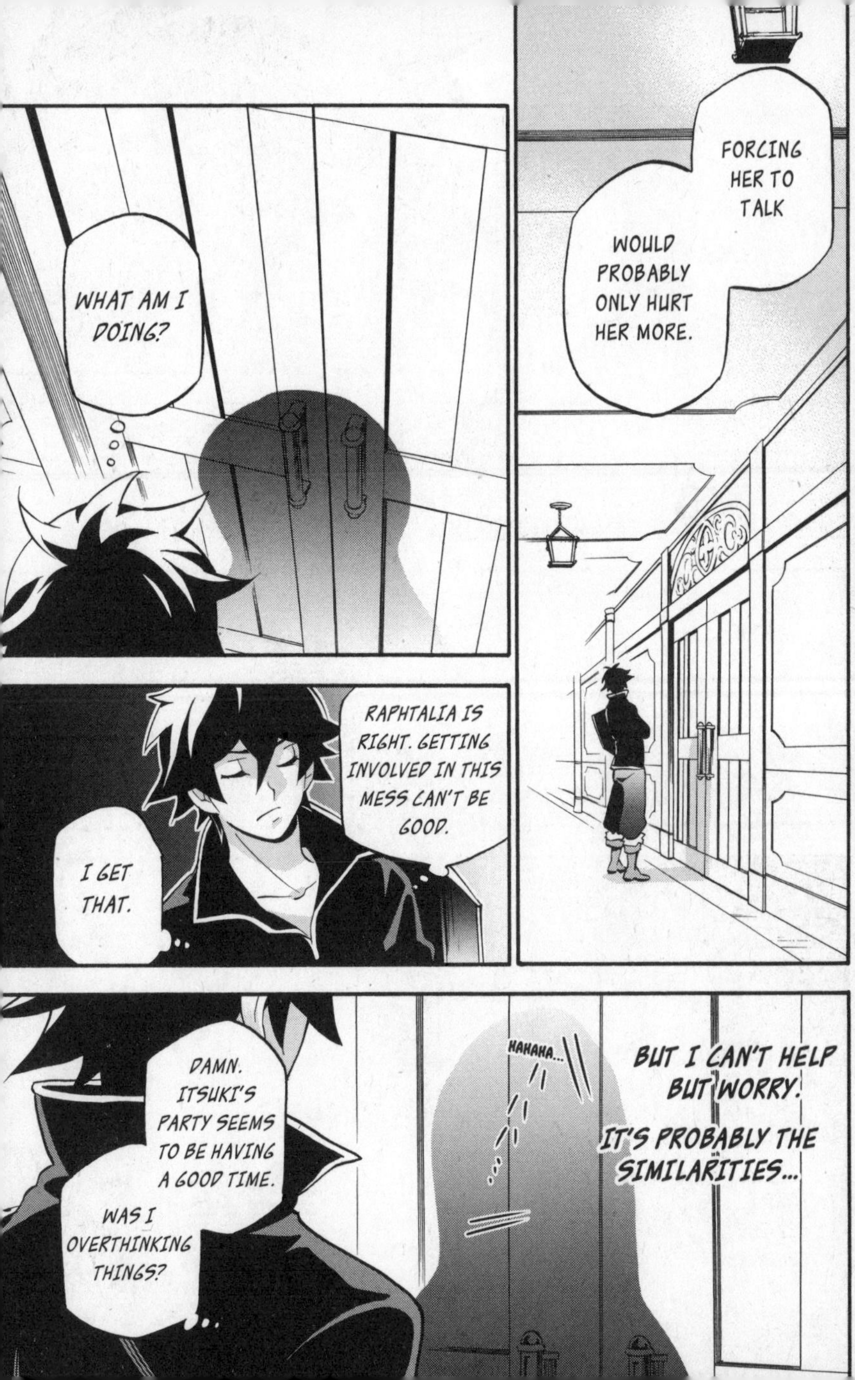
FORCING HER TO TALK
WOULD PROBABLY ONLY HURT HER MORE.
WHAT AM I DOING?
RAPHTALIA IS RIGHT. GETTING INVOLVED IN THIS MESS CAN'T BE GOOD.
I GET THAT.
BUT I CAN'T HELP BUT WORRY.
IT'S PROBABLY THE SIMILARITIES...
HAHAHA...
DAMN. ITSUKI'S PARTY SEEMS TO BE HAVING A GOOD TIME.
WAS I OVERTHINKING THINGS?

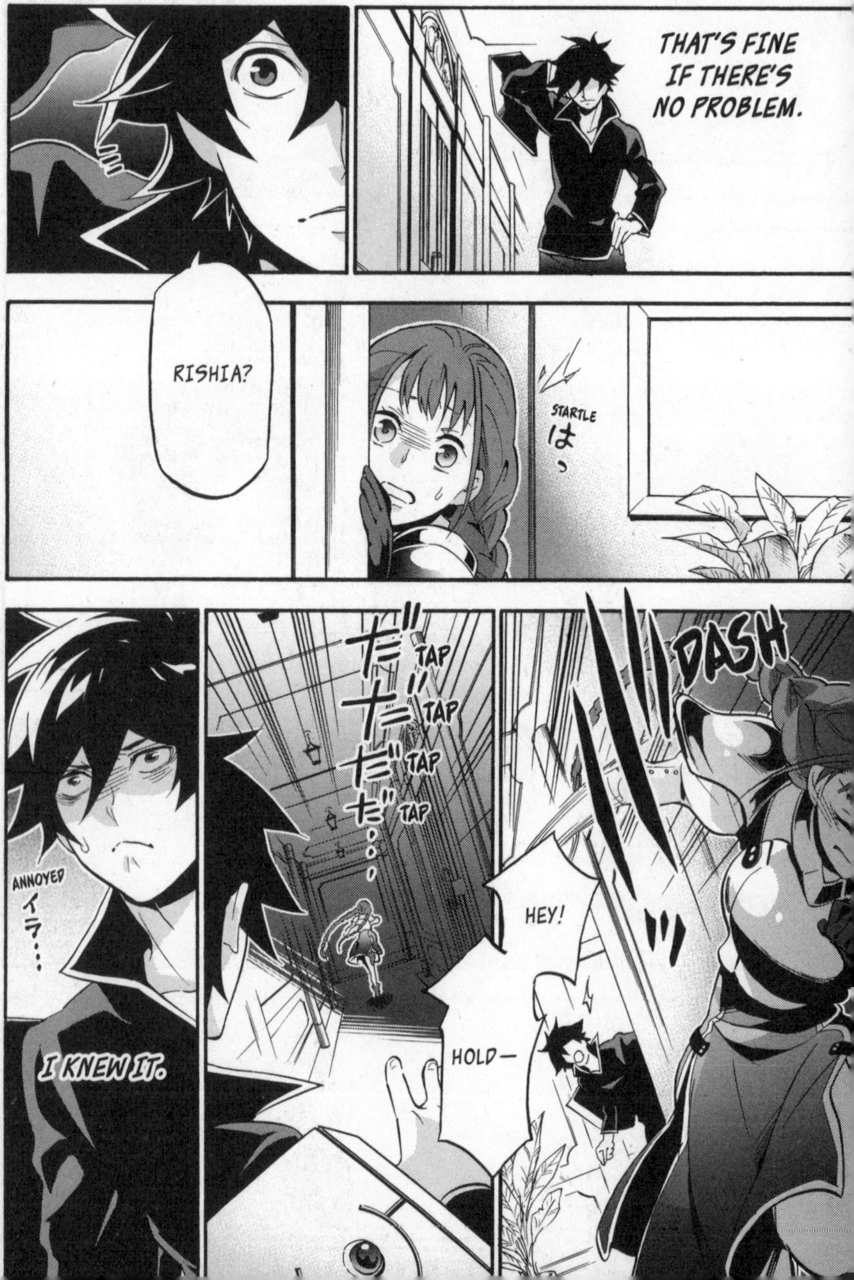
THAT'S FINE IF THERE'S NO PROBLEM.
RISHIA?
STARTLE
はっ
DASH
HEY!
HOLD—
だだだだ…
TAP TAP TAP TAP
ANNOYED
イラ…
I KNEW IT.

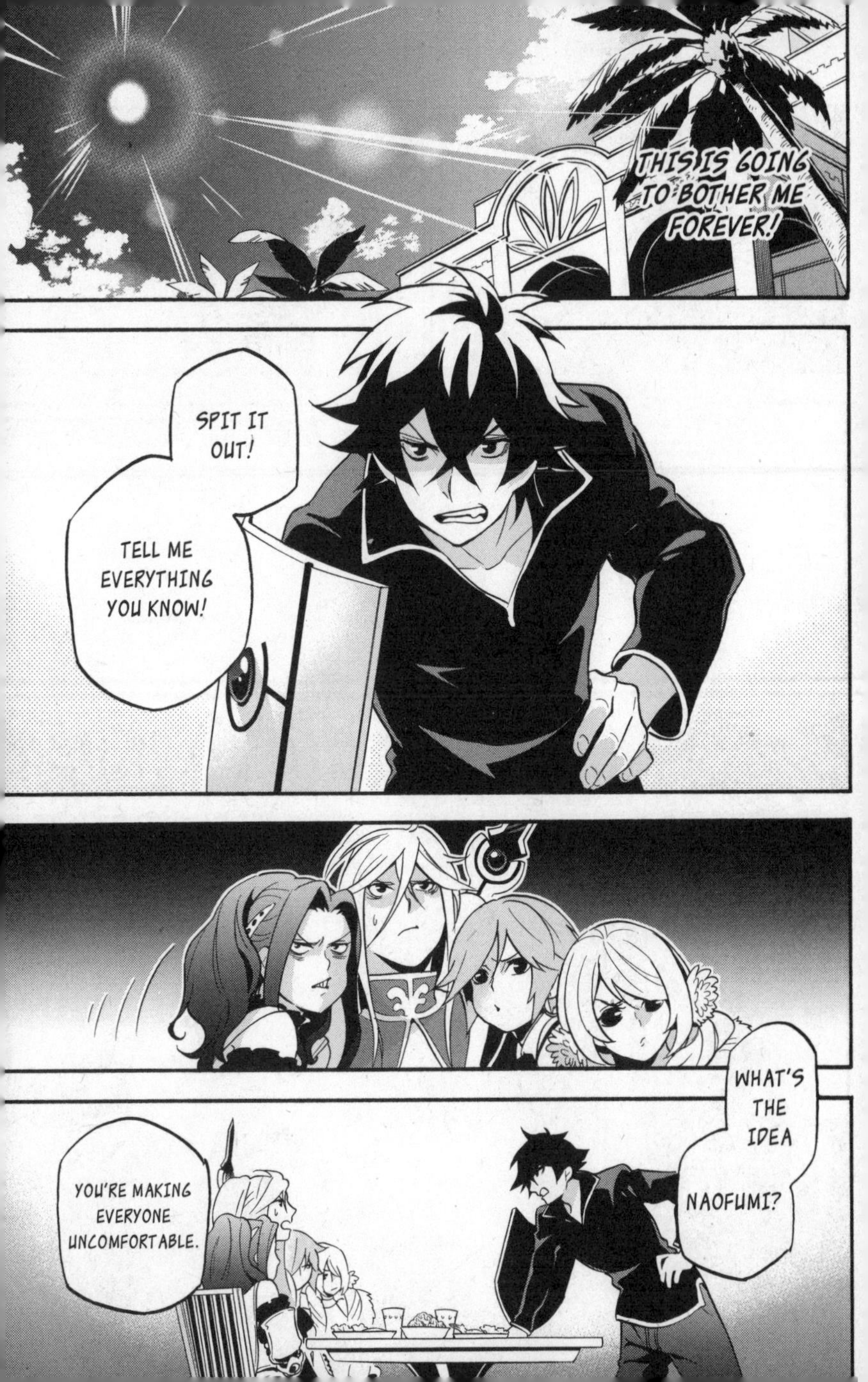
THIS IS GOING TO BOTHER ME FOREVER!
SPIT IT OUT!
TELL ME EVERYTHING YOU KNOW!
WHAT'S THE IDEA
NAOFUMI?
YOU'RE MAKING EVERYONE UNCOMFORTABLE.

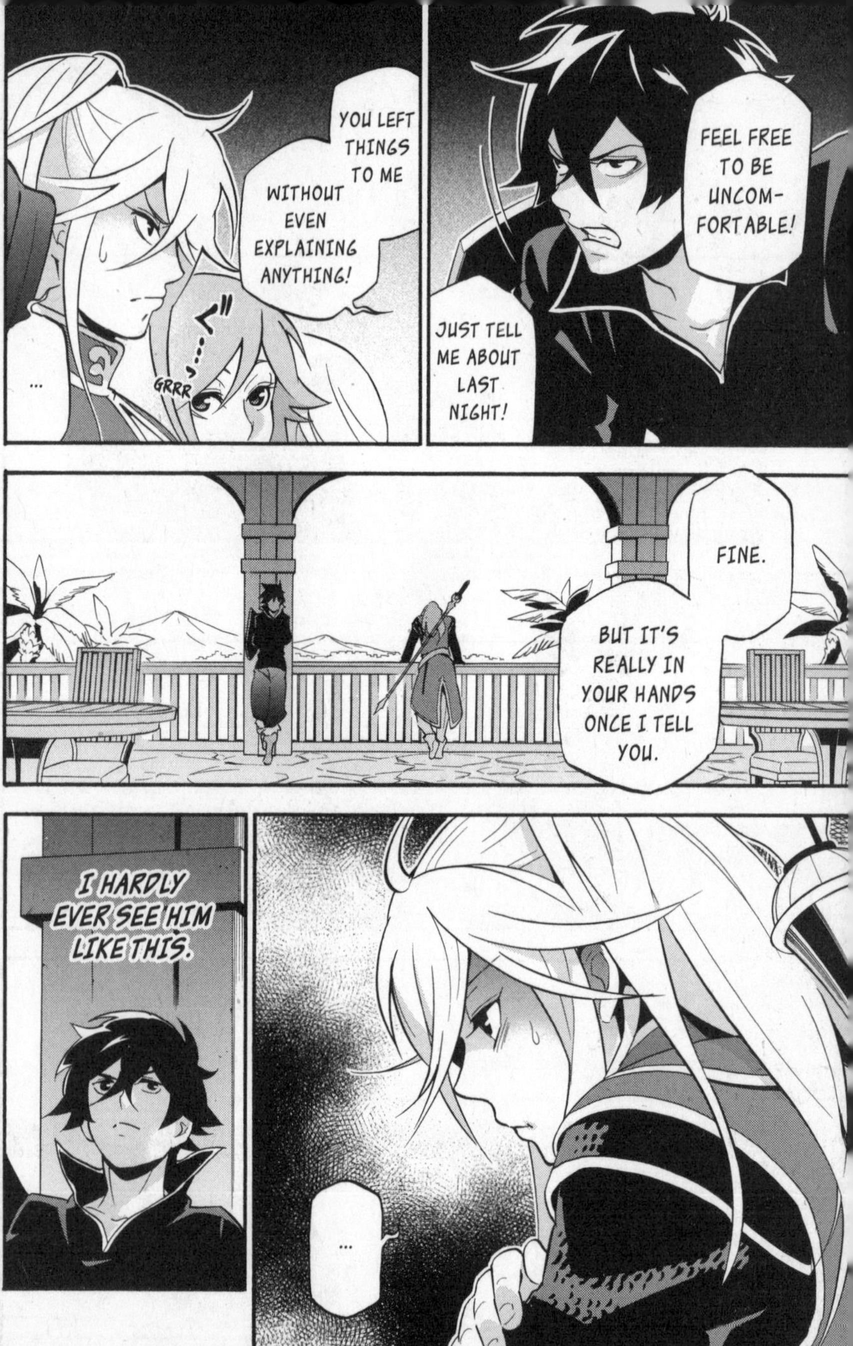
FEEL FREE TO BE UNCOM-FORTABLE!
JUST TELL ME ABOUT LAST NIGHT!
YOU LEFT THINGS TO ME WITHOUT EVEN EXPLAINING ANYTHING!
GRRR
...
FINE.
BUT IT'S REALLY IN YOUR HANDS ONCE I TELL YOU.
...
I HARDLY EVER SEE HIM LIKE THIS.

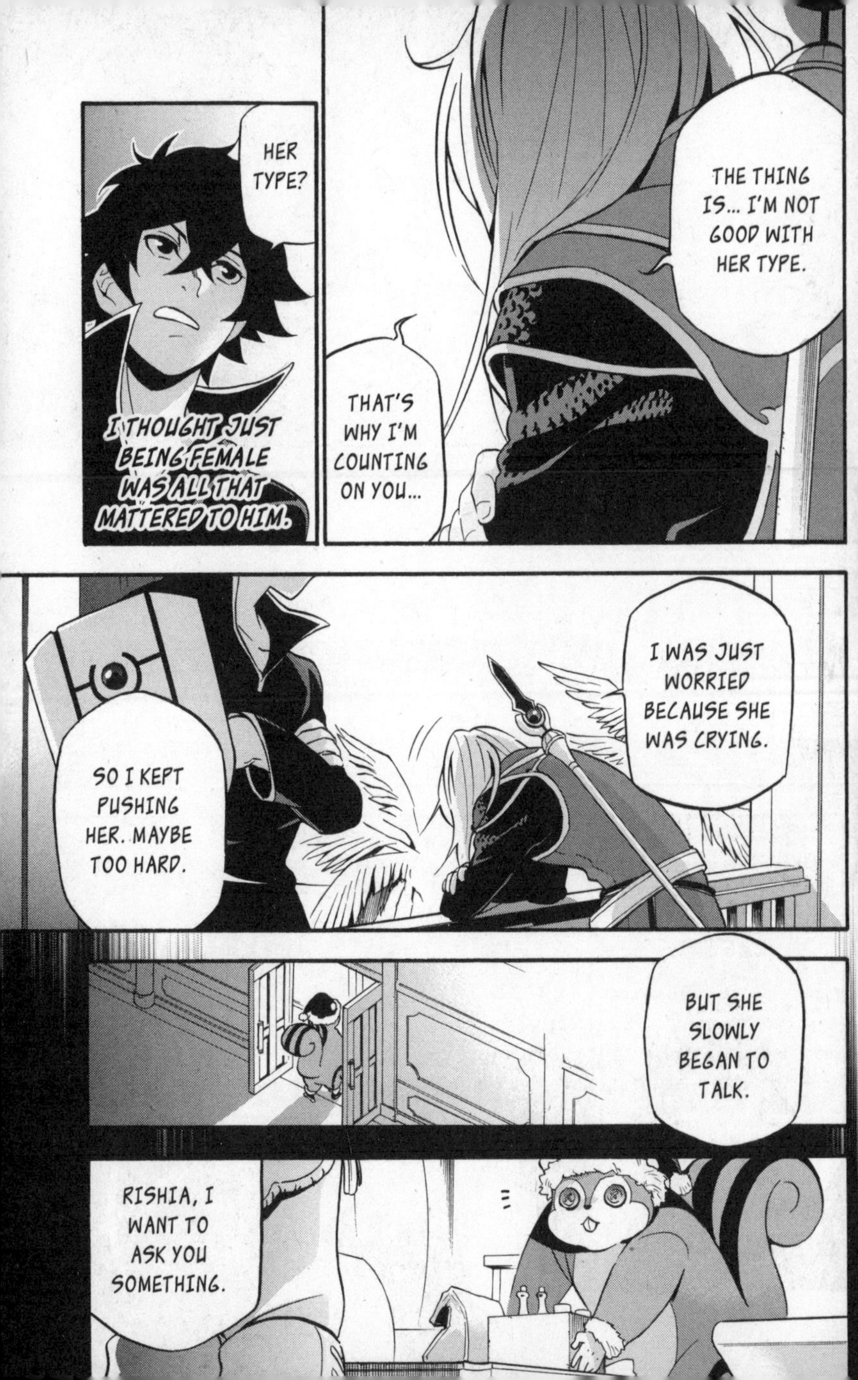
THE THING IS... I'M NOT GOOD WITH HER TYPE.
THAT'S WHY I'M COUNTING ON YOU...
HER TYPE?
I THOUGHT JUST BEING FEMALE WAS ALL THAT MATTERED TO HIM.
I WAS JUST WORRIED BECAUSE SHE WAS CRYING.
SO I KEPT PUSHING HER. MAYBE TOO HARD.
BUT SHE SLOWLY BEGAN TO TALK.
RISHIA, I WANT TO ASK YOU SOMETHING.

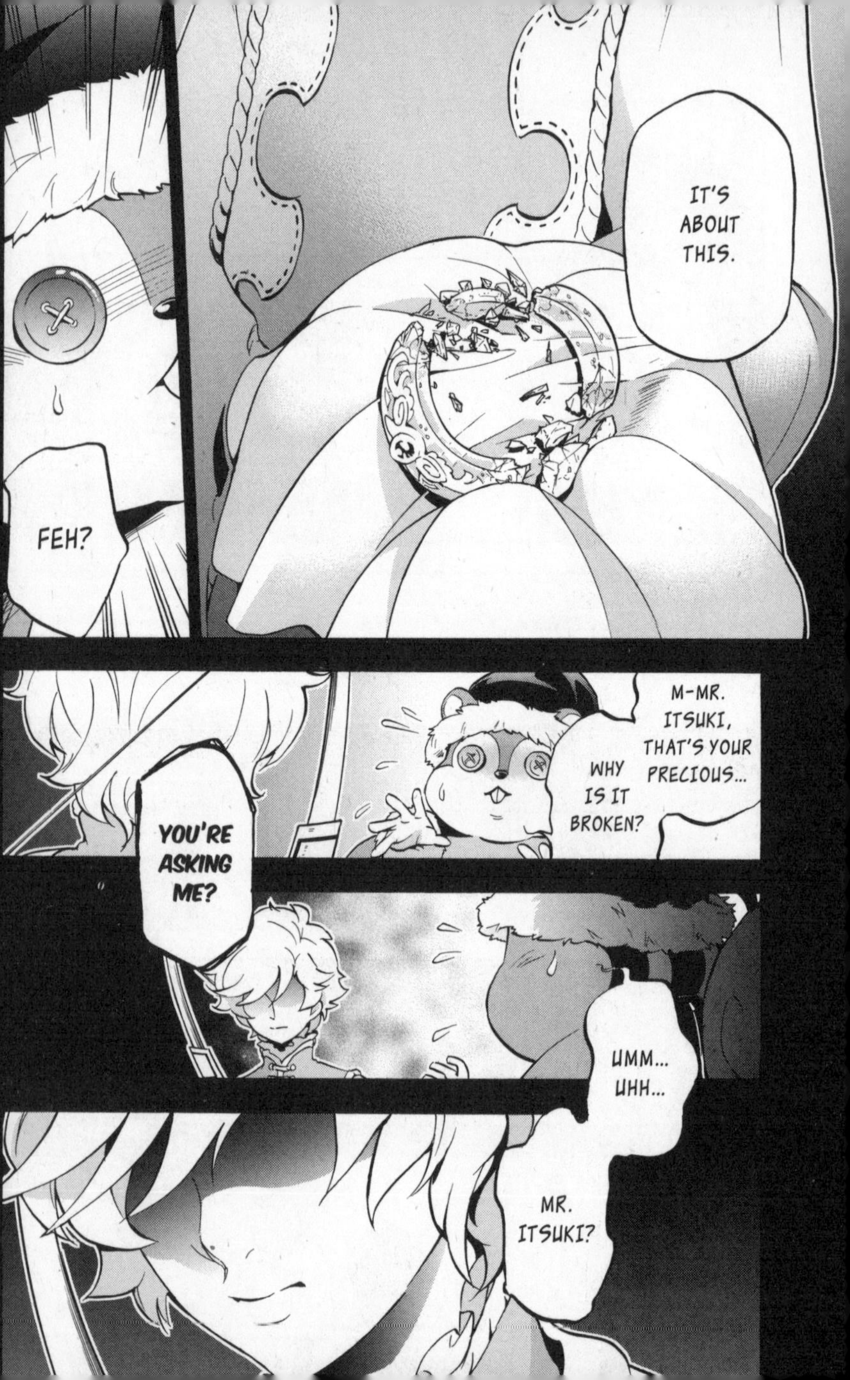
IT'S ABOUT THIS.
FEH?
M-MR. ITSUKI, THAT'S YOUR PRECIOUS...
WHY IS IT BROKEN?
YOU'RE ASKING ME?
UMM... UHH...
MR. ITSUKI?

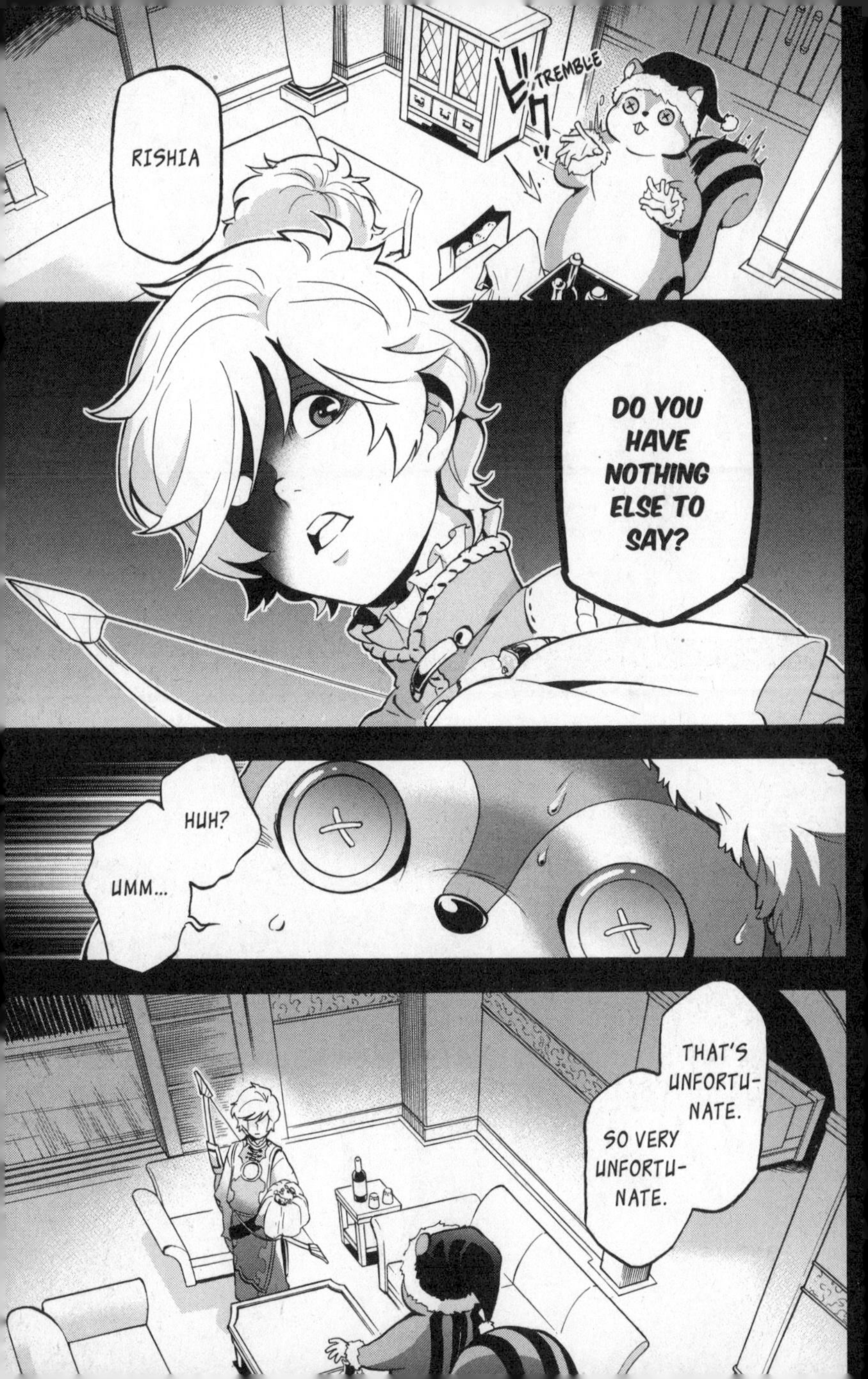
TREMBLE
RISHIA
DO YOU HAVE NOTHING ELSE TO SAY?
HUH?
UMM...
THAT'S UNFORTU- NATE.
SO VERY UNFORTU- NATE.

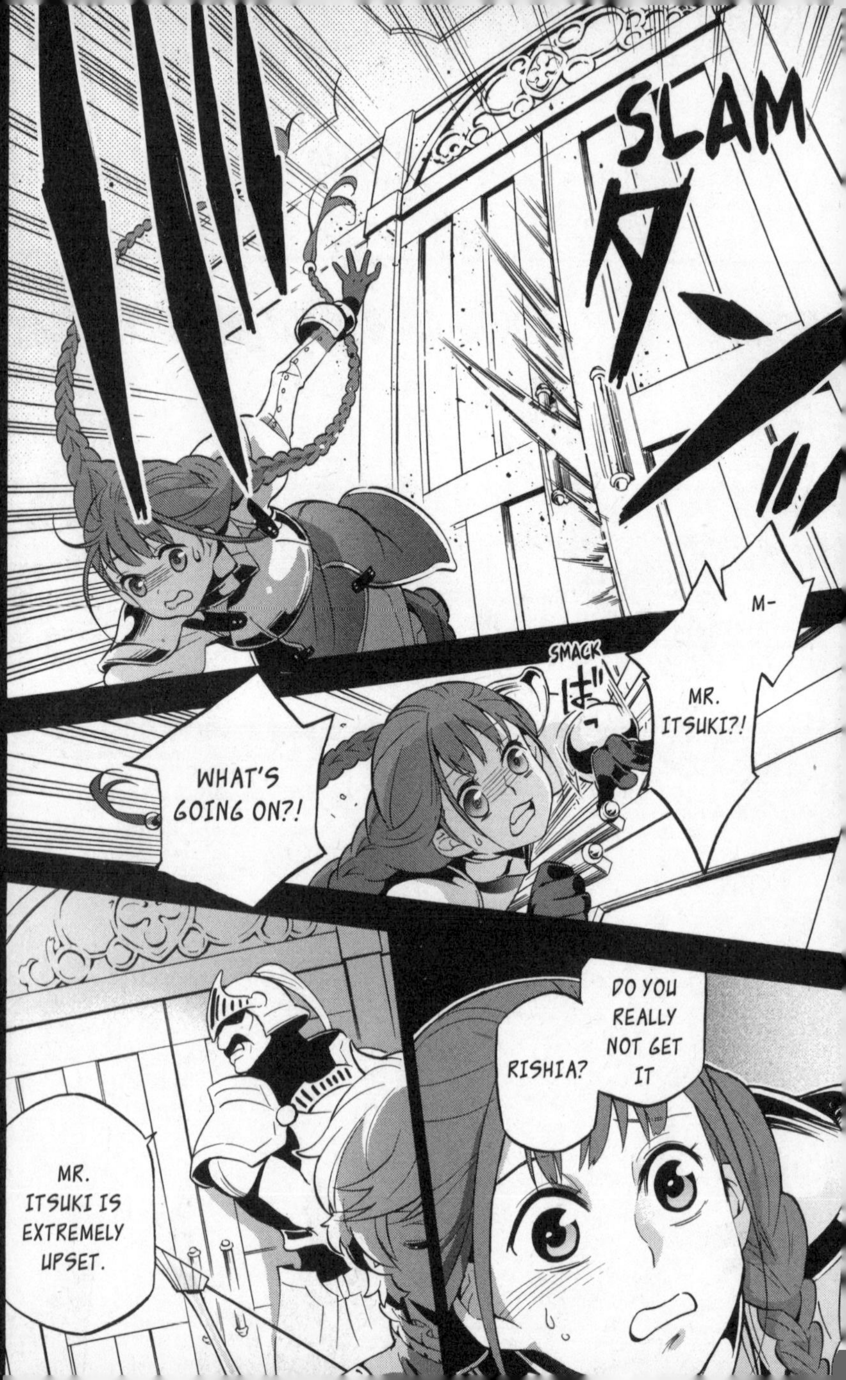
SLAM
M-
MR. ITSUKI?!
SMACK
WHAT'S GOING ON?!
DO YOU REALLY NOT GET IT RISHIA?
MR. ITSUKI IS EXTREMELY UPSET.

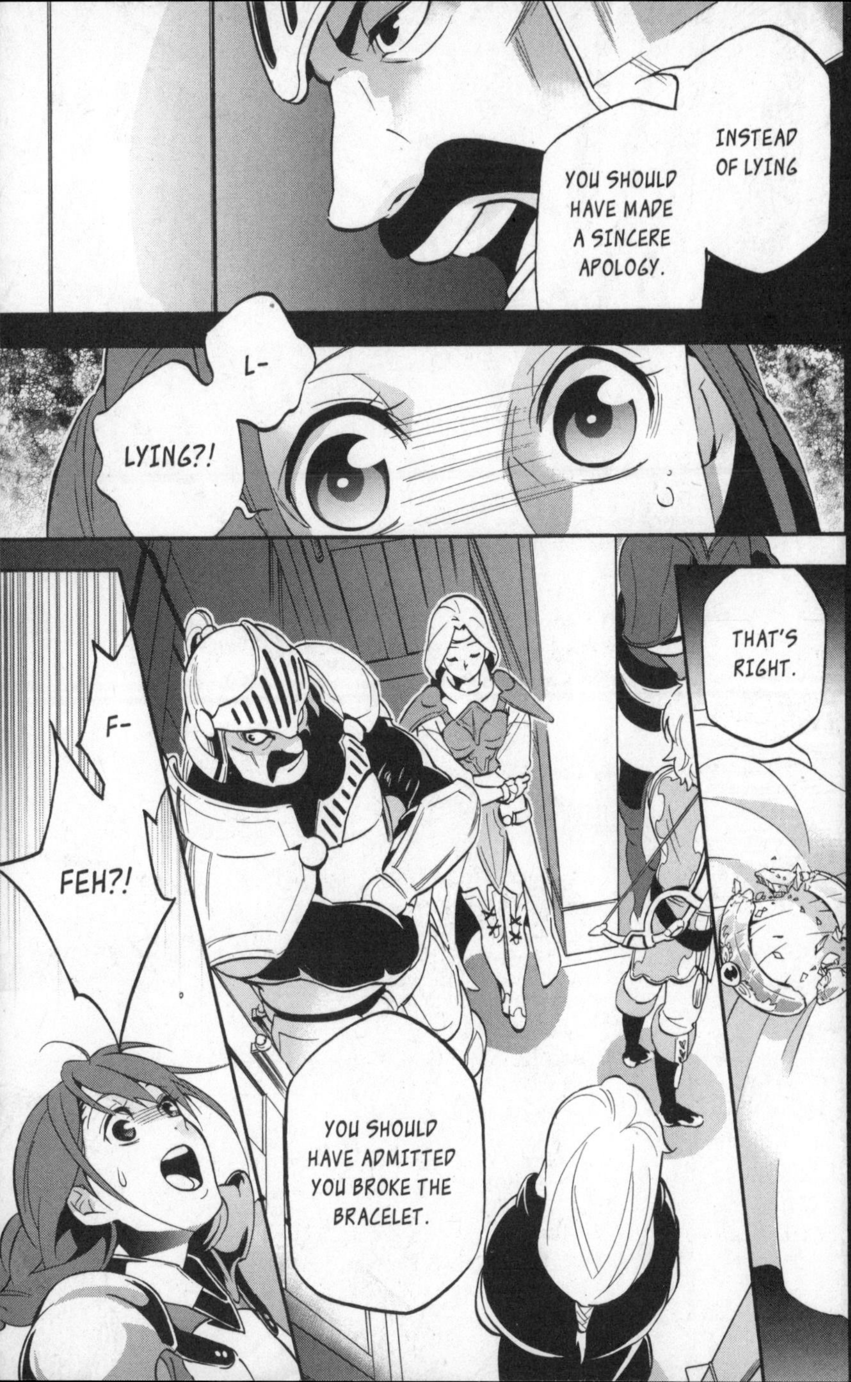
INSTEAD OF LYING
YOU SHOULD HAVE MADE A SINCERE APOLOGY.
L-
LYING?!
THAT'S RIGHT.
YOU SHOULD HAVE ADMITTED YOU BROKE THE BRACELET.
F-
FEH?!

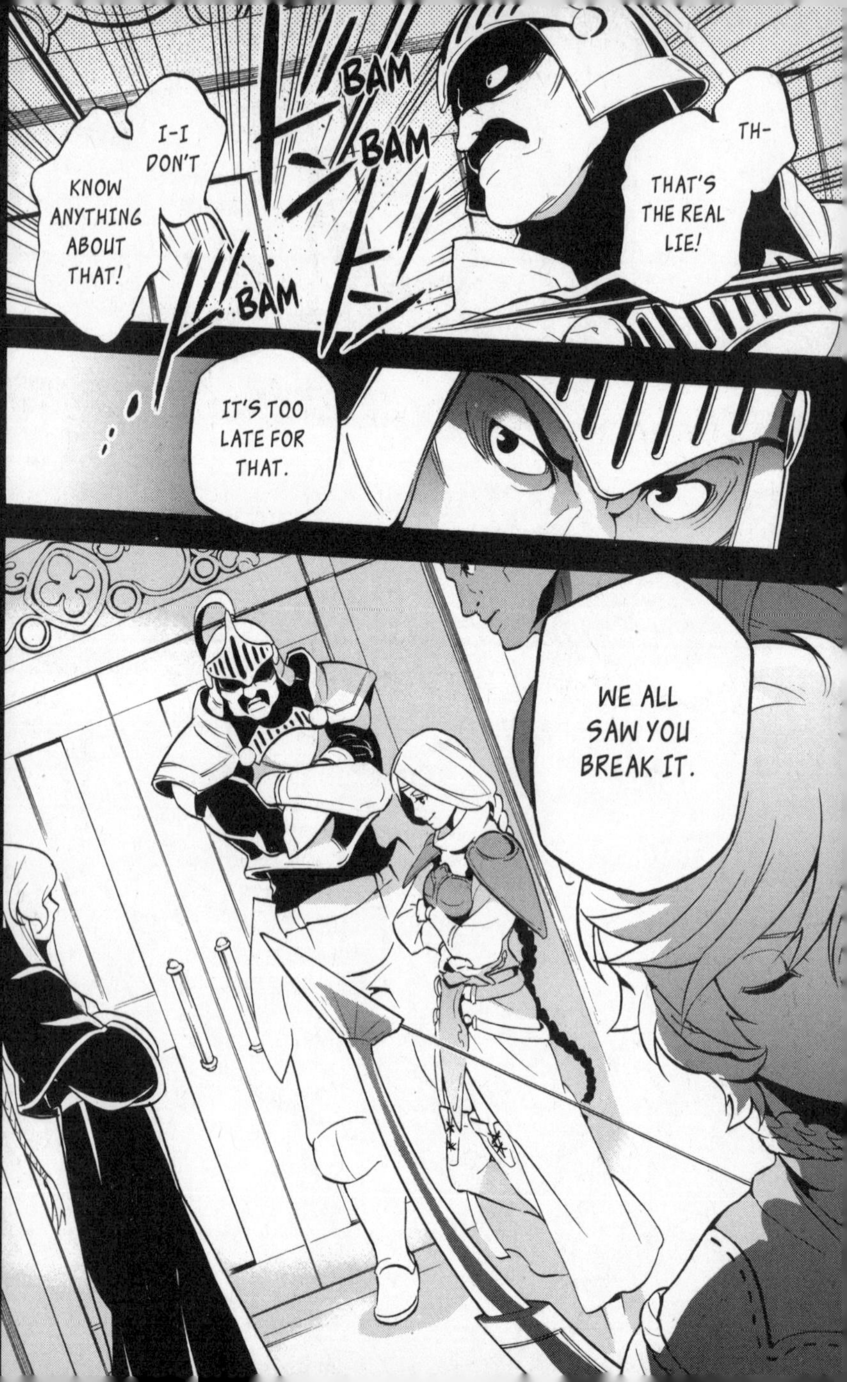
TH- THAT'S THE REAL LIE!
BAM
BAM
I-I DON'T KNOW ANYTHING ABOUT THAT!
BAM
IT'S TOO LATE FOR THAT.
WE ALL SAW YOU BREAK IT.

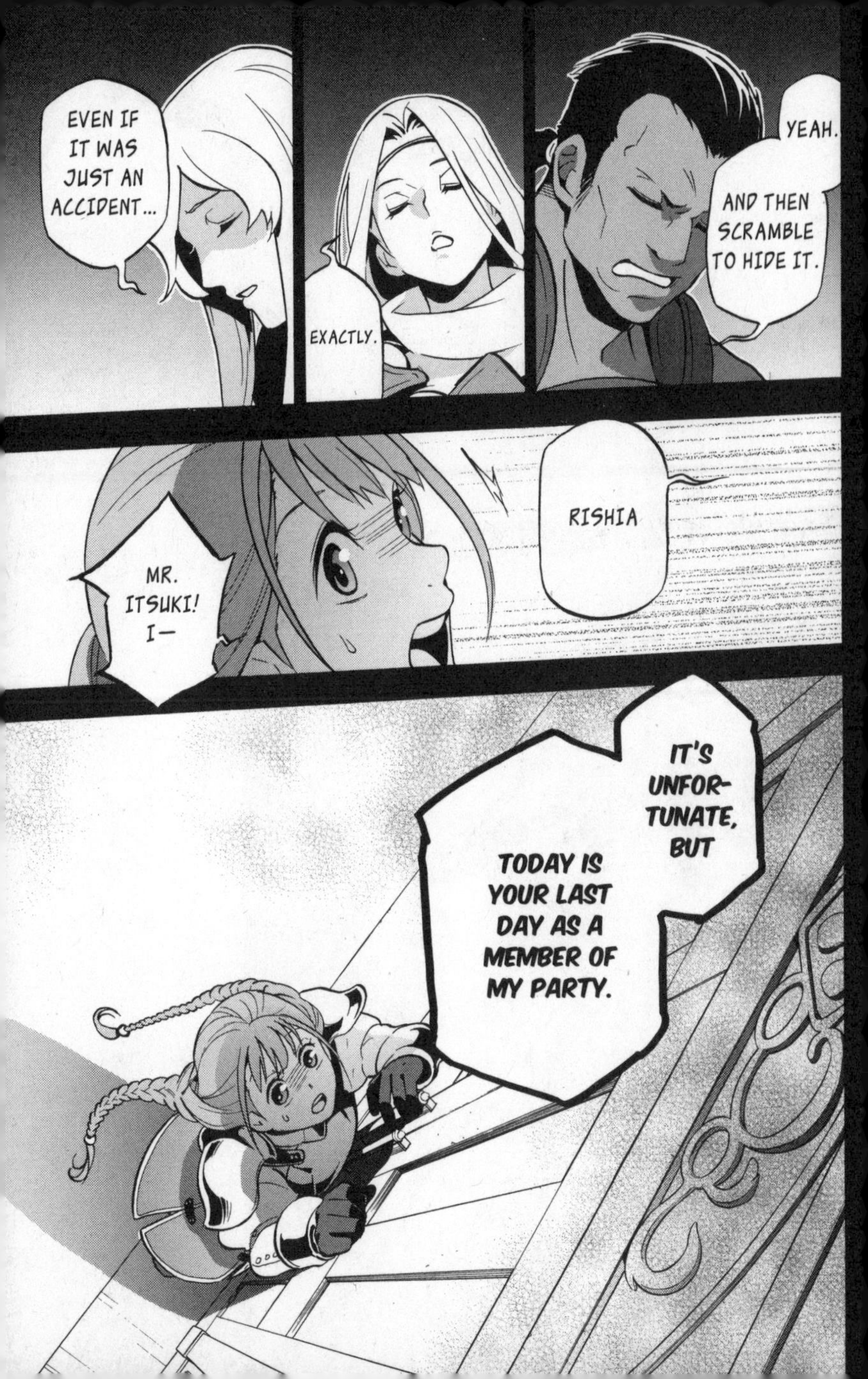
YEAH.
AND THEN SCRAMBLE TO HIDE IT.
EXACTLY.
EVEN IF IT WAS JUST AN ACCIDENT...
RISHIA
MR. ITSUKI! I—
IT'S UNFORTUNATE, BUT
TODAY IS YOUR LAST DAY AS A MEMBER OF MY PARTY.

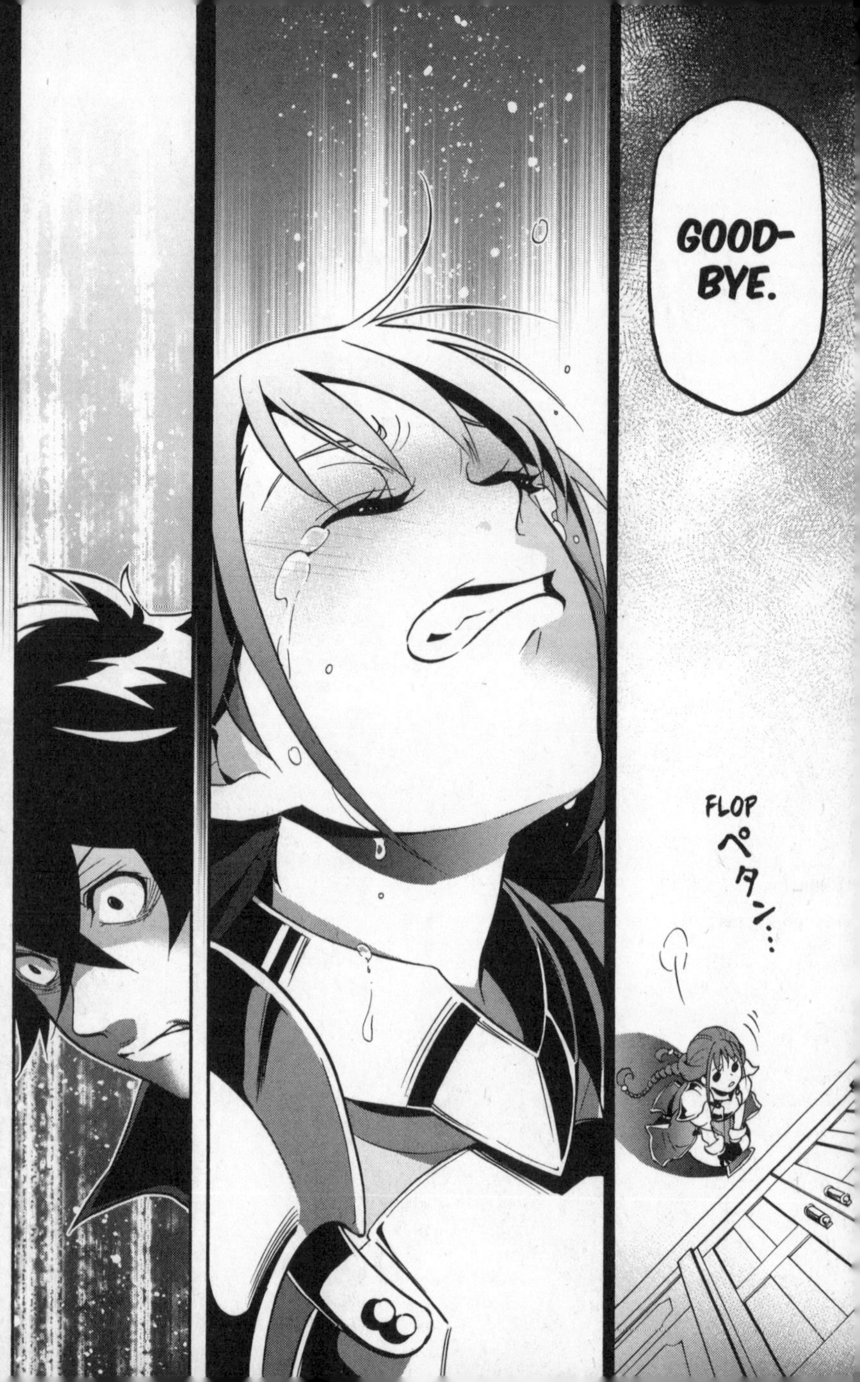
GOOD-BYE.
FLOP
ペタン…

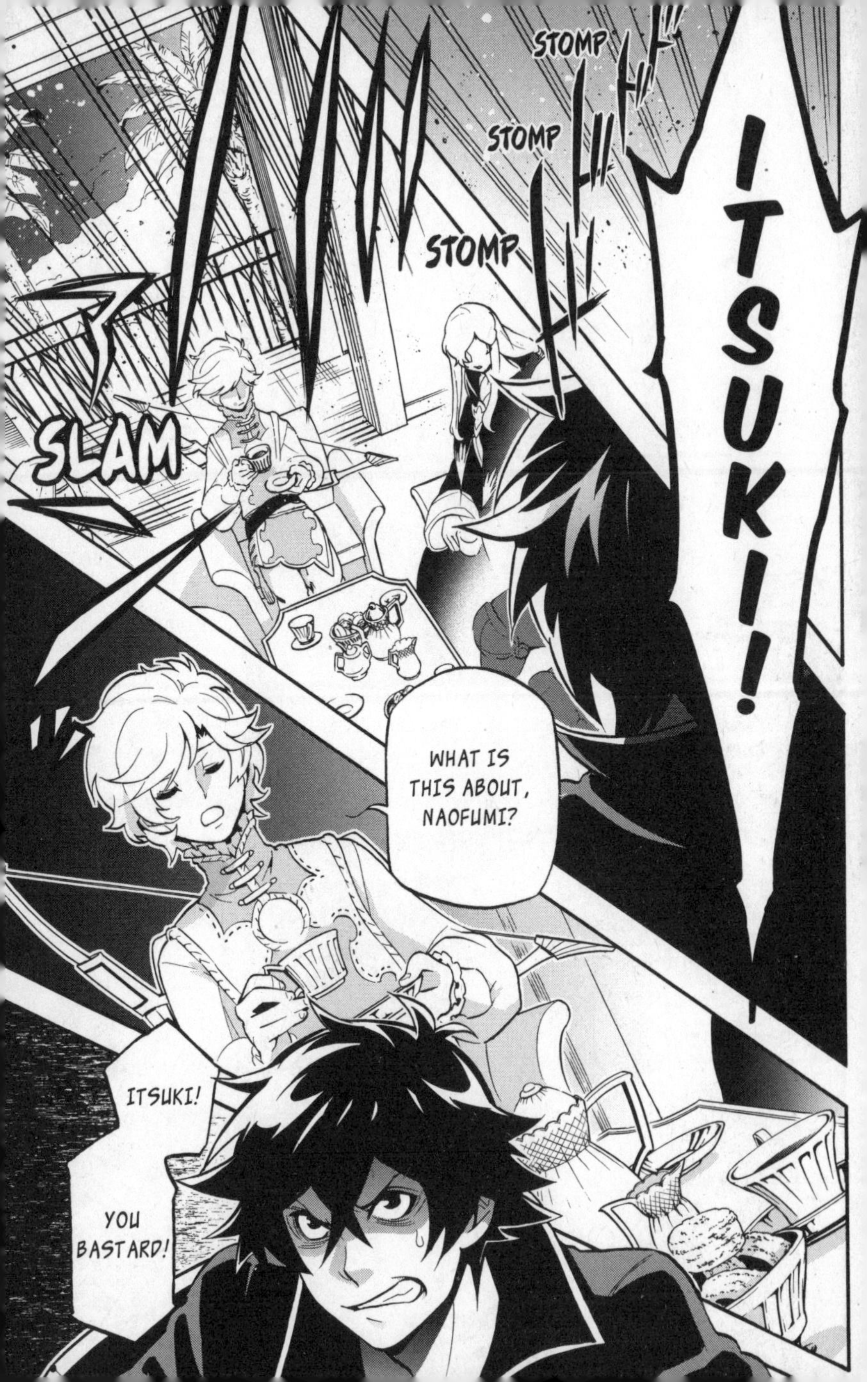
ITSUKI!!
STOMP
STOMP
STOMP
SLAM
WHAT IS THIS ABOUT, NAOFUMI?
ITSUKI!
YOU BASTARD!

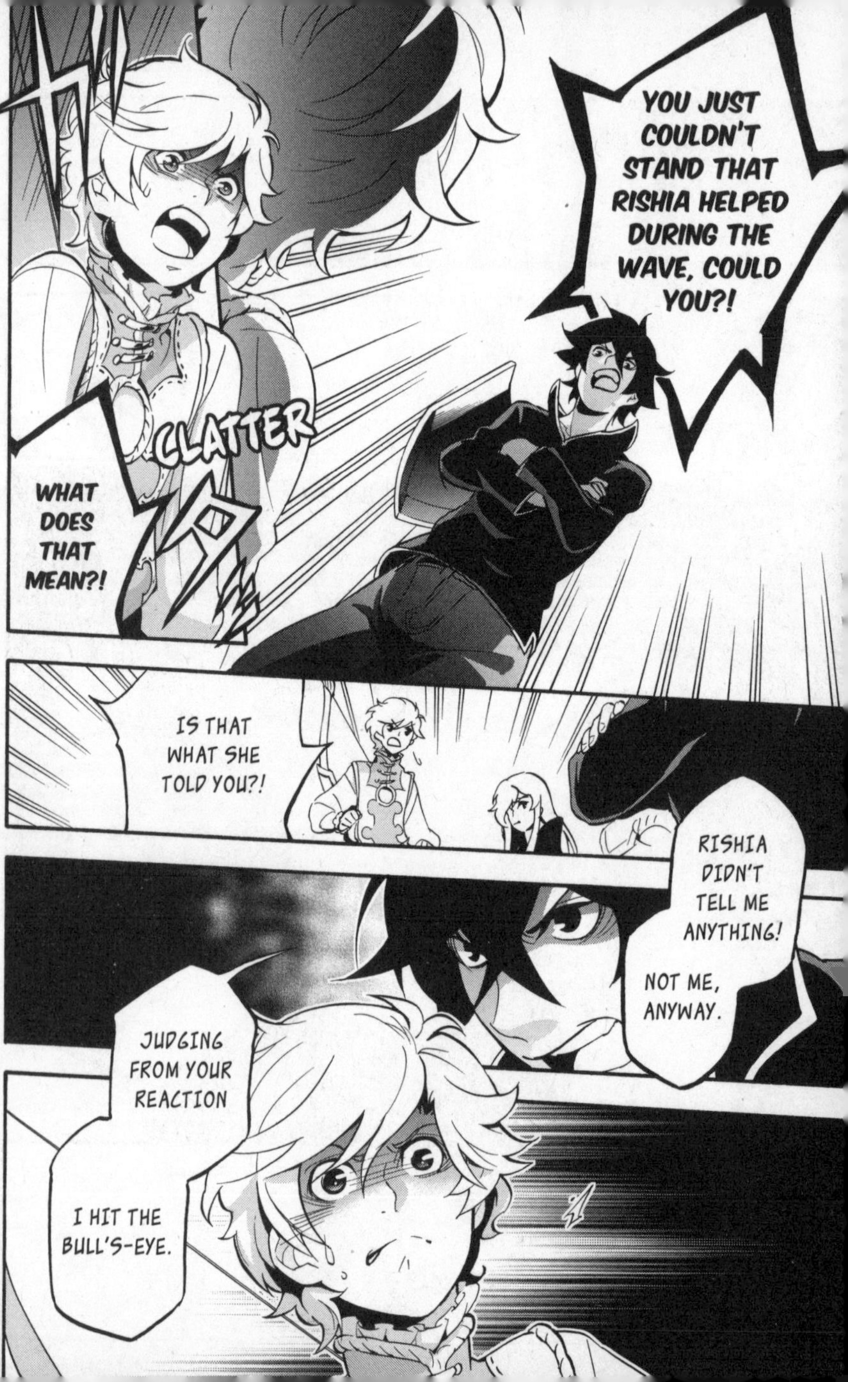
YOU JUST COULDN'T STAND THAT RISHIA HELPED DURING THE WAVE, COULD YOU?!
CLATTER
WHAT DOES THAT MEAN?!
IS THAT WHAT SHE TOLD YOU?!
RISHIA DIDN'T TELL ME ANYTHING!
NOT ME, ANYWAY.
JUDGING FROM YOUR REACTION
I HIT THE BULL'S-EYE.

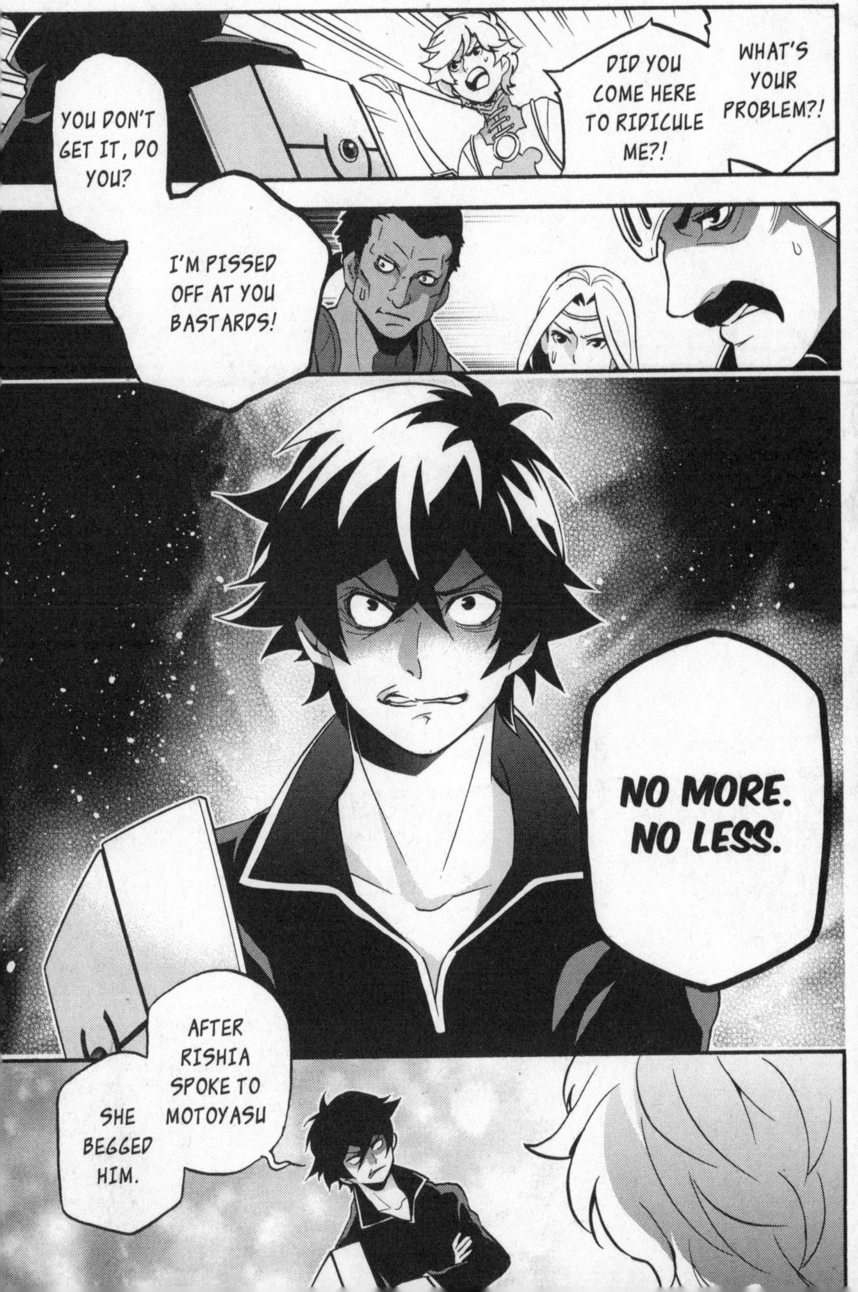
WHAT'S YOUR PROBLEM?!
DID YOU COME HERE TO RIDICULE ME?!
YOU DON'T GET IT, DO YOU?
I'M PISSED OFF AT YOU BASTARDS!
NO MORE. NO LESS.
AFTER RISHIA SPOKE TO MOTOYASU
SHE BEGGED HIM.

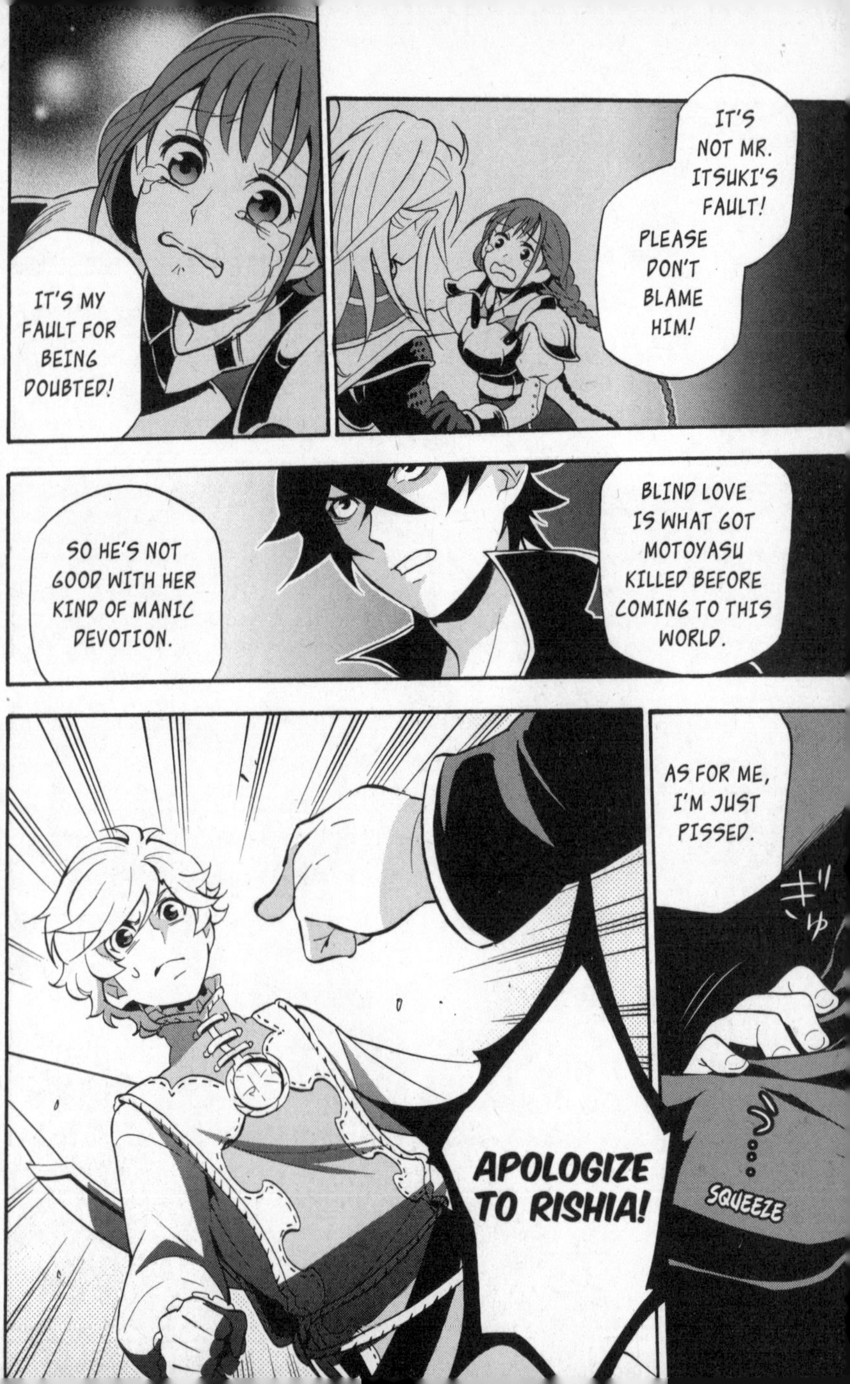
IT'S NOT MR. ITSUKI'S FAULT!
PLEASE DON'T BLAME HIM!
IT'S MY FAULT FOR BEING DOUBTED!
BLIND LOVE IS WHAT GOT MOTOYASU KILLED BEFORE COMING TO THIS WORLD.
SO HE'S NOT GOOD WITH HER KIND OF MANIC DEVOTION.
AS FOR ME, I'M JUST PISSED.
ぎゅ
SQUEEZE
APOLOGIZE TO RISHIA!

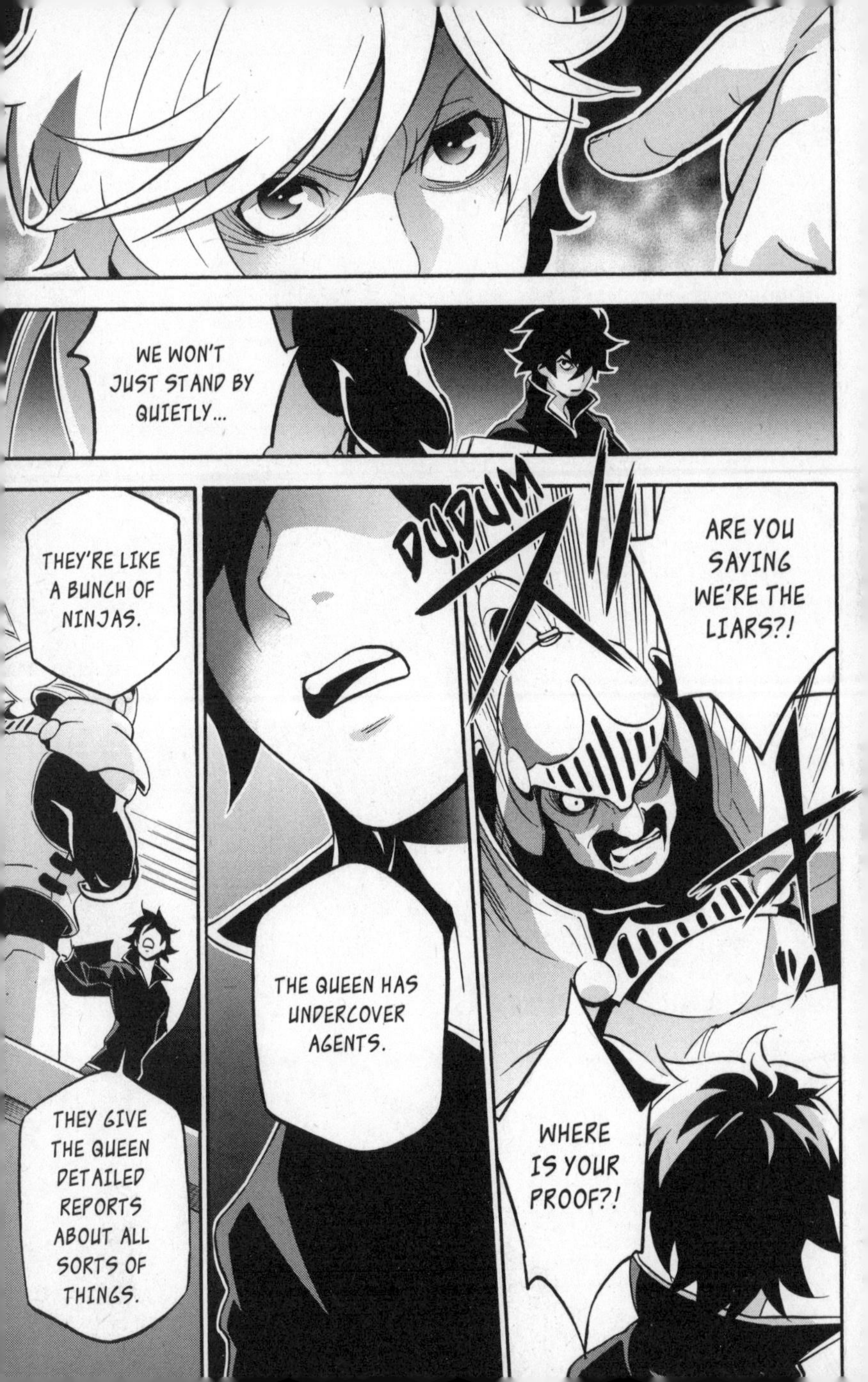
WE WON'T JUST STAND BY QUIETLY...
DUDUM
ARE YOU SAYING WE'RE THE LIARS?!
WHERE IS YOUR PROOF?!
THE QUEEN HAS UNDERCOVER AGENTS.
THEY'RE LIKE A BUNCH OF NINJAS.
THEY GIVE THE QUEEN DETAILED REPORTS ABOUT ALL SORTS OF THINGS.

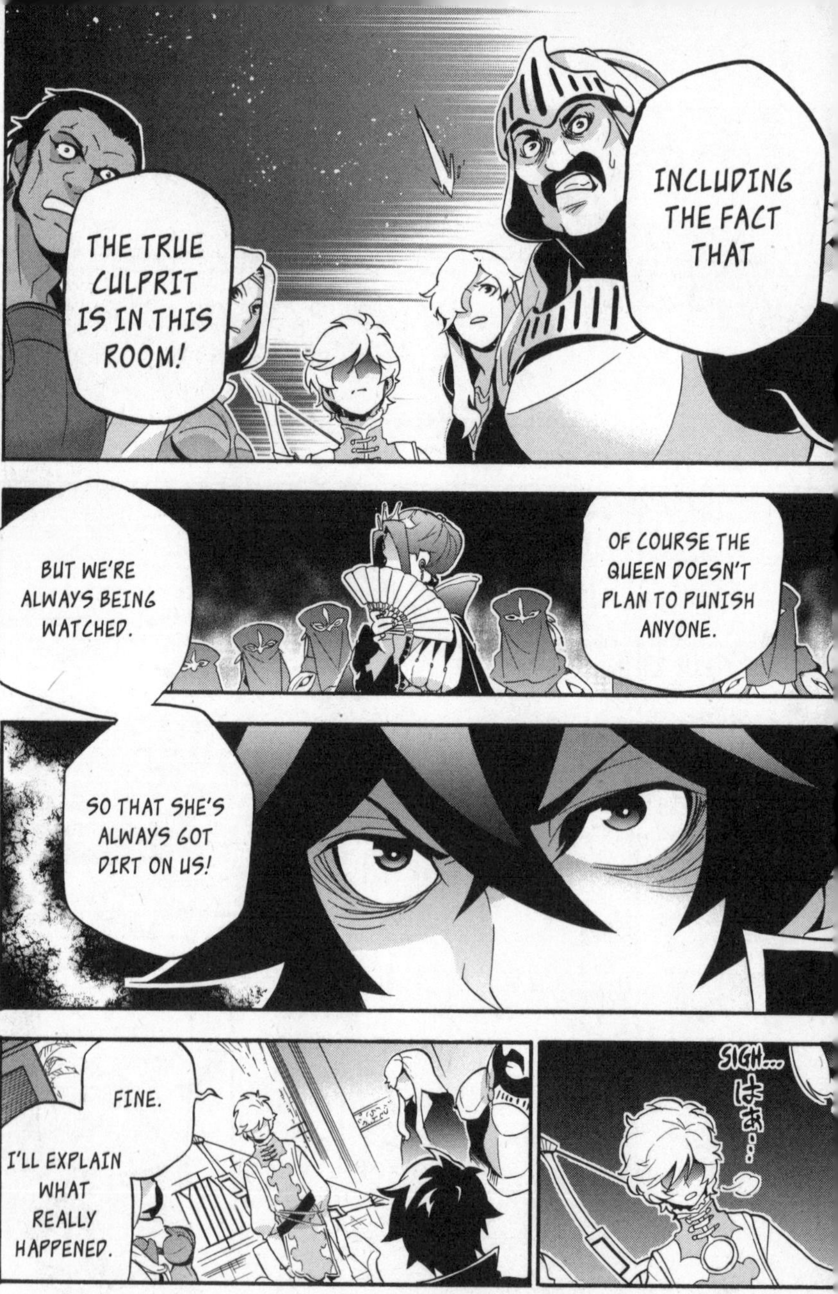
INCLUDING THE FACT THAT
THE TRUE CULPRIT IS IN THIS ROOM!
OF COURSE THE QUEEN DOESN'T PLAN TO PUNISH ANYONE.
BUT WE'RE ALWAYS BEING WATCHED.
SO THAT SHE'S ALWAYS GOT DIRT ON US!
SIGH...
はぁ…
FINE.
I'LL EXPLAIN WHAT REALLY HAPPENED.

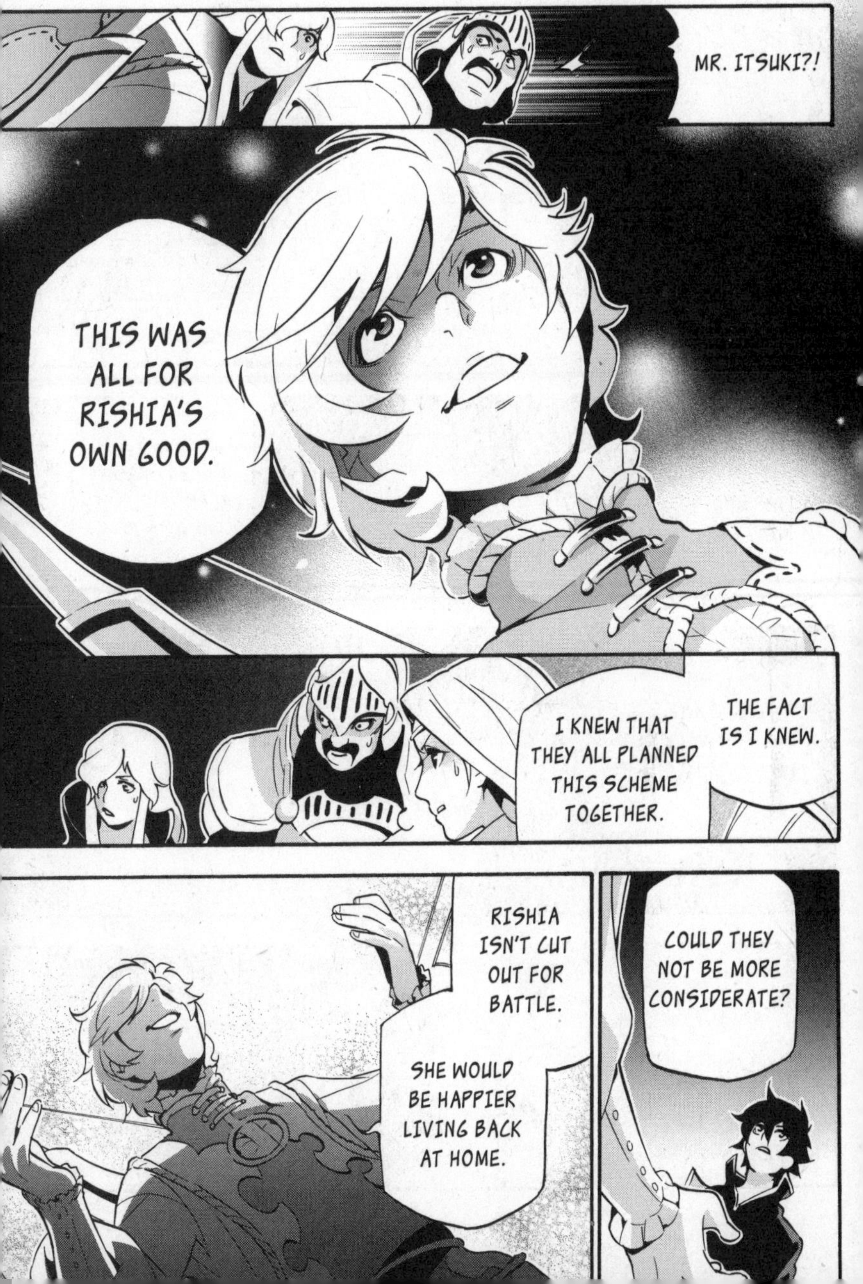
MR. ITSUKI?!
THIS WAS ALL FOR RISHIA'S OWN GOOD.
THE FACT IS I KNEW.
I KNEW THAT THEY ALL PLANNED THIS SCHEME TOGETHER.
COULD THEY NOT BE MORE CONSIDERATE?
RISHIA ISN'T CUT OUT FOR BATTLE.
SHE WOULD BE HAPPIER LIVING BACK AT HOME.

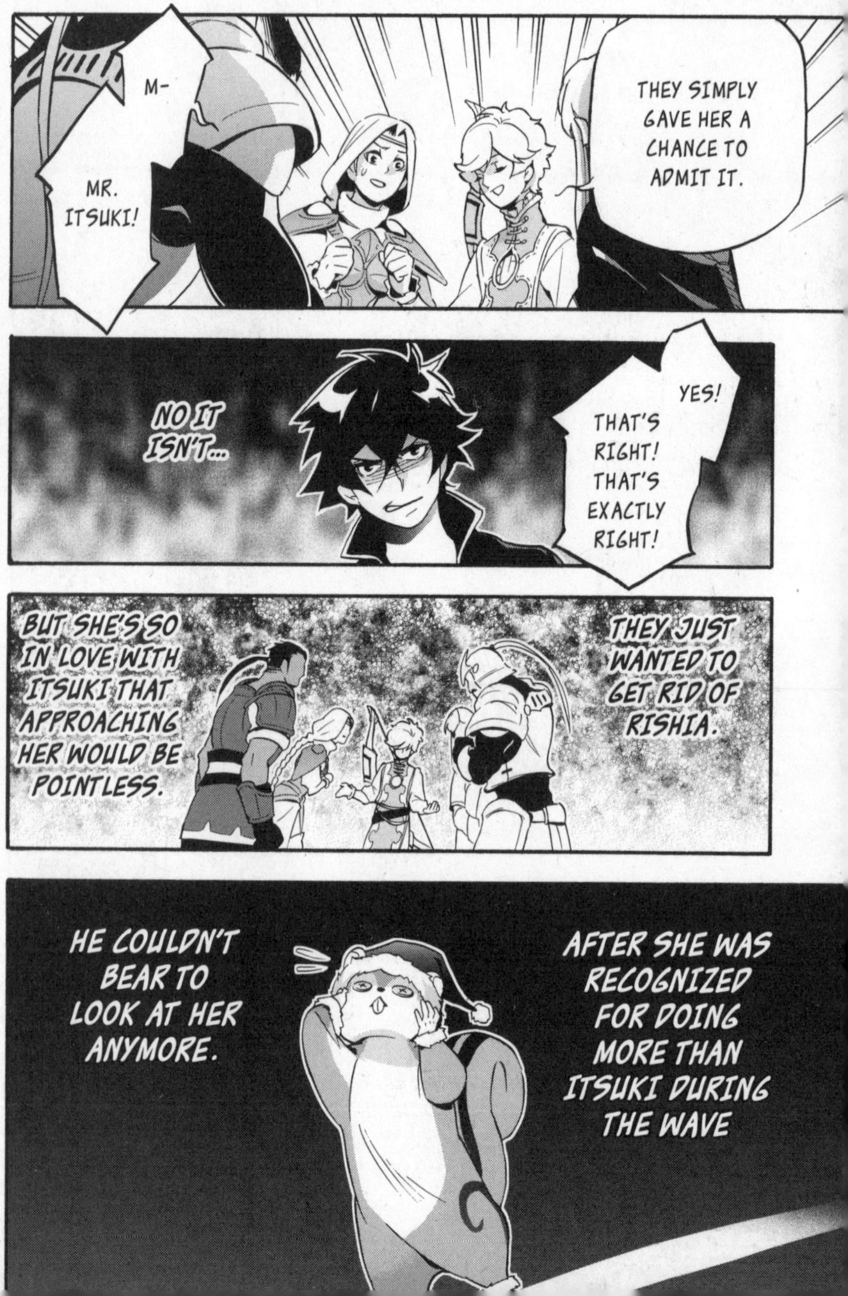
THEY SIMPLY GAVE HER A CHANCE TO ADMIT IT.
M-
MR. ITSUKI!
YES!
THAT'S RIGHT! THAT'S EXACTLY RIGHT!
NO IT ISN'T...
THEY JUST WANTED TO GET RID OF RISHIA.
BUT SHE'S SO IN LOVE WITH ITSUKI THAT APPROACHING HER WOULD BE POINTLESS.
AFTER SHE WAS RECOGNIZED FOR DOING MORE THAN ITSUKI DURING THE WAVE
HE COULDN'T BEAR TO LOOK AT HER ANYMORE.

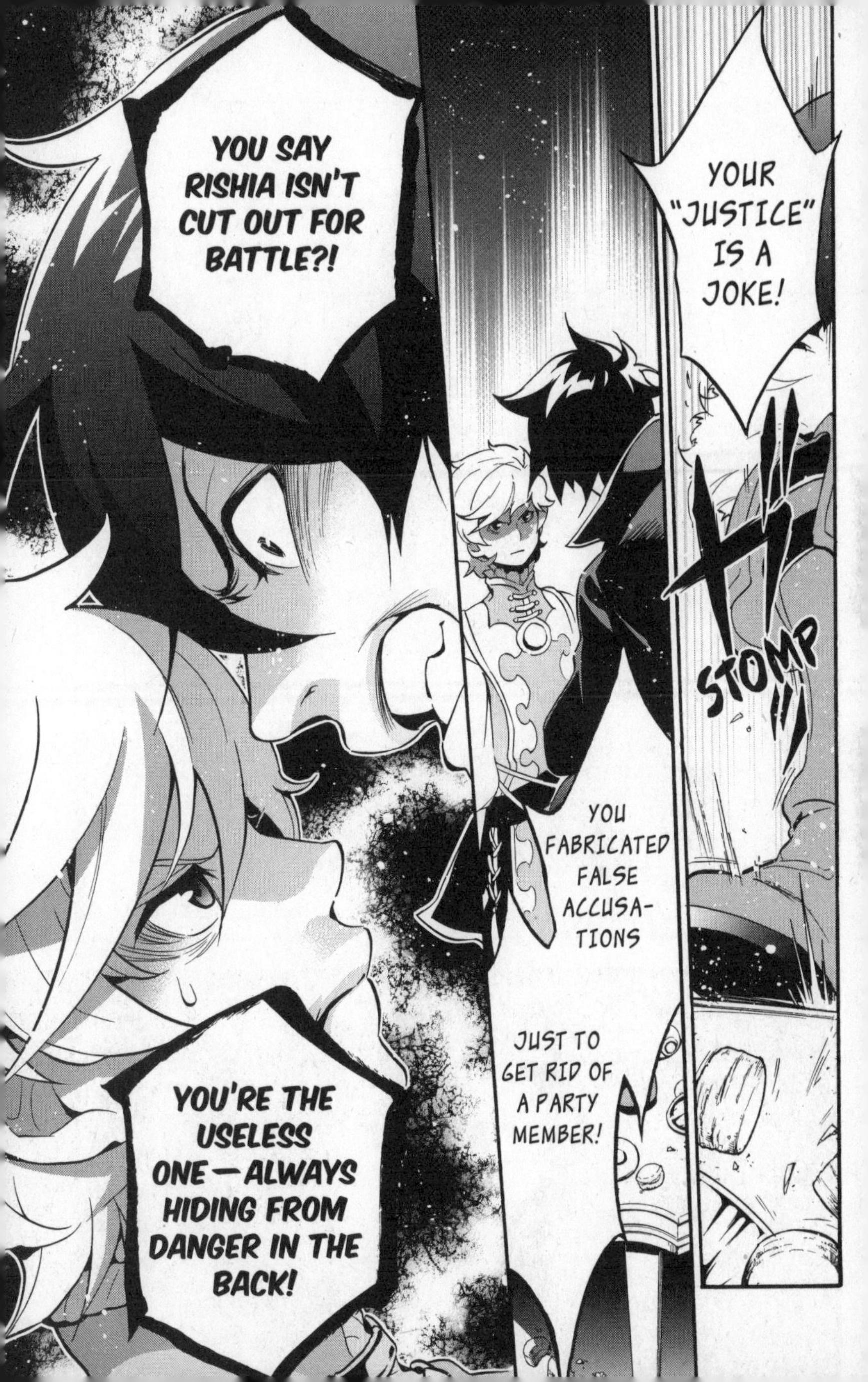
YOUR "JUSTICE" IS A JOKE!
STOMP
YOU FABRICATED FALSE ACCUSA-TIONS
JUST TO GET RID OF A PARTY MEMBER!
YOU SAY RISHIA ISN'T CUT OUT FOR BATTLE?!
YOU'RE THE USELESS ONE—ALWAYS HIDING FROM DANGER IN THE BACK!

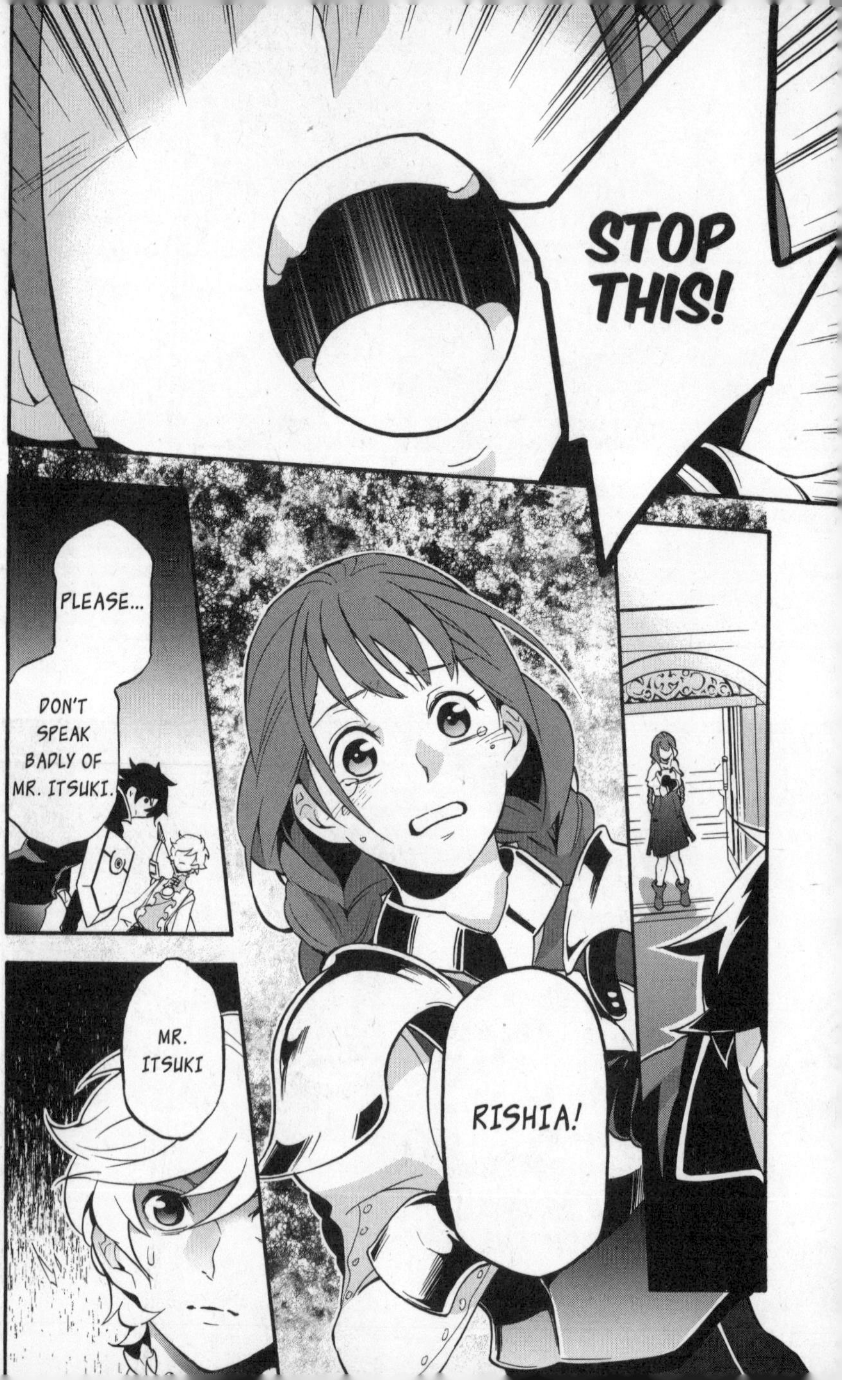
STOP THIS!
PLEASE...
DON'T SPEAK BADLY OF MR. ITSUKI.
RISHIA!
MR. ITSUKI

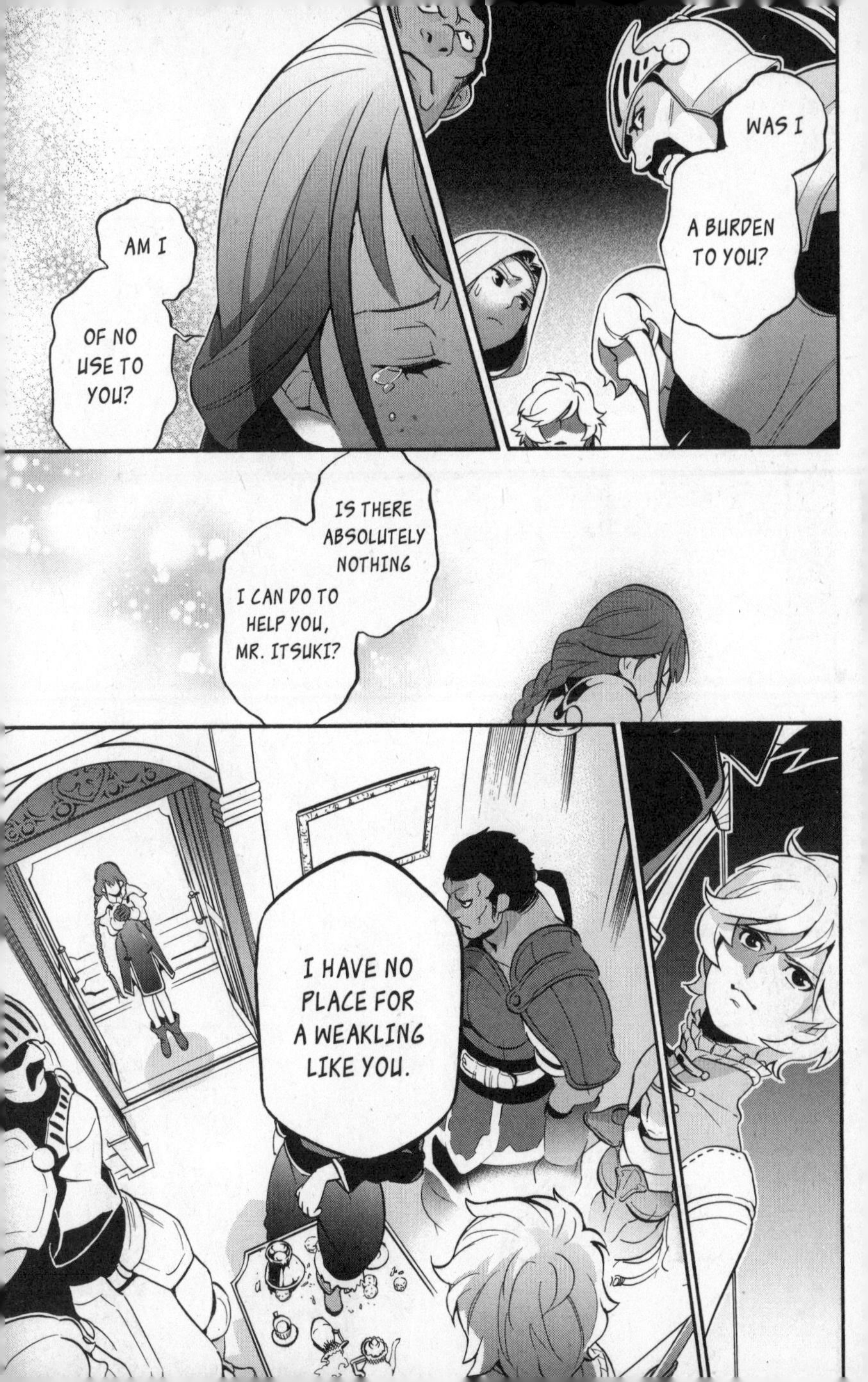
WAS I
A BURDEN TO YOU?
AM I
OF NO USE TO YOU?
IS THERE ABSOLUTELY NOTHING
I CAN DO TO HELP YOU, MR. ITSUKI?
I HAVE NO PLACE FOR A WEAKLING LIKE YOU.

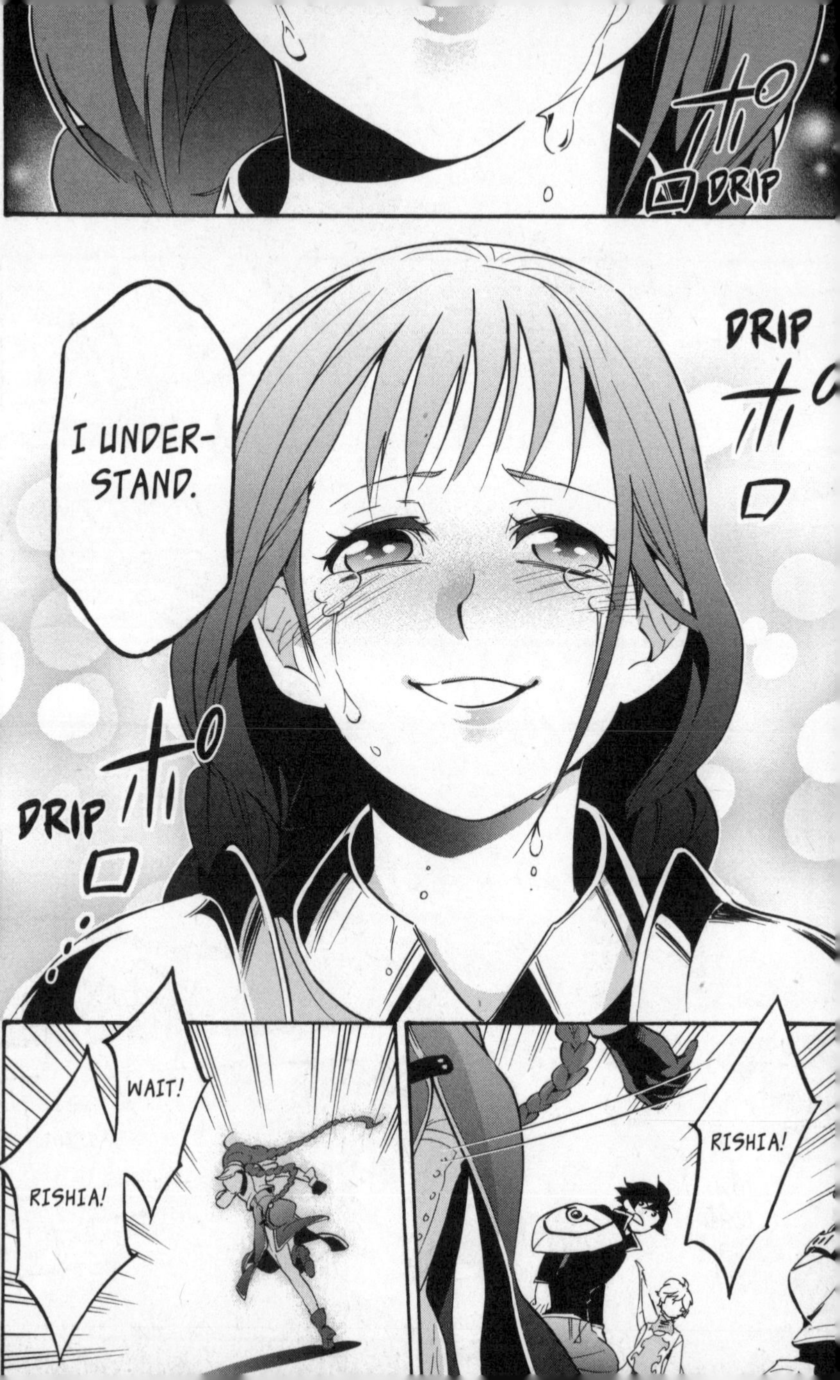
DRIP
DRIP
I UNDER-
STAND.
DRIP
RISHIA!
WAIT!
RISHIA!

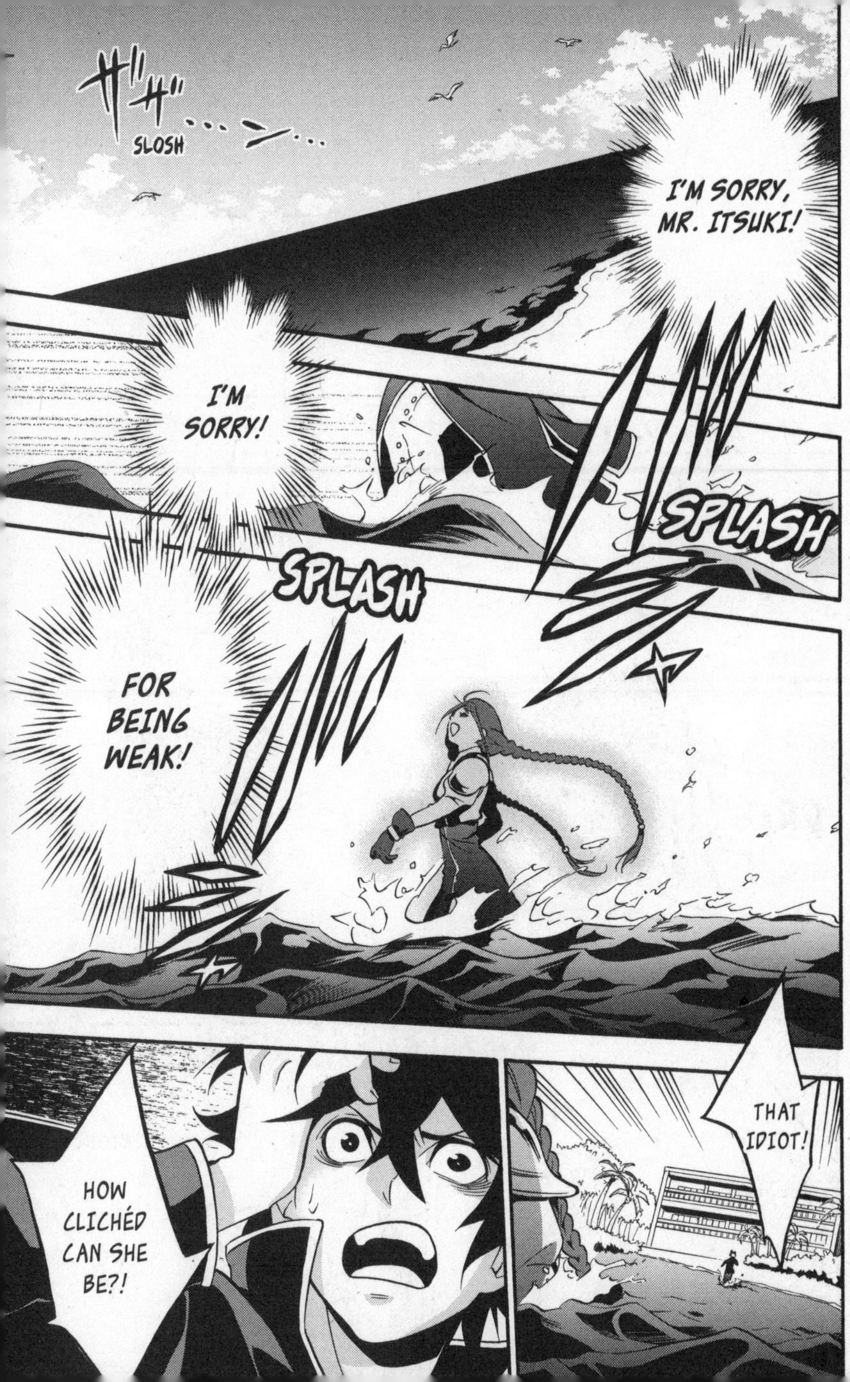
ザザ…ン…
SLOSH
I'M SORRY, MR. ITSUKI!
I'M SORRY!
SPLASH
SPLASH
FOR BEING WEAK!
THAT IDIOT!
HOW CLICHÉD CAN SHE BE?!

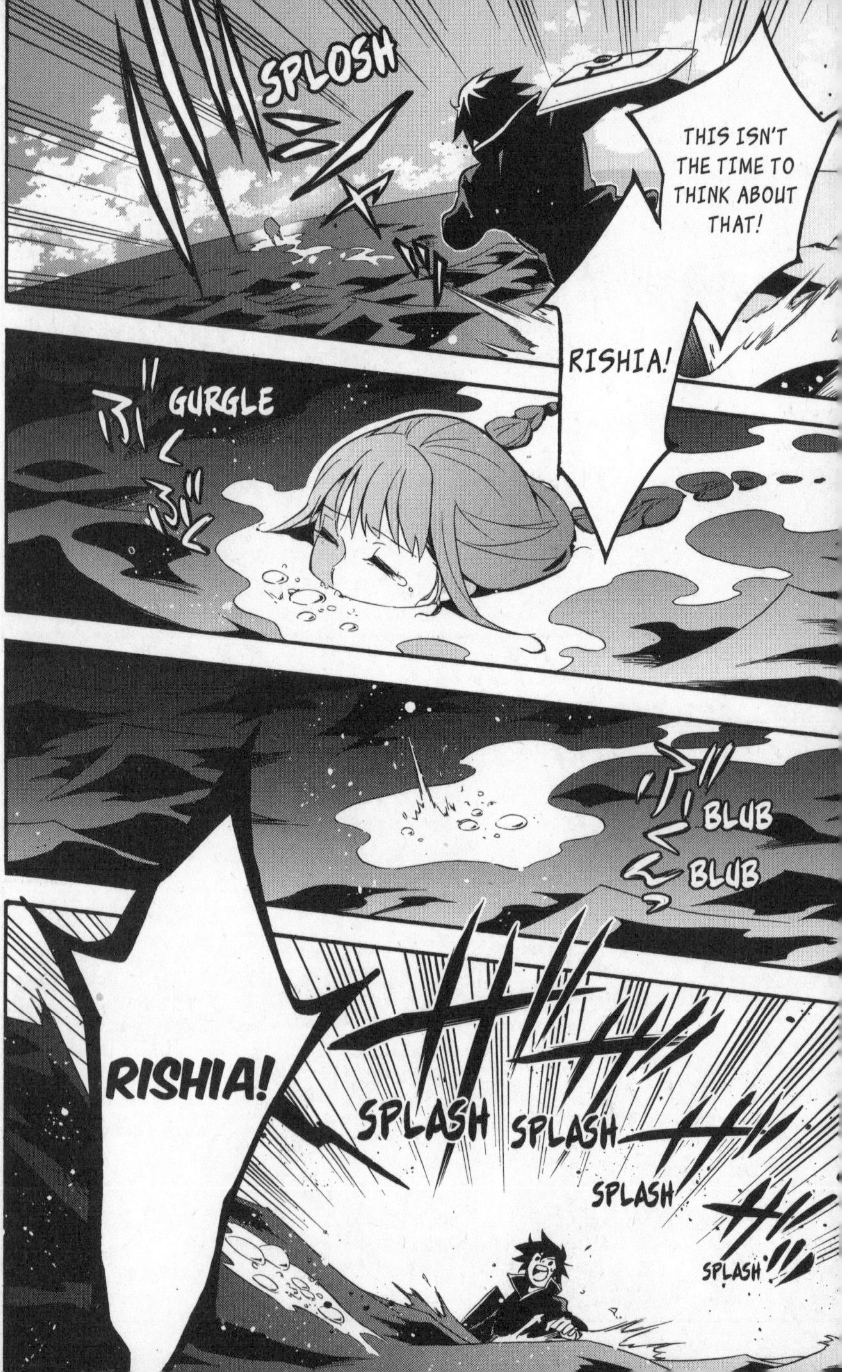
THIS ISN'T THE TIME TO THINK ABOUT THAT!
SPLOSH
RISHIA!
GURGLE
BLUB
BLUB
RISHIA!
SPLASH
SPLASH
SPLASH
SPLASH

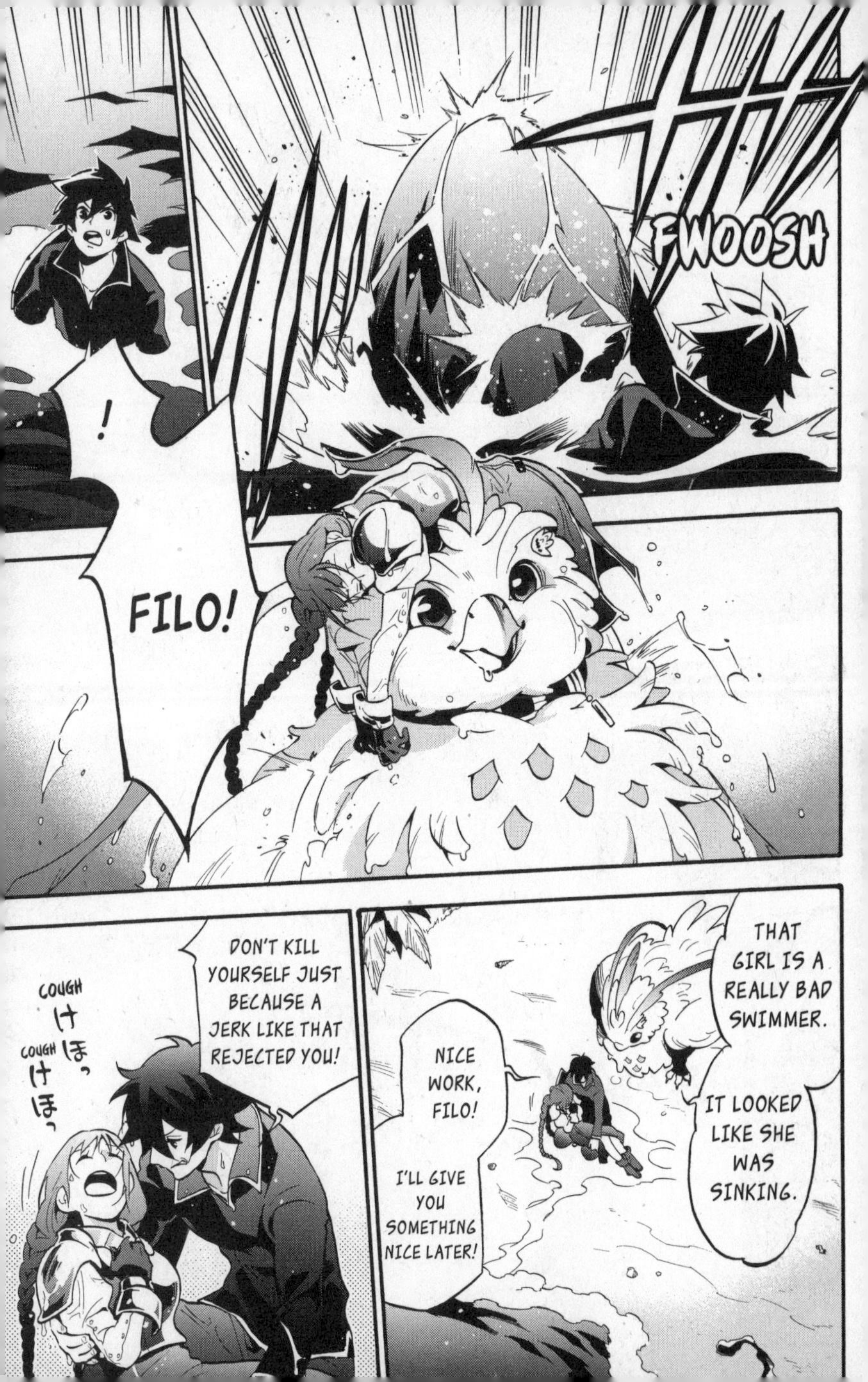
FWOOSH
!
FILO!
THAT GIRL IS A REALLY BAD SWIMMER.
IT LOOKED LIKE SHE WAS SINKING.
NICE WORK, FILO!
I'LL GIVE YOU SOMETHING NICE LATER!
DON'T KILL YOURSELF JUST BECAUSE A JERK LIKE THAT REJECTED YOU!
COUGH けほっ
COUGH けほっ

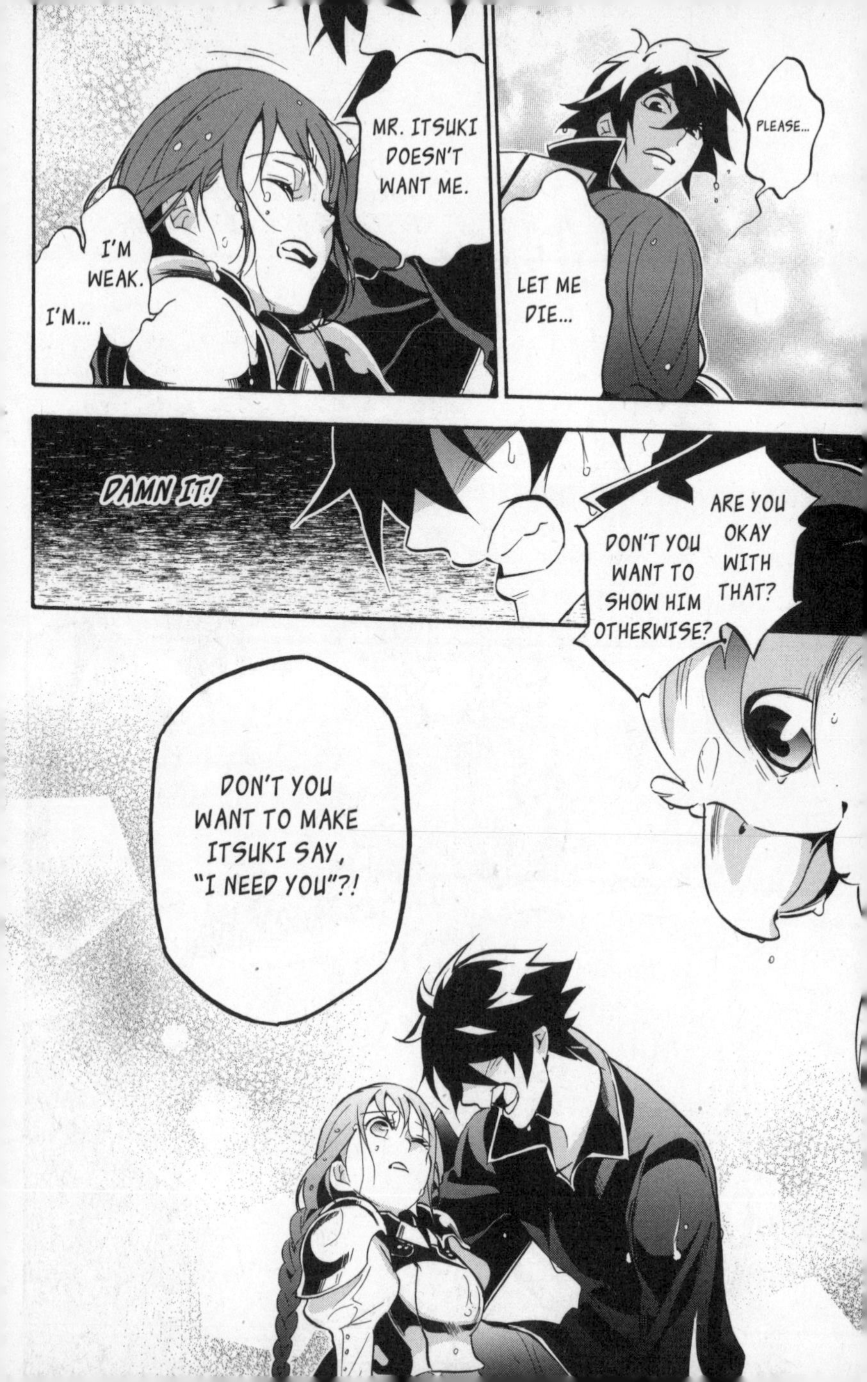
PLEASE...
LET ME DIE...
MR. ITSUKI DOESN'T WANT ME.
I'M WEAK. I'M...
DAMN IT!
ARE YOU OKAY WITH THAT?
DON'T YOU WANT TO SHOW HIM OTHERWISE?
DON'T YOU WANT TO MAKE ITSUKI SAY, "I NEED YOU"?!

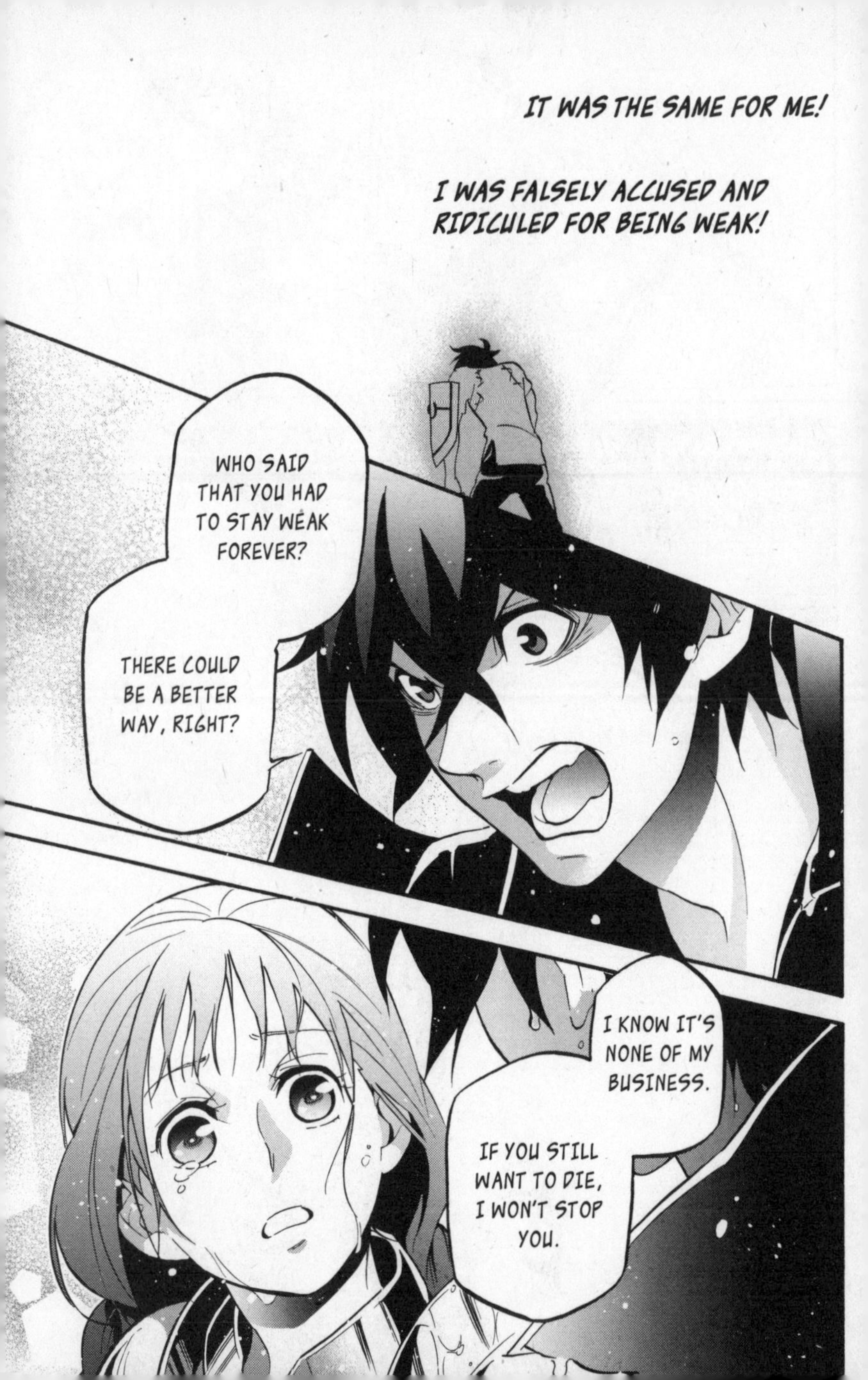
IT WAS THE SAME FOR ME!
I WAS FALSELY ACCUSED AND RIDICULED FOR BEING WEAK!
WHO SAID THAT YOU HAD TO STAY WEAK FOREVER?
THERE COULD BE A BETTER WAY, RIGHT?
I KNOW IT'S NONE OF MY BUSINESS.
IF YOU STILL WANT TO DIE, I WON'T STOP YOU.

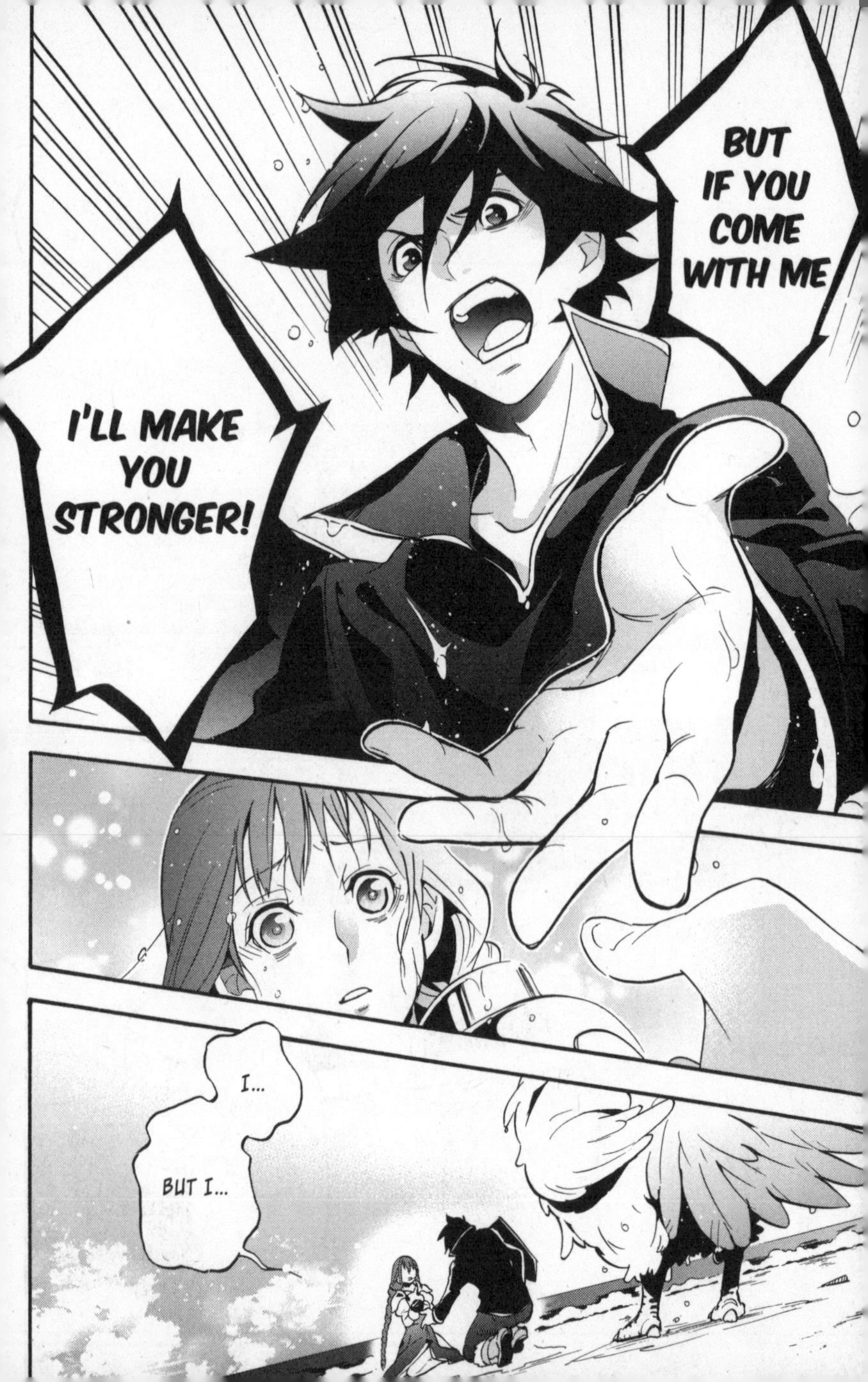
BUT IF YOU COME WITH ME
I'LL MAKE YOU STRONGER!
I...
BUT I...

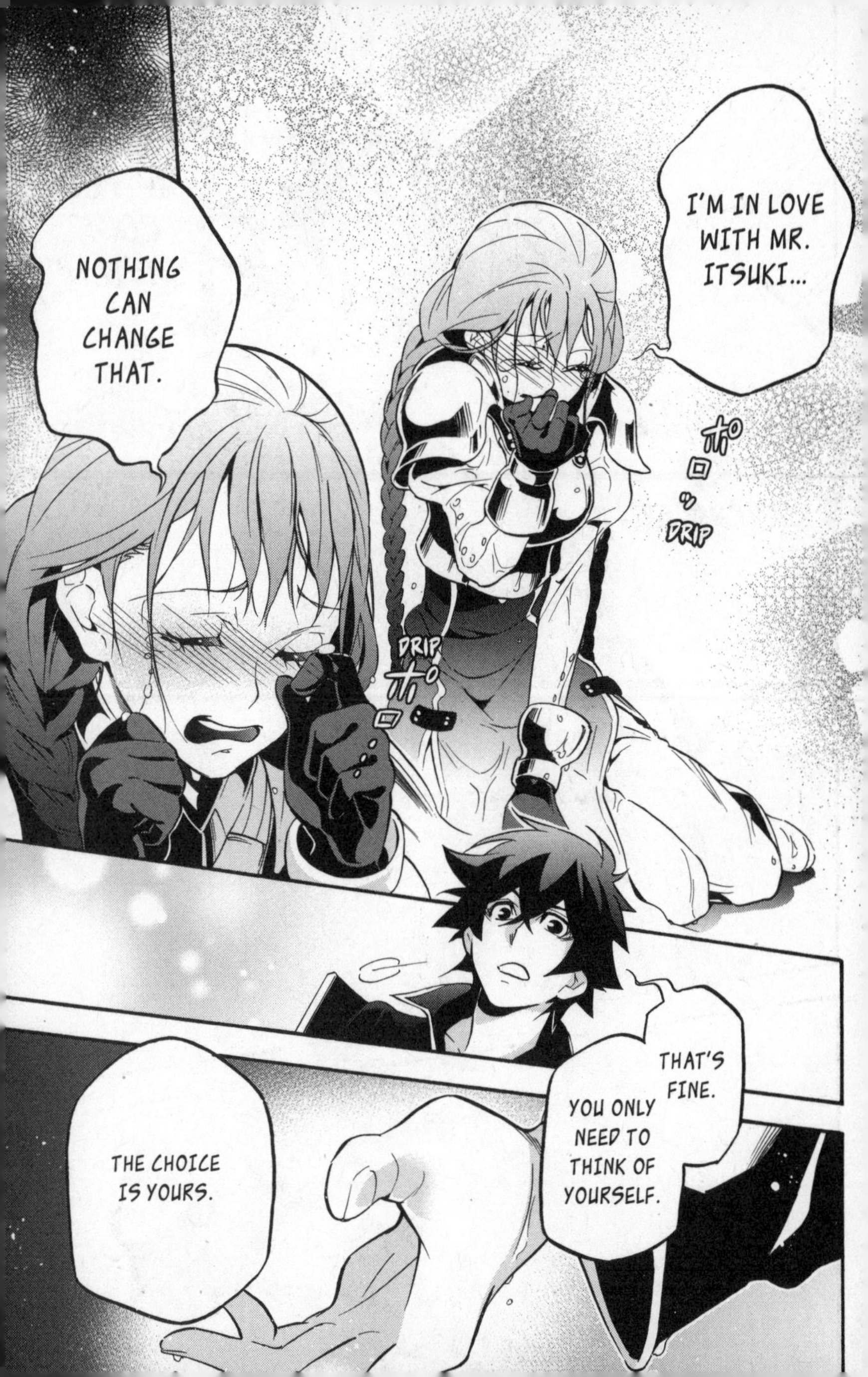
I'M IN LOVE WITH MR. ITSUKI...
DRIP
NOTHING CAN CHANGE THAT.
DRIP
THAT'S FINE.
YOU ONLY NEED TO THINK OF YOURSELF.
THE CHOICE IS YOURS.

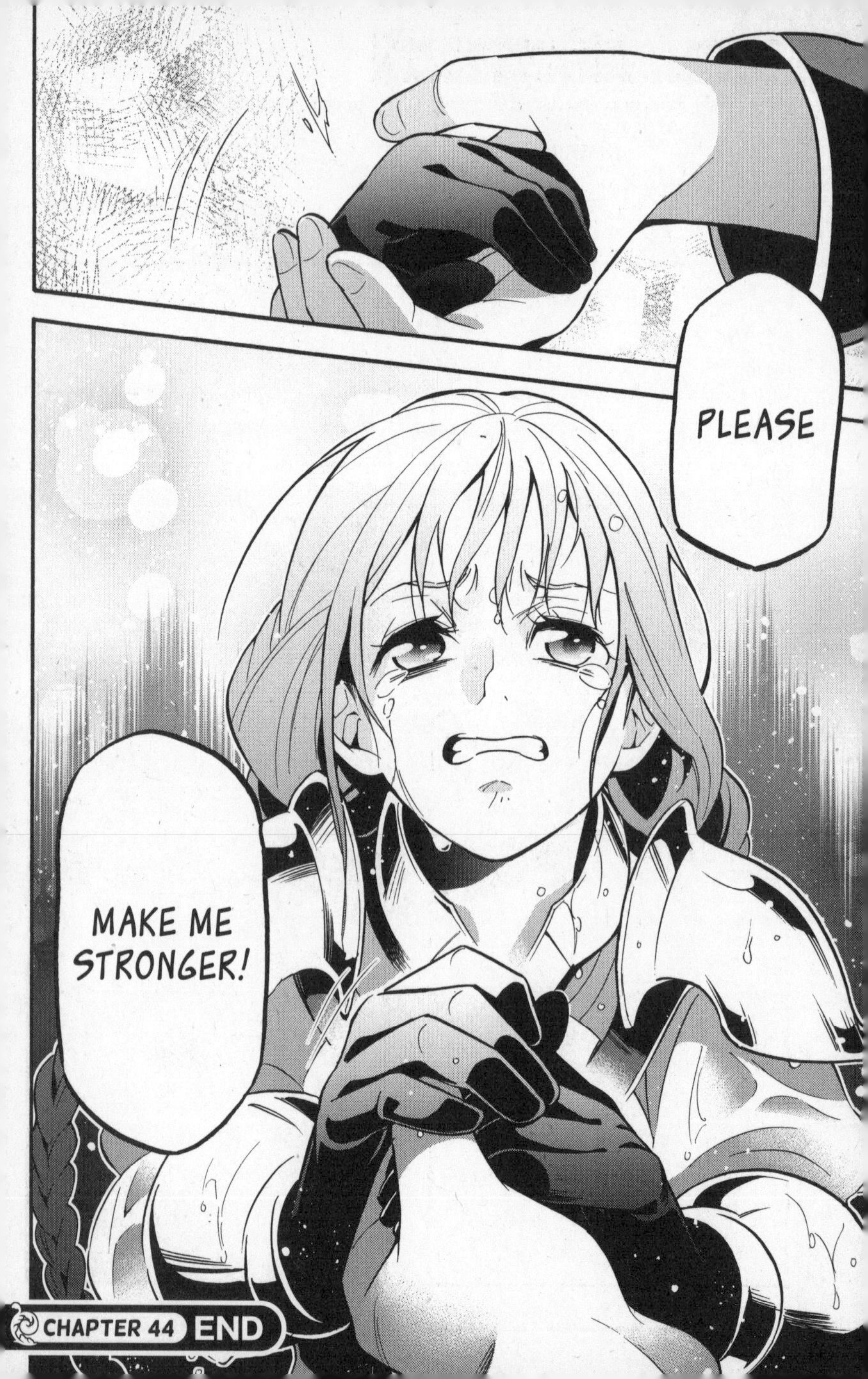
PLEASE
MAKE ME STRONGER!
CHAPTER 44 END

## EXTRA THE CAL MIRA HOT SPRINGS

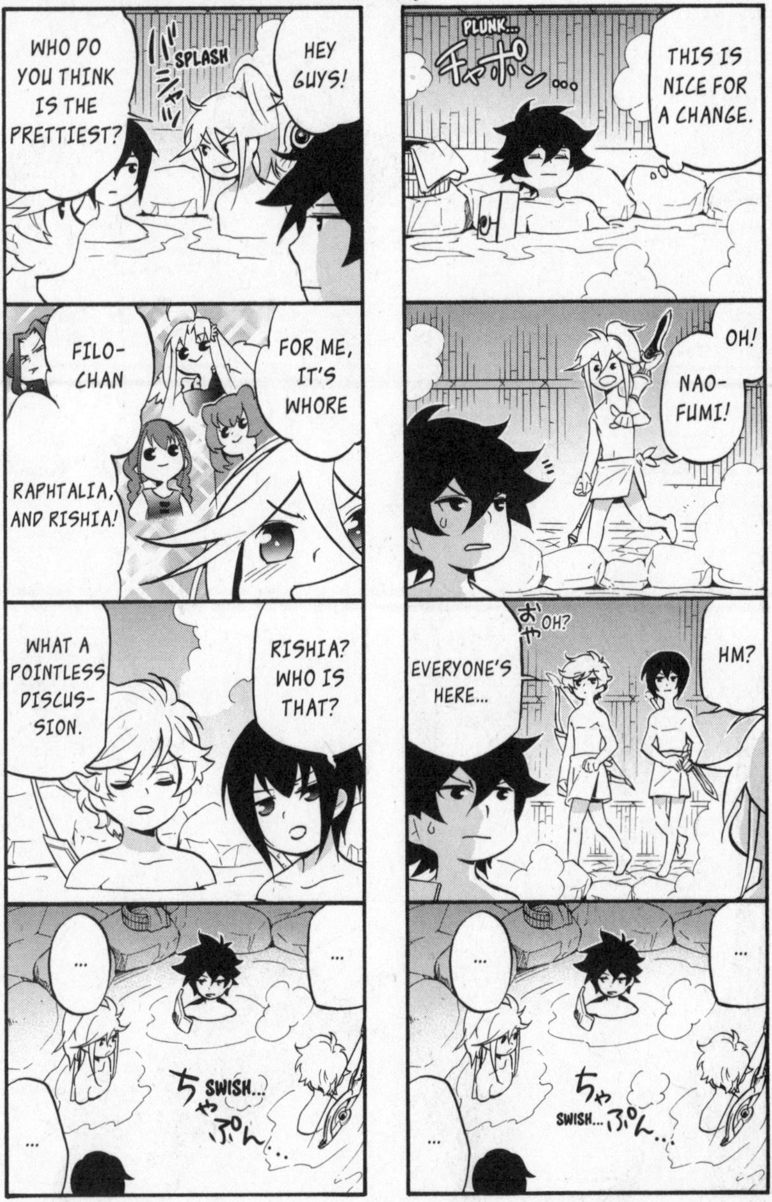
PLUNK...
チャポーン...
THIS IS NICE FOR A CHANGE.
OH!
NAO-FUMI!
HM?
おや
OH?
EVERYONE'S HERE...
...
...
...
ちゃぷん...
SWISH...
HEY GUYS!
バシャッ
SPLASH
WHO DO YOU THINK IS THE PRETTIEST?
FOR ME, IT'S WHORE
FILO-CHAN
RAPHTALIA, AND RISHIA!
RISHIA? WHO IS THAT?
WHAT A POINTLESS DISCUSSION.
...
...
...
ちゃぷん...
SWISH...

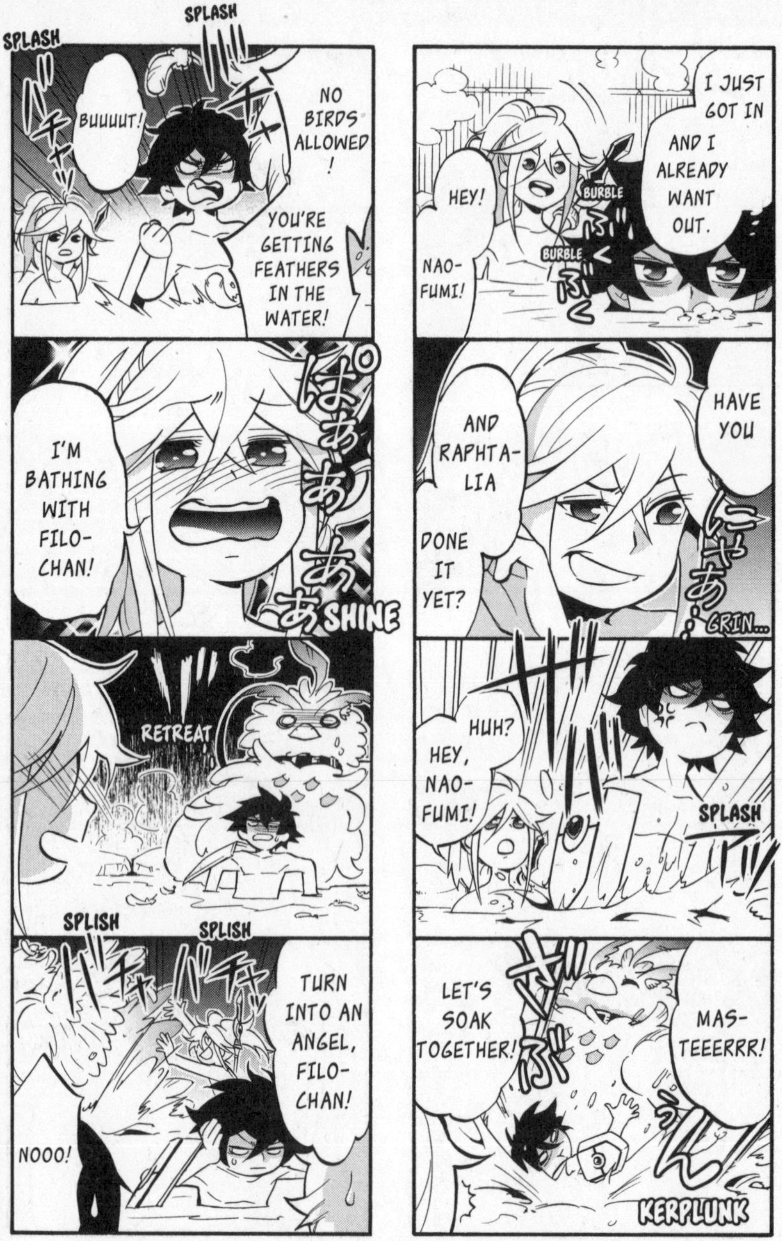
I JUST GOT IN
AND I ALREADY WANT OUT.
BURBLE
HEY!
BURBLE
NAO-FUMI!
HAVE YOU
AND RAPHTA-LIA
DONE IT YET?
GRIN...
SPLASH
HUH?
HEY, NAO-FUMI!
MAS-TEEERRR!
LET'S SOAK TOGETHER!
KERPLUNK
SPLASH
NO BIRDS ALLOWED!
YOU'RE GETTING FEATHERS IN THE WATER!
BUUUUT!
SPLASH
SHINE
I'M BATHING WITH FILO-CHAN!
RETREAT
SPLISH
SPLISH
TURN INTO AN ANGEL, FILO-CHAN!
NOOO!

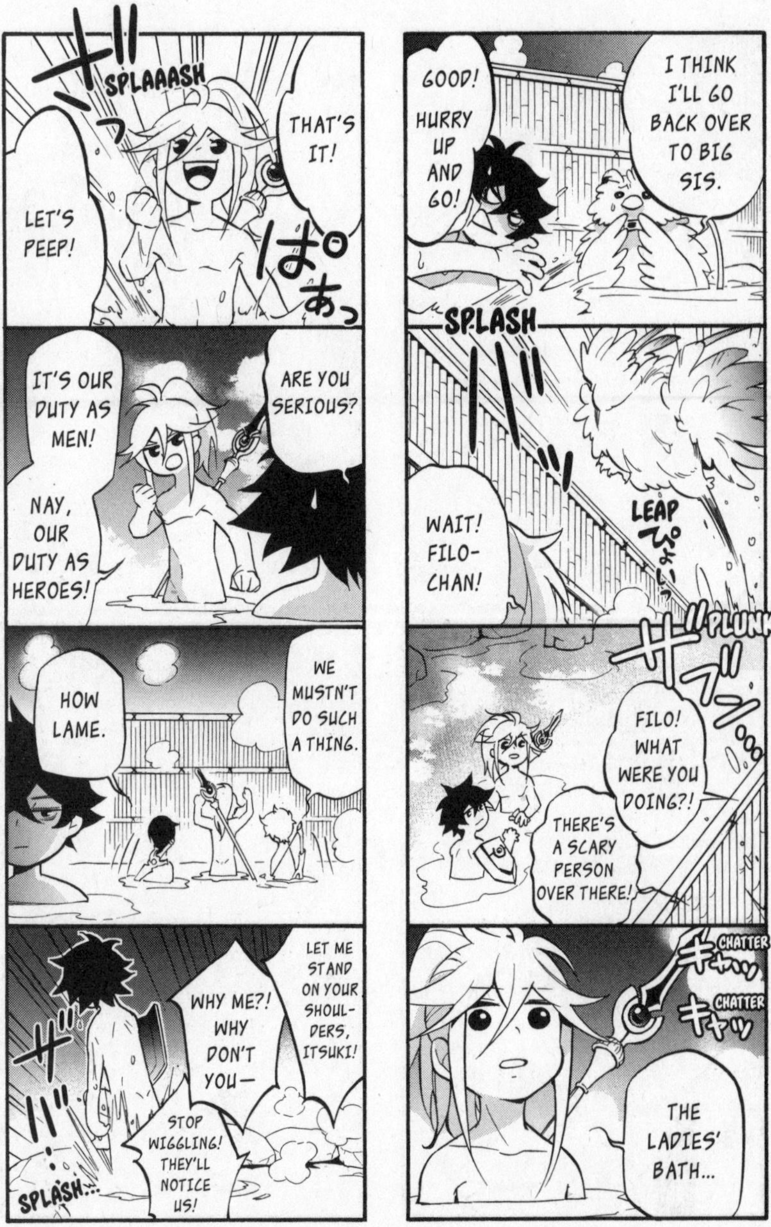
I THINK I'LL GO BACK OVER TO BIG SIS.
GOOD! HURRY UP AND GO!
SPLASH
LEAP
ぴょいっ
WAIT! FILO-CHAN!
PLUNK...
FILO! WHAT WERE YOU DOING?!
THERE'S A SCARY PERSON OVER THERE!
CHATTER
キャッ
CHATTER
キャッ
THE LADIES' BATH...
SPLAAASH
THAT'S IT!
LET'S PEEP!
ぱあっ
ARE YOU SERIOUS?
IT'S OUR DUTY AS MEN!
NAY, OUR DUTY AS HEROES!
WE MUSTN'T DO SUCH A THING.
HOW LAME.
LET ME STAND ON YOUR SHOULDERS, ITSUKI!
WHY ME?! WHY DON'T YOU—
STOP WIGGLING! THEY'LL NOTICE US!
SPLASH...

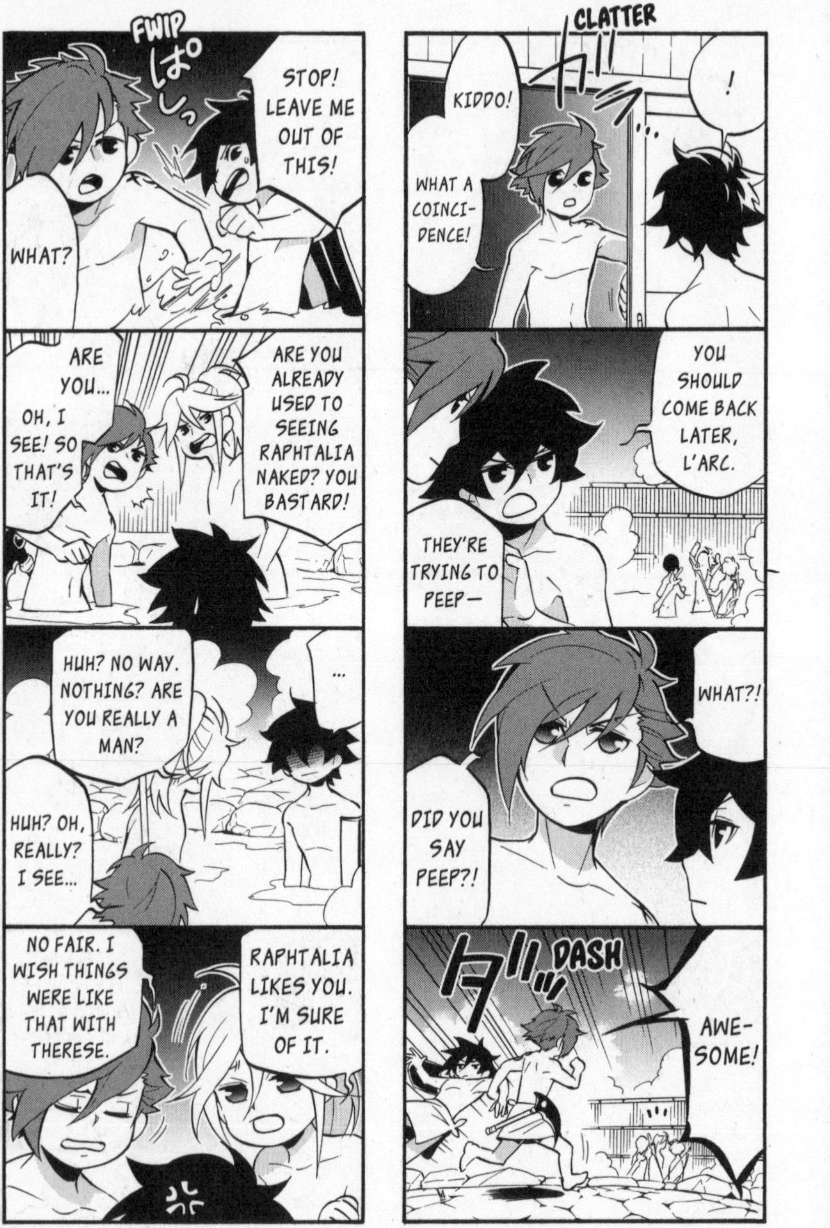
CLATTER
ガラ…
!
KIDDO!
WHAT A COINCI-DENCE!
YOU SHOULD COME BACK LATER, L'ARC.
THEY'RE TRYING TO PEEP—
WHAT?!
DID YOU SAY PEEP?!
DASH
タッ
AWE-SOME!
FWIP
ぱしっ
STOP! LEAVE ME OUT OF THIS!
WHAT?
ARE YOU ALREADY USED TO SEEING RAPHTALIA NAKED? YOU BASTARD!
ARE YOU...
OH, I SEE! SO THAT'S IT!
...
HUH? NO WAY. NOTHING? ARE YOU REALLY A MAN?
HUH? OH, REALLY? I SEE...
RAPHTALIA LIKES YOU. I'M SURE OF IT.
NO FAIR. I WISH THINGS WERE LIKE THAT WITH THERESE.

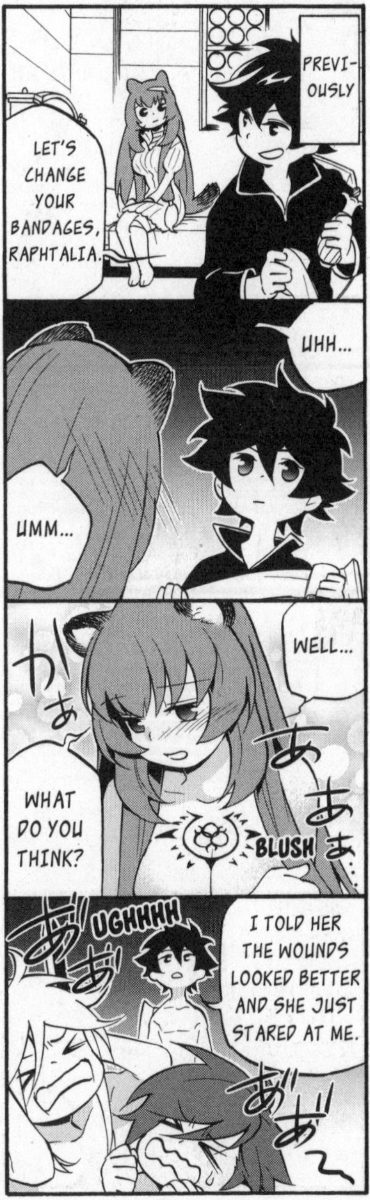
PREVIOUSLY
LET'S CHANGE YOUR BANDAGES, RAPHTALIA.
UHH...
UMM...
WELL...
BLUSH
WHAT DO YOU THINK?
UGHHHH
I TOLD HER THE WOUNDS LOOKED BETTER AND SHE JUST STARED AT ME.
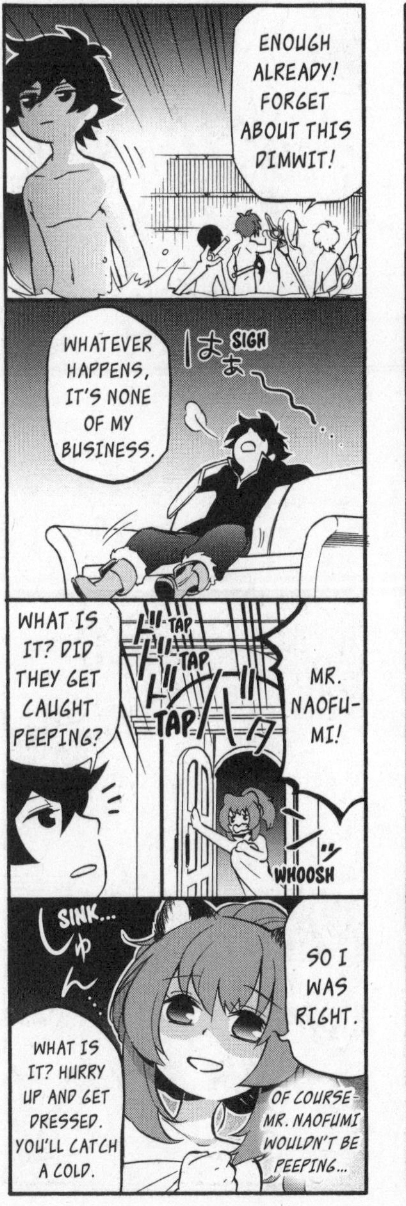
ENOUGH ALREADY! FORGET ABOUT THIS DIMWIT!
SIGH
WHATEVER HAPPENS, IT'S NONE OF MY BUSINESS.
MR. NAOFUMI!
TAP
TAP
TAP
WHAT IS IT? DID THEY GET CAUGHT PEEPING?
WHOOSH
SO I WAS RIGHT.
SINK...
OF COURSE MR. NAOFUMI WOULDN'T BE PEEPING...
WHAT IS IT? HURRY UP AND GET DRESSED. YOU'LL CATCH A COLD.

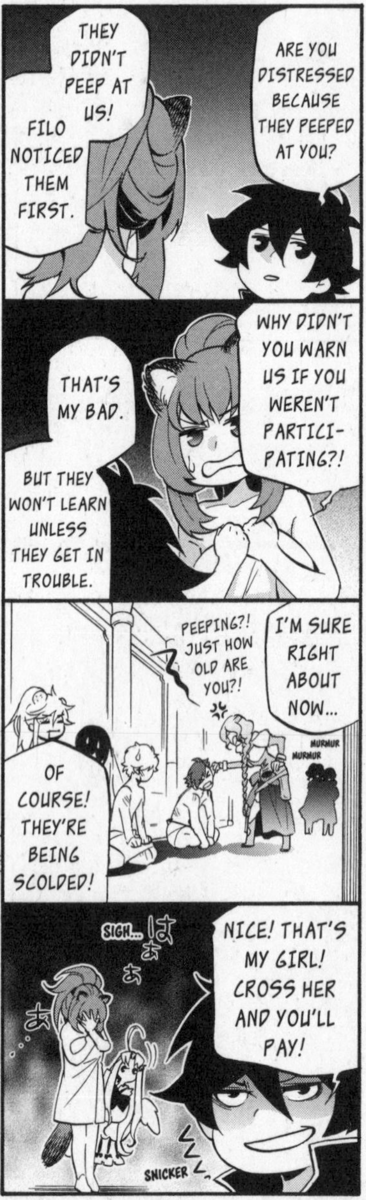
ARE YOU DISTRESSED BECAUSE THEY PEEPED AT YOU?
THEY DIDN'T PEEP AT US!
FILO NOTICED THEM FIRST.
WHY DIDN'T YOU WARN US IF YOU WEREN'T PARTICI-PATING?!
THAT'S MY BAD.
BUT THEY WON'T LEARN UNLESS THEY GET IN TROUBLE.
I'M SURE RIGHT ABOUT NOW...
PEEPING?! JUST HOW OLD ARE YOU?!
MURMUR MURMUR
OF COURSE! THEY'RE BEING SCOLDED!
NICE! THAT'S MY GIRL! CROSS HER AND YOU'LL PAY!
SIGH... はあああ
SNICKER

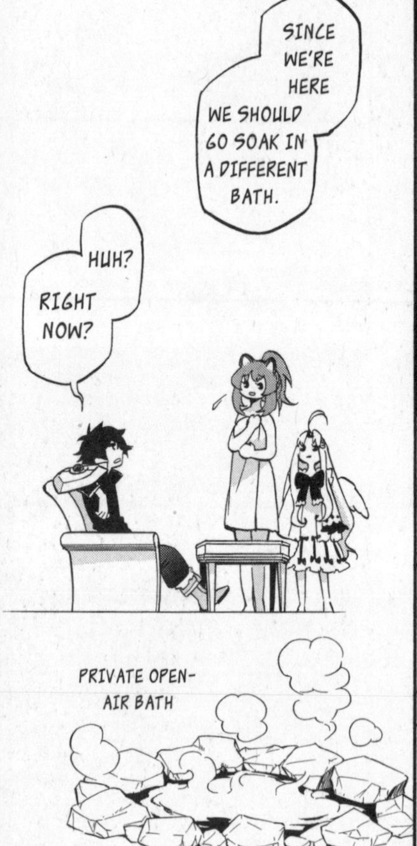
SINCE WE'RE HERE WE SHOULD GO SOAK IN A DIFFERENT BATH.
HUH? RIGHT NOW?
PRIVATE OPEN-AIR BATH

• SPECIAL THANKS •

ANEKO YUSAGI
MINAMI SEIRA
THE EDITORIAL STAFF
AKANO AMAMICHI, KAMIHITOE
SAMBUBEBE, AND WATANABE YUKO